Financial Shock
Updated Edition

Financial Shock

Updated Edition

Global Panic and Government Bailouts—How We Got Here and What Must Be Done to Fix It

Mark Zandi

Vice President, Publisher: Tim Moore
Associate Publisher and Director of Marketing: Amy Neidlinger
Executive Editor: Jim Boyd
Editorial Assistant: Myesha Graham
Operations Manager: Gina Kanouse
Digital Marketing Manager: Julie Phifer
Publicity Manager: Laura Czaja
Assistant Marketing Manager: Megan Colvin
Cover Designer: Chuti Prasertsith
Managing Editor: Kristy Hart
Project Editor: Anne Goebel
Copy Editor: Krista Hansing Editorial Services
Proofreader: Apostrophe Editing Services
Indexer: Lisa Stumpf
Senior Compositor: Jake McFarland
Manufacturing Buyer: Dan Uhrig

© 2009 by Pearson Education, Inc.
Publishing as FT Press
Upper Saddle River, New Jersey 07458

FT Press offers excellent discounts on this book when ordered in quantity for bulk purchases or special sales. For more information, please contact U.S. Corporate and Government Sales, 1-800-382-3419, corpsales@pearsontechgroup.com. For sales outside the U.S., please contact International Sales at international@pearson.com.

Company and product names mentioned herein are the trademarks or registered trademarks of their respective owners.

Printed in the United States of America

First Printing April 2009

ISBN-10: 0-13-701663-8
ISBN-13: 978-0-13-701663-1

Pearson Education LTD.
Pearson Education Australia PTY, Limited.
Pearson Education Singapore, Pte. Ltd.
Pearson Education North Asia, Ltd.
Pearson Education Canada, Ltd.
Pearson Educación de Mexico, S.A. de C.V.
Pearson Education—Japan
Pearson Education Malaysia, Pte. Ltd.

Library of Congress Cataloging-in-Publication Data on file.

For Ava, Bill, Anna, and Lily

Contents

Acknowledgments

This book would not have been possible without the support and help of a number of people.

Paul Getman, my friend, business partner, and sounding board for a quarter-century, has been instrumental in guiding me through the tricky parts of putting this work together. He taught me the basics of banking back in the 1980s, when it wasn't taught in graduate school. His insights have been key to guiding my thinking on the topics addressed in this book.

Andy Cassel also deserves a substantial amount of credit for his tireless efforts turning my prosaic prose into something hopefully worth reading.

I had invaluable help from Zoltan Pozsar, who culled through endless reports and documents and hunted down the most arcane of information. His enthusiasm and interest in the topic made my job much more interesting.

I would also like to thank Jim Boyd, my editor, who gave me very kind encouragement throughout the entire process. His cool demeanor was important to keeping my cool.

To my father and my brothers and sister, Richard, Karl, Peter, and Meriam: My father has been the proverbial, loving pain in the side, cajoling me to write a book; I surely wouldn't have done it otherwise. I haven't lived with my brothers and sisters for almost 30 years, but I think of them every day, and their influence is enduring.

Finally, I must acknowledge my dear wife and children. Their love and patience is key to anything I'm able to accomplish.

About the Author

Mark Zandi is chief economist and cofounder of Moody's Economy.com, where he directs the firm's research and consulting activities. Moody's Economy.com is an independent subsidiary of the Moody's Corporation and provides economic research and consulting services to global businesses, governments, and other institutions. His research interests include macroeconomic and financial economics, and his recent areas of research include an assessment of the economic impacts of various tax and government spending policies, the incorporation of economic information into credit risk analysis, and an assessment of the appropriate policy response to real estate and stock market bubbles. He earned his Ph.D. from the University of Pennsylvania, where he did his Ph.D. research with Gerard Adams and Nobel Laureate Lawrence Klein, and his Bachelor of Science degree from the Wharton School at the University of Pennsylvania.

Introduction

"If it's growing like a weed, it's probably a weed." So I was once told by the CEO of a major financial institution. He was talking about the credit card business in the mid-1990s, a time when lenders were mailing out new cards with abandon and cardholders were piling up huge debts. He was worried, and correctly so. Debt-swollen households were soon filing for bankruptcy at a record rate, contributing to the financial crisis that ultimately culminated in the collapse of mega hedge fund Long-Term Capital Management. The CEO's bank didn't survive.

A decade later, the world was engulfed by an even more severe financial crisis. This time the weed was the subprime mortgage: a loan to someone with a less-than-perfect credit history.

Financial crises are disconcerting events. At first they seem impenetrable, even as their damage undeniably grows and becomes increasingly widespread. Behind the confusion often lie esoteric and complicated financial institutions and instruments: program trading during the 1987 stock market crash, junk corporate bonds in the savings and loan debacle in the early 1990s, the Thai baht and Russian bonds in the late 1990s, and the technology-stock bust at the turn of the millennium.

Yet the genesis of the subprime financial shock has been even more baffling than past crises. Lending money to American home buyers had been one of the least risky and most profitable businesses a bank could engage in for nearly a century. How could so many mortgages have gone bad? And even if they did, how could even a couple of trillion dollars in bad loans derail a global financial system that is valued in the hundreds of trillions?

Adding to the puzzlement is the complexity of the financial institutions and securities involved in the subprime financial shock. What are subprime, Alt-A, and jumbo IO mortgages; asset-backed securities; CDOs; CPDOs; CDSs; and SIVs? How did this mélange of acronyms lead to plunging house prices, soaring foreclosures, wobbling stock markets, inflation, and recession? Who or what is to blame?

The reality is that there's plenty of blame to go around. A financial calamity of this magnitude could not have taken root without a great many hands tilling the soil and planting the seeds. Among the elements that fed the crisis are a rapidly evolving financial system, an eroding sense of responsibility in the lending process among both lenders and borrowers, the explosive growth of new and emerging economies amassing cash for their low-cost goods, lax oversight by policymakers skeptical of market regulation, incorrect ratings, and, of course, what economists call the "animal spirits" of investors and entrepreneurs.

America's financial system had long been the envy of the world. It had invested the nation's savings incredibly efficiently—so efficiently, in fact, that although our savings are meager by world standards, they bring returns greater than those in nations that save many times more. So it wasn't surprising when Wall Street engineers devised a new and ingenious way for global money managers to finance ordinary Americans buying homes: bundle the mortgages and sell them as securities. Henceforth, when the average family in Anytown, U.S.A., wrote a monthly mortgage check, the cash would become part of a money machine as sophisticated as anything ever designed in any of the world's financial capitals.

But the machine didn't work as so carefully planned. First it spun out of control, turning U.S. housing markets white-hot. Then it broke, its financial nuts and bolts seizing up while springs and wires flew out, spreading damage in all directions.

What went wrong? First and foremost, the risks inherent in mortgage lending became so widely dispersed that no one was forced to worry about the quality of any single loan. As shaky mortgages were combined, diluting any problems into a larger pool, the incentive for responsibility was undermined. At every point in the financial system, there was a belief that someone—*someone else*—would catch mistakes and preserve the integrity of the process. The mortgage lender counted on the Wall Street investment banker, who counted on the regulator or the ratings analyst, who assumed global investors were doing their own due diligence. As the process went badly awry, everybody assumed someone else was in control. No one was.

Global investors weren't cognizant of the true risks of the securities they had bought from Wall Street. Investors were awash in cash because global central bankers had opened the money spigots wide in the wake of the dotcom bust, 9/11, and the invasion of Iraq. The stunning economic ascent of China, which had forced prices lower for so many manufactured goods, also had central bankers focused on fighting deflation, which meant keeping interest rates low for a long time. A ballooning U.S. trade deficit, driven by a strong dollar and America's appetite for cheap imports, was also sending a flood of dollars overseas.

The recipients of all those dollars needed some place to put them. At first, U.S. Treasury bonds seemed an easy choice; they were safe and liquid, even if they didn't pay much in interest. But after accumulating hundreds of billions of dollars in low-yielding Treasuries, investors began to worry less about safety and more about returns. On the surface, Wall Street's new designer mortgage securities were an attractive alternative. Investors were told they were safe—at most, a step or two riskier than a U.S. Treasury bond, but with significantly higher returns—which itself should have served as a warning signal to investors. But with more U.S. dollars to invest, the quest for higher returns became more concerted, and investors warmed to increasingly sophisticated and complex mortgage and corporate securities, indifferent to the risks they were taking.

The financial world was stunned when U.S. homeowners began defaulting on their mortgages in record numbers. Some likened it to the mid-1980s, when a boom in loans to Latin American nations (financed largely with Middle Eastern oil wealth) went bust. That financial crisis had taken more than a decade to sort through. Few thought that subprime mortgages from across the United States could have so much in common with those third-world loans of yesteryear.

Still more disconcerting was the notion that the subprime mortgage losses meant investors had badly misjudged the level of risk in all their investments. The mortgage crisis crystallized what had long been troubling many in the financial markets: Assets of all types were overvalued, from Chinese stocks to Las Vegas condominiums. The subprime meltdown began a top-to-bottom reevaluation of the risks inherent in financial markets and, thus, a repricing of all investments, from stocks to insurance. That process would affect every aspect of economic life, from the cost of starting a business to the value of retirees' pensions, for years to come.

Policymakers and regulators had an unappreciated sense of the flaws in the financial system, and those few who felt something was amiss lacked the authority to do anything about it. A deregulatory zeal had overtaken the federal government, including the Federal Reserve, the nation's key regulator. The legal and regulatory fetters that had been placed on financial institutions since the Great Depression had broken. There was a new faith that market forces would impose discipline; lenders didn't need regulators telling them what loans to make or not make. Newly designed global capital standards and the credit rating agencies would substitute for the discipline of the regulators.

Even after mortgage loans started going bad en masse, the confusing mix of federal and state agencies that made up the nation's regulatory structure had difficulty responding. When regulators finally began to speak up about subprime and the other types of mortgage loans that had spun out of control, such lending was already on its way to extinction. What regulators had to say was all but irrelevant.

Yet even the combination of a flawed financial system, cash-flush global investors, and lax regulators could not itself have created the subprime financial shock. The essential final ingredient was hubris: a belief that the ordinary rules of economics and finance no longer applied. Everyone involved—home buyers, mortgage lenders, builders, regulators, ratings agencies, investment bankers, central bankers—believed they had a better formula, used a more accurate model, or would just be luckier than their predecessors. Even the bursting tech stock bubble just a few years earlier seemed to hold no particular lessons for the soaring housing market. This time, the thinking went, things were truly different. Though house prices shot up far faster than household incomes or rents—just as dotcom-era stock prices had left corporate earnings far behind—markets were convinced that, for a variety of reasons, houses weren't like stocks, so they could skyrocket in price without later falling back to Earth, as the Dow and NASDAQ had.

Skyrocketing house prices fed many dreams and papered over many ills. Households long locked out of the American dream finally saw a way in. Although most were forthright and prudent, too many weren't. Borrowers and lenders implicitly or explicitly conspired to fudge or lie on loan applications, dismissing any moral qualms with the thought that appreciating property values would make it all right in the end. Rising house prices would allow homeowners to refinance again and again, freeing cash while keeping mortgage payments low. That meant more fees for lenders as well. Empowered by surging home values, investment bankers invented increasingly sophisticated and complex securities that kept the money flowing into ever-hotter and faster-growing housing markets.

In the end, there was far less difference between houses and stocks than the markets thought. In many communities, houses were being traded like stocks, bought and sold purely on speculation that they would continue to go up. Builders also got the arithmetic wrong as they calculated the number of potential buyers for their new homes. Most of the mistakes made in the tech-stock bubble were repeated in the housing bubble and became painfully obvious in the subsequent bust and crash. The housing market fell into a self-reinforcing vicious cycle as house price declines begat defaults and foreclosures, which begat more house price declines.

It's probably no coincidence that financial crises occur about every ten years. It takes about that long for the collective memory of the previous crisis to fade and confidence to become all-pervasive again. It's human nature. Future financial shocks are assured.

A few naysayers popped up along the way. Some on Wall Street and in banks became visibly uncomfortable as the housing boom and bubble intensified. But it was hard to stand against the tide: Too much money was being made, and if you wanted to keep doing business, you had little choice but to hold your nose. As another Wall Street CEO famously said just before the bust, "As long as the music was playing, you had to get up and dance." A few government officials did some public hand-wringing, but their complaints lacked much force. Perhaps they were hamstrung by their own self-doubts, or perhaps their timing was off. Perhaps history demanded the dramatic and inevitable arrival of the subprime financial shock to finally make the point that it wasn't different this time.

I take some pride in being one of those who warned of the problems developing in the housing and mortgage markets and financial system more broadly, but I was early in expressing my doubts and had lost some credibility by the time the housing market unraveled and the financial shock hit. I certainly also misjudged the scale of what eventually happened. I expected house prices to decline and for Wall Street and investors to take losses, but I never expected the financial system to effectively collapse and precipitate the worst global economic downturn since the 1930s' Great Depression. Indeed, as I was finishing the first version of this book in July 2008, I penned this sentence: "As this is being written, about a year after the subprime financial shock hit, the worst of the crisis appears to be over." This was after the Bear Stearns collapse but before a string of fatal policy errors beginning with the government takeover of Fannie Mae and Freddie Mac, and the collective decision by the Bush Administration and the Federal Reserve to allow Lehman Brothers to go bankrupt.

These mistakes and a few others turned a serious yet manageable financial crisis into an out-of-control financial panic.

Any full assessment of the subprime fiasco must also consider the role of the credit rating agencies. Critics argue that the methods and practices of these firms contributed to the crisis by making exotic mortgage securities seem much safer than they ultimately proved to be. Others see a fatal flaw in the agencies' business model, under which the issues of securities pay the agencies to rate these securities. Three firms dominate the global business of rating credit securities: Moody's, Standard & Poor's, and Fitch. In 2005, Moody's purchased the company I cofounded, and I have been an employee of that firm since then. To avoid any appearance of a conflict of interest, I have no choice but to leave discussion of this facet of the subprime shock to others. The views expressed in this book are mine alone and do not represent those held or endorsed by Moody's. It is also important for you, the reader, to know that I am donating my royalties from the book to a Philadelphia-based nonprofit, The Reinvestment Fund (TRF). TRF invests in inner-city projects in the Northeast United States.

Understanding the roots of the subprime financial shock is necessary to better prepare for the next financial crisis. Policymakers must use its lessons to reevaluate the regulatory framework that oversees the financial system. The Federal Reserve should consider whether its hands-off policy toward asset-price bubbles is appropriate. Bankers must build better systems for assessing and managing risk. Investors must prepare for the wild swings in asset prices that are sure to come, and households must relearn the basic financial principles of thrift and portfolio diversification.

The next financial crisis, however, won't likely involve mortgage loans, credit cards, junk bonds, or even those odd-sounding financial securities. The next crisis will be related to our own federal government's daunting fiscal challenges. The United States is headed inexorably toward record budget deficits, measured both in total dollars and in proportion to the economy. Global investors are already growing disaffected with U.S. debt, and even the Treasury will have a difficult time finding buyers for all the bonds it will be trying to sell if nothing changes soon. Hopefully, the lessons learned from the subprime financial shock will be the catalyst for making better choices regarding taxes and government spending that we collectively will have to make in the not-too-distant future.

This book isn't filled with juicy financial secrets; it might not even spin a terribly dramatic yarn. Instead, it is an attempt to make sense of what has been a complex and confusing period, even for a professional economist with 25 years at his craft. I hope you find it organized well enough to come away with a better understanding of what has happened. Although nearly every event feels like the most important ever when you are close to it, I'm confident that the subprime financial shock will be judged the most significant financial event in our nation's economic history.

1

Subprime Précis

Until recent events, few outside the real estate industry had even heard of a subprime mortgage. But this formerly obscure financial vehicle has grabbed the world's attention because of its ravaging effect on the global economy and financial system.

Simply defined, a subprime mortgage is just a loan made to someone with a weak or troubled credit history. Historically, it has been a peripheral financial phenomenon, a marginal market involving few lenders and few borrowers. However, subprime home buyers unable to make good on their mortgage payments set off a financial avalanche in 2007 that pushed the global economy into its worst downturn since the Great Depression of the 1930s. Financial markets and the economy will ultimately recover, but the subprime financial shock will go down as a major inflection point in economic history.

Genesis

The fuse for the subprime financial shock was set early in this decade, following the tech-stock bust, 9/11, and the invasions of Afghanistan and Iraq. With stock markets plunging and the nation in shock after the attack on the World Trade Center, the Federal Reserve Board (the Fed) slashed interest rates. By summer 2003, the federal funds rate—the one rate the Fed controls directly—was at a record low. Fearing that their own economies would slump under the weight of the faltering U.S. economy, other major central banks around the world soon followed the Fed's lead.

In normal times, central bankers worry that lowering interest rates too much might spark inflation. If they worried less this time, a major factor was China. Joining the World Trade Organization in November 2001 not only ratified China's arrival in the global market, but it lowered trade barriers and accelerated a massive shift of global manufacturing to the formerly closed communist mainland. As low-cost Chinese-made goods flooded markets, prices fell nearly everywhere and inflation seemed a remote concern. Policymakers even worried publicly about deflation, encouraging central banks to push rates to unprecedented lows.

China's explosive growth, driven by manufacturing and exports, boosted global demand for oil and other commodities. Prices surged higher. This pushed up the U.S. trade deficit, as hundreds of billions of dollars flowed overseas to China, the Middle East, Russia, and other commodity-producing nations. Many of these dollars returned to the United States as investments, as Asian and Middle Eastern producers parked their cash in the world's safest, biggest economy. At first they mainly bought U.S. Treasury bonds, which produced a low but safe return. Later, in the quest for higher returns, they expanded to riskier financial instruments, including bonds backed by subprime mortgages.

Frenzied Innovation

The two factors of extraordinarily low interest rates and surging global investor demand combined with the growth of Internet technology to produce a period of intense financial innovation. Designing new ways to invest had long been a Wall Street specialty: Since the 1970s, bankers and traders had regularly unveiled new futures, options, and derivatives on government and corporate debt— even bonds backed by residential mortgage payments. But now the

financial innovation machine went into high gear. Wall Street produced a blizzard of increasingly complex new securities.

These included bonds based on pools of mortgages, auto loans,
credit card debt, and commercial bank loans, sliced and sorted
according to their presumed levels of risk. Sometimes these securities
were resliced and rebundled yet again or packaged into risk-swapping
agreements whose terms remained arcane to all but their authors.

Yet the underlying structure had a basic theme. Financial engineers start with a simple credit agreement, such as a home mortgage
or a credit card. Not so long ago, such arrangements were indeed
simple, involving an individual borrower and a single lender. The
bank loaned you money to buy a house or a car, and you paid back the
bank over time. This changed when Wall Street bankers realized that
many individual mortgages or other loans could be tied together and
"securitized"—transformed from a simple debt agreement into a
security that could be traded, just as with other bonds and stocks,
among investors worldwide.

Now a monthly mortgage payment no longer made a simple trip
from a homeowner's checking account to the bank. Instead, it was
pooled with hundreds of other individual mortgage payments, forming a cash stream that flowed to the investors who owned the new
mortgage-backed bonds. The originator of the loan—a bank, a mortgage broker, or whoever—might still collect the cash and handle the
paperwork, but it was otherwise out of the picture.

With mortgages or consumer loans now bundled as tradable
securities, Wall Street's second idea was to slice them up so they carried different levels of risk. Instead of pooling all the returns from a
given bundle of mortgages, for example, securities were tailored so
that investors could receive payments based on how much risk they
were willing to take. Those seeking a safe investment were paid first,
but at a lower rate of return. Those willing to gamble most were paid
last but earned a substantially higher return. At least, that was how it
worked in theory.

By mid-decade, such financial innovation was in full frenzy. Any asset with a cash flow seemed to qualify for such slice-and-dice treatment. Residential mortgage loans, merger-and-acquisition financing, and even tolls generated by public bridges and highways were securitized in this way. As designing, packaging, and reselling such newfangled investments became a major source of profit for Wall Street, bankers and salesmen successfully marketed them to investors from Perth to Peoria.

The benefits of securitization were substantial. In the old days, credit could be limited by local lenders' size or willingness to take risks. A homeowner or business might have trouble getting a loan simply because the local bank's balance sheet was fully subscribed. But with securitization, lenders could originate loans, resell them to investors, and use the proceeds to make more loans. As long as there were willing investors anywhere in the world, the credit tap could never run dry.

On the other side, securitization gave global investors a much broader array of potential assets and let them precisely calibrate the amount of risk in their portfolios. Government regulators and policymakers also liked securitization because it appeared to spread risk broadly, which made a financial crisis less likely. Or so they thought.

Awash in funds from growing world trade, global investors gobbled up the new securities. Reassured by Wall Street, many believed they could successfully manage their risks while collecting healthy returns. Yet as investors flocked to this market, their returns grew smaller relative to the risks they took. Just as at any bazaar or auction, the more buyers that crowd in, the less likely they are to find a bargain. The more investors there were seeking high yields, the more those yields fell. Eventually, a high-risk security—say, a bond issued by the government of Venezuela, or a subprime mortgage loan—brought barely more than a U.S. Treasury bond or a mortgage insured by Fannie Mae.

Starved for greater returns, investors began using an old financial trick for turning small profits into large ones: leverage—that is, investing with borrowed money. With interest rates low all around the world, they could borrow cheaply and thus magnify returns many times over. Investors could also sell insurance to each other, collecting premiums in exchange for a promise to cover the losses on any securities that went bad. Because that seemed a remote possibility, such insurance seemed like an easy way to make extra money.

As time went on, the market for these new securities became increasingly esoteric. Derivatives such as collateralized debt obligations, or CDOs, were particularly attractive. A CDO is a bondlike security whose cash flow is derived from other bonds, which, in turn, might be backed by mortgages or other loans. Evaluating the risk of such instruments was difficult, if not impossible; yet investors took comfort in the high ratings given by analysts at the ratings agencies, who presumably were in the know. To further allay any worries, investors could even buy insurance on the securities.

Housing Boom

Global investors were particularly enamored of securities backed by U.S. residential mortgage loans. American homeowners were historically reliable, paying on their mortgages even in tough economic times. Certainly, some cities or regions had seen falling house prices and rising mortgage defaults, but these were rare. Indeed, since the Great Depression, house prices nationwide had not declined in a single year. And U.S. housing produced trillions of dollars in mortgage loans, a huge source of assets to securitize.

With funds pouring into mortgage-related securities, mortgage lenders avidly courted home buyers. Borrowing costs plunged and mortgage credit was ample. Housing was as affordable as it had been since just after World War II, particularly in areas such as California and the Northeast, where homeownership had long been a stretch for most renters. First-time home buyers also benefited as the Internet transformed the mortgage industry, cutting transaction costs and boosting competition. New loan products were invented for house-holds that had historically had little access to standard forms of credit, such as mortgages. Borrowers with less than perfect credit history—or no credit history—could now get a loan. Of course, a subprime borrower needed a sizable down payment and a sturdy income, but even that changed quickly.

Home buying took on an added sheen after 9/11, as Americans grew wary of travel, with the hassles of air passenger screening and code-orange alerts. Tourist destinations struggled. Americans were staying home more, and they wanted those homes to be bigger and nicer. Many traded up.

As home sales took off, prices began to rise more quickly, particu-larly in highly regulated areas of the country. Builders couldn't put up houses quickly enough in California, Florida, and other coastal areas, which had tough zoning restrictions, environmental requirements, and a long and costly permitting process.

The house price gains were modest at first, but they appeared very attractive compared with a still-lagging stock market and the rock-bottom interest rates banks were offering on savings accounts. Home buyers saw a chance to make outsized returns on homes by taking on big mortgages. Besides, interest payments on mortgage loans were tax deductible, and since the mid-1990s, even capital gains on most home sales haven't been taxed.

It didn't take long for speculation to infect housing markets. Flip-pers—housing speculators looking to buy and sell quickly at a large profit—grew active. Churning was especially rampant in condo-minium, second-home, and vacation-home markets, where a flipper could always rent a unit if it didn't sell quickly. Some of these investors were disingenuous or even fraudulent when applying for loans, telling lenders they planned to live in the units so they could obtain better mortgage terms. Flippers were often facilitated by home builders who turned a blind eye in the rush to meet ever-rising home sales projections.

Speculation extended beyond flippers, however. Nearly all home-owners were caught up in the idea that housing was a great invest-ment, possibly the best they could make. The logic was simple: House prices had risen strongly in the recent past, so they would continue to rise strongly in the future.

Remodeling and renovations surged. By mid-decade, housing markets across much of the country were in a frenzied boom. House sales, construction, and prices were all shattering records. Prices more than doubled in such far-flung places as Providence, Rhode Island; Naples, Florida; Minneapolis, Minnesota; Tucson, Arizona; Salt Lake City, Utah; and Sacramento, California.

The housing boom did bring an important benefit: It jump-started the broader economy out of its early-decade malaise. Not only were millions of jobs created to build, sell, and finance homes, but homeowners were also measurably wealthier. Indeed, the seeming financial windfall for lower- and middle- American homeowners was arguably unprecedented. The home was by far the largest asset on most households' balance sheet.

Moreover, all this newfound wealth could be readily and cheaply converted into cash. Homeowners became adept at borrowing against the increased equity in their homes, refinancing into larger mortgages, and taking on big home equity lines. This gave the hous-ing boom even more economic importance as the extra cash financed a spending splurge.

Extra spending was precisely what the central bankers at the Fed-eral Reserve had in mind when they were slashing interest rates. After all, the point of adjusting monetary policy is to raise or lower the economy's speed by regulating the flow of credit through the financial system and economy. Nevertheless, by mid-2004, the booming hous-ing market and strong economy convinced policymakers it was time to throttle back by raising rates.

Housing Bust

Signs that the boom was ending appeared in spring 2005, in places such as Boston and San Diego. After several years of surging house prices and nearly a year of rising interest rates, many home buyers simply could no longer afford the outsized mortgages needed to buy. Homes that had been so affordable just a few years earlier were again out of reach.

The frenzy began to cool. Not only did bidding wars among home buyers vanish, but many sellers couldn't get their list prices as the number of properties for sale began to mount. Moreover, many sellers found it extraordinarily painful to cut prices. Flippers feared the loss of their capital, and other homeowners with big mortgages couldn't take less than they needed to pay off their existing mortgage loans. Realtors were loath to advise clients to lower prices, lest they destroy belief in the boom that had powered enormous realty fees and bonuses.

Underwriting Collapses

As they anxiously watched loan origination volumes top out, mortgage lenders searched for ways to keep the boom going. Adjustable-rate mortgage loans (ARMs) were a particularly attractive way to expand the number of potential home buyers. ARMs allowed for low monthly payments, at least for awhile.

Although borrowers have had access to such loans since the early 1980s, new versions of the ARM came with extraordinarily low initial rates, known as teasers. In most cases, the teaser rate was fixed for two years, after which it quickly adjusted higher, usually every six months, until it matched higher prevailing interest rates. Many of the homeowners who took on these exploding ARM loans were among the first to lose their homes in foreclosure.

Lenders also began to require smaller down payments. To allow home buyers to avoid paying mortgage insurance (generally required for large loans with low down payments), lenders counseled borrowers to take out second mortgages. For many such borrowers, the amount of the first and second mortgage together equaled the market value of the home, meaning there was no cushion in case that value declined. Moreover, although payments on the second mortgage may have been initially lower than the cost of the insurance, most loans also had adjustable rates, which moved higher as interest rates rose.

Such creative lending worked to support home sales for awhile, but it also further raised house prices. Rising prices together with higher interest rates (thanks to continued Fed tightening) undermined house affordability even more. Growing still more creative—or more desperate—lenders offered loans without requiring borrowers to prove they had sufficient income or savings to meet the payments. Such "stated income" loans had been available in the past, but only to a very few self-employed professionals. Now they went mainstream, picking up a new nickname among mortgage-industry insiders: liars' loans.

By 2006, most subprime borrowers were taking out adjustable-rate loans carrying teaser rates that would reset in two years, potentially setting up the borrowers for a major payment shock. Most of those borrowers had put down little or no money of their own on their homes, meaning they had little to lose. Many had overstated their incomes on the loan documents, often with their lenders' tacit approval. By any traditional standard, such lending would have been viewed as a prescription for financial disaster. But lenders argued that as long as house prices rose, homeowners could build enough home equity to refinance before disaster struck.

For their part, home appraisers were working to ensure that this came true. Typically, their appraisals were based on cursory drive-by inspections and comparisons with nearby homes that had recently been sold or refinanced—in some cases, homes they themselves had appraised. Lenders, meanwhile, were happy to see their subprime borrowers refinance; most subprime loans carried hefty penalties for paying off the mortgage early, and that meant more fee income for lenders.

Regulators and Rating Agencies

Federal and state regulators may have been nervous about runaway mortgage lending, but they failed to do much about it. They certainly had reason to worry; their own surveys showed that most mortgage borrowers understood little about the financial obligations they were taking on. Many ARM borrowers did not know their mortgage payments were likely to increase, much less when they would adjust higher or by how much.

Meanwhile, hamstrung government regulators couldn't keep up with lenders who were constantly devising ways to elude oversight. Some of the most egregious lending was done not by traditional mortgage lenders, such as commercial banks and savings and loans, but by real estate investment trusts (REITs). The Securities and Exchange Commission (SEC), the agency that regulates stock and bond sales, also regulates REITs. Yet the SEC was focused on insider trading at the time, not predatory mortgage lending. An even more important factor was a philosophical distaste for regulation that seemed to pervade the Federal Reserve, the nation's most important banking regulator. Without Fed leadership, the agencies that monitor smaller corners of the banking system, such as the Office of the Comptroller of the Currency, the Federal Deposit Insurance Corporation, and Office of Thrift Supervision, were deterred from taking action. State regulators also had a say, but they were no match for a globally wired financial industry.

Regulators' reluctance to intervene in the mortgage market may have also been based on their trust in the acumen of the rating agencies. These companies provide opinions about the creditworthiness of securities and are paid by the issuers of these securities. Global banking regulators had only recently given the agencies' opinions a quasi-official status, by making their opinions count toward determining whether banks had an appropriate amount of capital to safeguard depositors. The rating agencies were also the only institutions outside of the mortgage or banking business with enough data and information to make an informed judgment about the securities' safety. If the agencies gave them an A-rating (meaning that they saw very little chance of default), regulators weren't going to argue.

Yet the rating agencies badly misjudged the risks. Poor-quality data and information led to serious miscalculations. The agencies were not required to check what the originators or servicers of the mortgage loans told them, and this information was increasingly misleading. The agencies also had the difficult task of developing models to evaluate the risk of newfangled loan schemes that had never been through a housing slump or economic recession. Without that experience, the models were not up to the task they were asked to perform. The ratings were supposed to account for the range of things that could go wrong, from rising unemployment to falling house prices, but what went wrong was much worse than they had anticipated.

Delusional Home Builders

Despite the developing stress lines, home builders retained their congenital optimism about the housing market. Most could afford it; they still had plenty of cash and bank lines built up during the boom. So they kept on building, putting up a record number of homes through summer 2006. The home-building industry had been transformed during the previous decade, as large, publicly traded firms took market share away from smaller, privately held builders. The big builders now did most of the construction in the largest markets. Observers thought this would mean more disciplined building; the large builders would have better market information, and shareholders would demand that builders pull back at the first sign of weakness. That, too, turned out to be a delusion.

The big publicly held builders and their stockholders showed no such discipline. They ignored the weakening market, putting more shovels into the ground and projecting future sales growth to keep their stock prices up. When challenged by investment analysts or reporters, construction executives proffered theories about why the housing market would remain strong. Some said lots of immigrants were coming to the U.S. and would keep buying no matter what; unfortunately, after 9/11, there were fewer immigrants. There were also variations on the old saw about land—that they're not making more of it. True, in some places developable land was in increasingly short supply; many beachside resorts are short on spare lots. But, of course, developers don't need much vacant land to put up a condo tower, many of which were sprouting skyward along much of the nation's coasts.

Undaunted, some builders even established their own mortgage lending affiliates to ensure that credit kept flowing even if traditional lenders became skittish. These affiliates were particularly aggressive, even offering down payments to buyers as gifts. (They recouped the cost in a higher house price.) And if that still failed to entice purchasers, the builders could offer a marble counter top, a bigger deck, or a built-out basement to close a deal. Yet despite all their efforts, as spring 2006 turned to summer, fewer deals closed and cancellations ballooned.

Lenders Cave

Eventually, the mortgage lenders caved. With housing affordability collapsing, there was no longer a way to squeeze marginal home buyers into mortgages—at least, not without some disingenuous sleight of hand. Not only was it tough to make a new loan, but a growing number of recent borrowers, mostly flippers, weren't even making their first few mortgage payments. Even though the lenders didn't own the loans (they had already been sold for securitization), the terms of those deals left lenders on the hook for any losses that occurred soon after the sale. This was a modest attempt to dissuade fraud. Now these early-payment defaults became a call to arms for nervous regulators, who finally took action and issued new rules to limit some of the more aggressive types of lending.

As their losses began to mount, some mortgage lenders sold out and found buyers for their businesses in still-confident investment banks. The Wall Street firms calculated that the loan originators' losses would be short term and that they themselves would be well compensated in the long run through the extra securitization business their ownership would bring in. But by the end of 2006, even the investment banks began to lose heart, and loss-plagued loan companies found nobody wanted to buy them. The only recourse for many lenders was bankruptcy and, ultimately, liquidation.

Subprime Shock

Global investors were very slow to notice the mounting troubles in the U.S. housing and mortgage markets. After some volatility early in 2007, when the Chinese stock market briefly stumbled, global stock and bond prices rocketed to new highs. But fissures were developing in some esoteric corners of the financial markets, such as the credit default swap market (a market for insurance contracts on bonds—mostly corporate bonds, but also mortgage-backed bonds), but this meant little to all but the handful of investors who traded in them.

But by late spring, the cracks could no longer be ignored. A string of venerable investment banks, including the now-defunct Bear Stearns, announced that some of their hedge funds, which had invested aggressively in mortgage-related securities, were hemorrhaging cash and facing failure. Investors weren't prepared for the news. Most global stock, bond, and real estate markets were trading near record highs, reflecting investors' complacent view of the risks involved. As the extent of the financial system's exposure to subprime mortgages came into relief in the following weeks, these same investors began running for the door. By summer 2007, the subprime financial shock was reverberating across the globe.

Some parts of the market for mortgage-backed securities effectively shut down. Bonds backed by the Federal Housing Administration (which is part of the federal government) and Fannie Mae and Freddie Mac (which at the time were publicly traded companies but have since been nationalized and are now owned by taxpayers) continued to be issued. But banks abruptly stopped issuing other mortgage-backed bonds, especially those backed by subprime loans. At the peak of the boom, such bonds accounted for half of all mortgage originations.

Money Stops Flowing

The mortgage securities market wasn't the only casualty of the subprime shock. Very quickly, global money markets began to suffer as well, thanks to a complex chain of financial links that few outside these markets had noticed or understood previously. Over the course of several years, major U.S. and European money center banks had established so-called structured investment vehicles, or SIVs. These are entities set up to invest in a wide range of assets, including subprime mortgage securities, with money they raise by selling short-term commercial paper. Commercial paper (which businesses have historically used to purchase inventory that will soon be sold or for other short-term financing needs) is a mainstay of the money markets because it is regarded as both safe and liquid. Millions of savers who use money markets as an alternative to passbook bank accounts or certificates of deposit are investing in commercial paper, whether they know it or not.

In a time of low interest rates and easy credit, SIVs could easily and cheaply issue short-term commercial paper and use the proceeds to buy longer-term mortgage-backed securities. Now, however, money market funds and other investors began to lose faith in the commercial paper SIVs issued. The SIVs were effectively out of business.

It is a truism to say that financial markets work on trust. Each party to a deal must trust that the other side will honor its commitments.

Lenders must trust that their loans will be paid back; investors must trust that they will see a return on their investment. But no market depends more on trust than a money market, in which the transactions are large and are held for short periods of time. Without trust, money markets quickly break down. By late summer 2007, trust in the SIVs had evaporated. Investors shunned their commercial paper, forcing the SIVs to sell their assets at increasingly distressed prices, thus accelerating the downdraft in financial markets generally.

Short-term lending within the global banking system was also disrupted, as a string of banks began to report losses on their mortgage-related holdings. The distress appeared particularly acute in Europe, as several prominent German and British institutions stumbled. But these high-profile affairs were assumed to be just the tip of the iceberg. With U.S. mortgage security holdings so widely dispersed, and with little information about who was suffering losses and to what extent, banks shrank from doing business with each other. Fewer thought it prudent to borrow or lend, and those that would demanded substantially higher interest rates to compensate for the greater risk they now believed existed.

Banking Buckles

Pressure now mounted on the banks. Not only were they struggling to raise funds in money markets and to straighten out their troubled SIVs, but their mortgage holdings also suddenly turned toxic. They couldn't even count their losses because trading had collapsed in the mortgage securities market; thus, pricing their mortgage assets was all but impossible. Banks began feverishly writing down the value of these assets, although it was unclear how large those write-downs should be.

The banks were further hurt as investor angst over mortgage credit quality spilled over into corporate credit, particularly for lower-rated loans and bonds. These "junk" loans and bonds had financed a wave of leveraged corporate buyouts and had been lucrative for the banks, but they were supposed to be temporary; banks expected to quickly resell them to investors. Now investors stopped buying, so the loans were stuck on the banks' balance sheets. That put the banks at significant risk if the businesses involved in these leveraged buyouts began to falter, a growing likelihood in a weakening economy. At the very least, these loans tied up scarce capital—the dollars regulators require banks to set aside in case of credit problems. This impairs the bank's capability to extend credit to other borrowers. A bank's capability to lend depends on how much capital it has; less capital means less lending.

Other parts of the credit market were now feeling the stress, as investors grew wary of all risk. Prices for lower-quality bonds backed by auto and credit card loans fell sharply, as did prices for the commercial mortgage securities used to finance the purchase and construction of office towers, shopping malls, and hotels. Bond issuance declined substantially, with junk corporate bond issuance stalling and even well-performing emerging economies pulling back on the debt they were willing and able to sell.

Bond Insurers at the Brink

Financial guarantors faced especially sharp problems. These institutions sell insurance on bonds, guaranteeing to make investors whole if the bonds ever default. Providing insurance on municipal bonds has long been their principal business; because state and local governments almost never default, it has been very profitable, if a bit dull.

The government agencies that issue municipal bonds, from the Port Authority of New York to the state of California, are willing to insure their bonds only if such insurance costs less than the added interest they would pay with no insurance. The formula normally works because the guarantors have their own top-grade seal of approval, which the pension funds and endowments that invest in risk-free assets such as insured municipal bonds demand.

Now, however, it appeared that the guarantors had undermined their own financial viability by expanding beyond their core municipal insurance business. In search of bigger profits, the guarantors wrote hundreds of billions of dollars in insurance contracts in the credit default swap market, a market in which investors buy and sell insurance on a wide array of bonds and CDOs. They promised to compensate buyers if their mortgage-related bonds ever defaulted. As the calamity in the housing and mortgage markets unfolded, these payouts began to look as if they would cut deeply into the insurers' capital base. The most infamous of these insurers is AIG, whose gargantuan miscalculations in the CDS market ultimately cost U.S. taxpayers hundreds of billions of dollars. The retention bonuses it gave to many of the same CDS traders who made the failed bets came to epitomize the worst of the hubris and greed on Wall Street.

The rating agencies that rate the bond insurers' debt warned the guarantors to shore up their capital or see their ratings downgraded. Downgrades would almost certainly put the insurers out of business, rendering their insurance worthless. Investors with a mandate to purchase only risk-free assets would have no choice but to sell their insured municipal holdings, at whatever price they could get.

The formerly staid muni market launched into turmoil as the odds of this scenario rose. Rock-solid municipalities found themselves in the unlikely position of having to pay interest rates reserved for only high-risk borrowers. Waves from the subprime financial shock had reached so far that they had even engulfed state and local governments.

Liquidity-Squeezed Broker-Dealers

The financial shock hit Wall Street's so-called broker-dealers in spring 2008, when rumors swirled over their potential liquidity problems. These are investment firms that buy and sell securities both for customers and for themselves. They often are highly leveraged, borrowing to make big bets on securities ranging from U.S. Treasury bonds to exotic and risky securities backed by mortgages. When they bet right, their profits can be huge—but when they bet wrong, they can end up like Bear Stearns.

Bear Stearns bet big on the residential mortgage market. It not only issued mortgage securities, but it had acquired mortgage-lending firms that originated the loans that went into those securities. Bear "made a market" in mortgage securities, meaning it would either buy or sell, whichever a customer wanted. It prospered during the housing bubble, but as the housing and mortgage markets collapsed, each of Bear's various business segments soured in turn, and confidence in the firm's viability weakened. Unlike commercial banks that collect funds from depositors, a broker-dealer relies on other financial institutions to lend it the money it invests. If those other institutions lose faith and begin withdrawing their money, the broker-dealer's only options are filing bankruptcy or—as in Bear Stearns' case—selling out.

Over a tumultuous weekend in mid-March, the Federal Reserve engineered the sale of Bear Stearns to JPMorgan Chase. The Fed acted out of fear of what a bankruptcy could have meant for the financial system, given Bear's extensive relationships with banks, hedge funds, and other institutions around the world. Policymakers were legitimately worried that the financial system would freeze. To make the deal work, the Fed had agreed to absorb any losses on tens of billions of dollars in risky Bear Stearns securities that JPMorgan Chase had acquired in its takeover of the failed firm. The Fed also established new sources of cash for these hard-pressed institutions to forestall a similar fate befalling another one.

Financial Panic

The financial turmoil experienced a brief respite in summer 2008. The weak economy got a lift from the rebate checks taxpayers received as part of the first economic stimulus package quickly cobbled together by the Bush Administration and the Democratic

Congress. A few large financial institutions reported decent earnings, suggesting perhaps that with the resolution of Bear Stearns, the coast was clearing. Unfortunately, it was the proverbial calm before the storm.

Things took a dramatic turn for the worse when in early September, policymakers stumbled badly, beginning with the government takeover of Fannie Mae and Freddie Mac. Fannie and Freddie were publicly traded companies with a federal government charter to promote homeownership by providing ample and cheap credit to minorities and other disadvantaged groups. This became difficult to do during the height of the housing boom because subprime lenders were willing to provide even more—and cheaper—credit. Fannie and Freddie's share of mortgage lending fell sharply. The companies fought back; they had to, given the requirements of their charters and the demands of their profit-hungry shareholders. They didn't push all the way into the subprime market, but by the peak of the housing bubble, they had become sizable players in risky parts of the mortgage market. And although the dollar amount of this lending was small compared to the rest of their operations, it was large compared to their capital base. The companies' regulator had historically not required them to hold a lot of capital because they had made only safe mortgage loans; they didn't increase their capital commensurately when they moved into riskier lending.

As losses at Fannie and Freddie began to mount, their stock- and bondholders—including some of the largest and bluest of blue-chip institutional investors in the world—grew increasingly nervous. Fannie's and Freddie's stock prices fell, and their borrowing costs began to rise, increasing mortgage rates for home buyers. By the first week of September 2008, the Bush Administration felt it had no choice but to take over Fannie Mae and Freddie Mac. The Treasury Department put them into conservatorship. Shareholders were wiped out, and although bondholders were protected, the action crystallized in the minds of global investors that all financial institutions, no matter how large, were at significant threat of failure. Fannie and Freddie

probably would have been considered insolvent if their assets and liabilities were valued at market prices, but they still had sufficient regulatory capital, the amount of capital necessary to satisfy regulatory
requirements. In past financial crisis, policymakers had showed forbearance to large institutions in similar situations—Citigroup was
likely insolvent during the early 1990s Savings & Loan crisis but was
not taken over by regulators—so as not to unnerve investors. Treasury
Secretary Paulson didn't show the same forbearance with Fannie and
Freddie, and this spooked investors.

Investors' fears boiled over when policymakers allowed broker-
dealer Lehman Brothers to fail one week later. Lehman's problem
wasn't a lack of cash—it could use the credit facility the Fed had
established after the Bear Stearns collapse for just such a purpose.
But no other financial institution wanted to do business with a firm
that could soon be out of business. Hedge funds that had used
Lehman to execute their trades no longer did so, and other, bigger
financial institutions forced Lehman to put up more funds as collateral just in case something went wrong. A year earlier, Lehman
Brothers had been at the center for the financial system, but in what
seemed like just a few days, the system had shut Lehman out. The
company was careening toward bankruptcy.

The Treasury and the Federal Reserve worked feverishly to find a
buyer for Lehman, as they had done for Bear Stearns, but no one
stepped forward. Lehman's fate was in the hands of the Treasury and
the Fed. The Fed argued that it couldn't help because Lehman didn't
have enough assets to provide the collateral necessary to get a Fed
loan; by its charter, the Fed could provide only a fully collateralized
loan. The Treasury also said no, arguing that it couldn't bail out everyone, and the financial system had plenty of time, given the Bear collapse, to prepare for a Lehman failure.

Not forestalling a Lehman bankruptcy was a mistake; not everyone was prepared. The Reserve Primary Fund, one of the nation's
oldest and largest money market funds, had invested heavily in

Lehman debt. Lehman's bankruptcy forced them to write off that investment. The resulting losses caused them to break the buck: The value of the fund's assets fell below what it owed its investors. This was too much to bear for many mom-and-pop investors, who thought a money fund was as safe as putting their money in the mattress; they began withdrawing their funds. Money funds that are large investors in commercial paper—the short-term IOUs of major businesses— had no choice but to stop buying CP. What's more, they were forced to sell CP to meet the redemptions. Large businesses were immediately scrambling for ways to finance their basic operations. Equity investors realized that no business was immune from the fallout of the mounting credit crunch, and stock prices plunged.

The entire financial system was on the precipice of collapse. A rattled Treasury Secretary Paulson and Fed Chairman Bernanke came before Congress with a plan to save the system. The idea was for taxpayers to put up $700 billion in a Troubled Asset Relief Fund to buy the banking system's toxic assets. Neither the need for the $700 billion TARP nor how the money was to be used and overseen was well explained. Confusion circulated over just how purchasing distressed mortgage loans and securities would be conducted and why this would quell the financial panic. With taxpayers incensed that they were being asked to bail out bankers who had made terrible mistakes, in late September, Congress failed to muster enough votes to pass the TARP legislation. Financial markets were roiled. Congress passed TARP a few days later because they couldn't ignore the market turmoil, but the collective psyche had been badly damaged. There was no longer time to begin asset purchases, and the TARP monies were used instead to make direct capital infusions into the teetering financial institutions. Taxpayers now owned big stakes in the nation's biggest financial institutions.

Although TARP funds weren't being used for asset purchases, it was widely expected that they eventually would be. Investors were thus shocked when Secretary Paulson announced in November 2008 that the TARP fund would not be used for this purpose after all.

Depressed asset prices fell even more. If the government wasn't going to buy these assets, no one would. The collateral damage from this decision was the near-collapse of Citigroup, which held hundreds of billions in these bad loans and securities. Ironically, the only way to avert this calamity was for the Federal Reserve to guarantee Citi's troubled assets, the same assets the Treasury had decided not to buy.

A string of policy errors had turned a severe yet manageable financial crisis into an inherently unpredictable and even uncontrollable financial panic. The longer the panic continued, the darker the economic outlook became.

The Great Recession

With the entire financial system hemorrhaging losses, and with every corner of the credit markets in disarray, loans to consumers, businesses, and even state and local governments became scarcer and more costly. Banks aggressively ratcheted up their lending standards; borrowers who normally were considered good credits and could readily get a loan, now could not. Not only was a subprime loan out of the question, but even prime borrowers were struggling to get credit.

Without credit, home sales buckled, and subprime borrowers who had hoped to refinance before their mortgage payments exploded higher could not do so. Foreclosure seemed the only option. Inventories of unsold homes surged and house prices collapsed.

Commercial property markets froze as tighter bank underwriting and problems in the commercial mortgage securities market undermined deals. Just a year earlier, transaction volumes and real estate prices had been at record highs. Now property deals could not be consummated, weighing on commercial real estate prices and impairing developers' ability to finance new projects.

Even small and midsize companies in far-flung businesses completely unrelated to housing or mortgage finance found themselves in tough negotiations, with lenders demanding more stringent and costly terms. Financing investment and hiring was suddenly more difficult. Credit is the mother's milk of a well-functioning economy, and with credit no longer flowing, the economy crumbled.

Previously stalwart stock investors, who had held on admirably through much of the turmoil in the credit markets, capitulated. Financial shares of commercial and investment banks, mortgage insurers, and financial guarantors collapsed. The financial system's problems were daunting when the economy was still growing; with the economy in a full-blown downturn, they were overwhelming. The massive losses financial institutions had already recognized on their mortgage holdings were now wholly inadequate. Shares in nonfinancial companies were crushed as investors factored in the implications of a worldwide downturn on corporate earnings. Stock prices that were at all-time highs in late 2007 had been halved by early 2009.

The carnage in the financial system convinced businesses that they needed to batten down the hatches. It was quickly becoming a matter of survival, as sales and prices fell, cash got tight, and getting a loan became all but impossible. Unemployment, which had started 2007 at just over 4%, had nearly doubled to more than 8% by the start of 2009. It seemed headed to double digits. To preserve cash, many businesses also required employees who still had jobs to cut their hours and even their pay. Travel budgets were slashed and investment plans shelved. Despite businesses' best efforts, corporate bankruptcies rose rapidly.

The massive job losses, cracked nest eggs, and financial turmoil were too much for households to bear; consumer confidence plunged to record lows. Christmas 2008 was about the worst Christmas for retailers in a quarter-century, and the automakers were suffering with sales they hadn't seen since World War II. All this made businesses even more nervous, prompting more cutting. A self-reinforcing vicious cycle had set it. This was the worst economic downturn since the Great Depression. There wouldn't be endless breadlines and the mass exodus of homeless families as in the 1930s, but the downturn was resulting in tremendous financial suffering. It was the Great Recession.

2

Sizing Up Subprime

Imagining how something as obscure as a subprime mortgage loan could have brought the global financial system to its knees and pushed the U.S. economy into a deep recession might be hard. It's particularly strange because such loans, designed for people with a dark mark on their credit records, were, at most, marginal financial products for most of their quarter-century history.

Yet the word *subprime* has come to stand for something much bigger: an unprecedented, broad-based erosion of credit standards. During the subprime lending frenzy, practically anyone could get a mortgage. Loans were streamlined, stripped of most controls, and offered freely under conditions that would have given most traditional bankers nightmares. Lenders even handed checks to people without requiring proof that they had a job or the income necessary to pay back the loan. The subprime phenomenon grew far beyond home mortgages, to include auto loans, credit cards, and even student loans.

Despite the clear risks, lenders also no longer required borrowers to obtain mortgage insurance. Such insurance used to be required of anyone attempting to buy a home without a substantial down payment. Instead, lenders advised borrowers to skirt the insurance requirement by taking out two loans: a first mortgage small enough not to need insurance, and a second to cover the rest of the purchase price. The borrowers' incentives were clear: Payments on the second mortgage were less than the insurance—at least for awhile.

A requirement that borrowers save for the expenses of home ownership also fell by the wayside. Lenders no longer required an escrow account for property taxes, which were rapidly escalating with housing values. The same applied to homeowners' insurance, which was growing more expensive, particularly in storm-prone coastal areas.

Mortgages grew more complex, evolving from plain-vanilla fixed-rate loans into myriad adjustable-rate and variable-payment form loans. Adjustable-rate mortgages (ARMs) that included only interest in the monthly payments—even loans in which such payments didn't cover the interest, with the difference added back to the principal—became increasingly common. Only someone adept at financial planning and spreadsheets could reasonably map out what these loans meant for a homeowner's future mortgage bill.

Examining the terms under which home buyers were able to get loans in the housing boom is essential to understanding why so many are now losing their homes. The smorgasbord of terms offered to borrowers during the boom is confusing but necessary to sort through.

Government Versus Private

The menu of mortgages available to home buyers begins with those the government offers. The government plays a surprisingly large role in the nation's housing market; more than 40% of all mortgage loans outstanding have some form of federal backing.[1]

Washington supports mortgage lending most directly through the Federal Housing Administration (FHA) and the Veterans Administration (VA).[2] These agencies don't make loans themselves; they insure lenders against default. In exchange, the agencies impose some modest standards covering down payments, income, and other conditions. Despite the easy terms, FHA and VA lending faded to a trickle during the housing boom, as private subprime lenders offered borrowers much more attractive terms. More recently, the agencies have made a comeback as subprime lending has evaporated and as policymakers have expanded the FHA's lending authority.

Government's role in the housing market is also evident in its relationship with Fannie Mae and Freddie Mac. The Federal National Mortgage Association (Fannie Mae, for short) was established during the Great Depression to improve the flow of mortgage credit and increase home ownership. The Federal Home Loan Mortgage Corp. (Freddie Mac) was set up in 1970 to do essentially the same thing: to provide competition to Fannie Mae. Both were subsequently so successful that they were spun into publicly traded companies in 1989.

The two were still heavily regulated, and their charters required them to promote home ownership among lower-income and disadvantaged groups. As such, they were barred from backing very large or "jumbo" loans. Loans that fall below a certain size (the largest currently being $729,000 in the nation's highest-priced markets) and that also conform to other Fannie and Freddie requirements are known as "conforming" loans.

The government no longer formally backed Fannie and Freddie and had no legal obligation to help if they stumbled. Investors firmly believed that if push came to shove, Washington would be there if needed—so much so that Fannie and Freddie were able to raise funds more cheaply than other private financial institutions. As is clear from recent events, investors were right that the federal government would not let either company go down. Fannie and Freddie had become two of the largest global financial institutions and were so important to the U.S. housing market and economy that they were too big to fail.

Fannie and Freddie came full circle when, in early September 2008, the Bush Administration determined that they were headed toward insolvency and put them into conservatorship. That is, the government took control of the institutions, effectively wiping out the company's shareholders.

Fannie and Freddie were not key drivers of the subprime frenzy, but they did participate in it. They couldn't help themselves from investing in riskier mortgage loans, partly because of their need to generate profits for their shareholders and partly because of their charters, which required that they provide mortgage credit to borrowers that subprime lenders were taking from them. Even though Fannie and Freddie suffered modest losses on their mortgage investments (at least, compared to other mortgage lenders), the losses were large enough to overwhelm their capital. Policymakers felt they had no choice but to take them over; allowing them to fail was just not an option. The FHA, Fannie Mae, and Freddie Mac—all part of the federal government—now account for most of the nation's mortgage lending.

Prime Versus Subprime

Government's role in the mortgage market rapidly diminished during the height of the housing boom and bubble. At its peak in 2007, private sources of mortgage credit overtook government sources of mortgage credit and accounted for some 60% of outstanding mortgage debt.

The private mortgage market can be sliced in numerous ways. The most obvious is based on borrowers' credit scores. The market distinguishes between prime and subprime borrowers using such scores, which reflect how an individual has managed his debts in the past. Scores are derived using statistical techniques based on information in borrowers' credit files. Borrowers with a record of late debt payments receive a lower score. Borrowers with a lot of credit cards and other financial obligations receive lower scores, as do borrowers who actively use most of the credit lines available to them.

Many types of credit scores exist—almost as many as there are lenders—but the most common is the FICO score, named after the firm, which was the first to successfully commercialize its use. The FICO[3] score ranges from a low of 300 to a perfect 850. The lower the score, the higher the likelihood that the borrower will not manage new credit well. Until recent years, credit scores were primarily used to make decisions about credit cards. In the past decade, however, scoring has become common across all consumer lending, including mortgage loans.

As the term suggests, a prime borrower is someone lenders are eager to do business with because the person has a good history of debt repayment. Prime borrowers might have missed a payment or two in the past, but never by more than a month. A bill two months past due causes borrowers' credit scores to drop, jeopardizing their prime status. By contrast, a subprime borrower has a significantly blemished credit history, or none at all. During the housing boom, many first-time home buyers had never received credit.

A wide range of in-betweens exists—not quite prime, not quite subprime. Some of these borrowers receive labels such as "alternative-A," or eligible for an A or prime loan, but with something not quite right. These alt-A borrowers generally have solid credit scores, but another credit issue precludes them from being considered prime. For example, an investor or borrower whose income has not been documented and verified might be classified as alt-A.

No credit score officially distinguishes a prime borrower from a subprime borrower, but most lenders and regulators consider someone with a score of less than 620 subprime. (The average national credit score across all borrowers is about 700.) Credit scores for subprime borrowers moved higher during the housing boom, but largely because lenders were aggressively pushing subprime loans—loans that carried higher rates and fees—to people who might well have been eligible for cheaper conventional mortgages. The average FICO score among subprime borrowers who took out loans to purchase homes in 2006 had risen to about 650 (see Table 2.1).

TABLE 2.1 What Is a Subprime Mortgage? Characteristics of Securitized Mortgage Purchase Loans, 2006

	Subprime	Alt-A	Jumbo
Basic Characteristics			
Avg. FICO Score	646	717	748
Avg. Combined Loan-to-Value Ratio	95.0%	89.0%	79.0%
Avg. Debt-to-Income Ratio	42.0%	38.0%	36.0%
Avg. Loan Size	$205,410	$302,404	$584,545
Product Type			
Interest-Only Fixed Rate	1.0%	13.2%	15.1%
Other Fixed Rate	8.5%	7.5%	40.5%
Interest-Only ARM	22.0%	39.6%	38.4%
Negative Amortization ARM	0.0%	23.2%	0.2%
Other ARM	68.5%	6.5%	5.9%
Type			
Fixed Rate	9.4%	30.7%	55.6%
1-Year ARM	0.7%	21.1%	0.3%
2-Year ARM	75.9%	2.1%	0.0%
3-Year ARM	10.5%	4.1%	0.9%
5-Year ARM	2.8%	31.5%	21.5%
7-Year ARM	0.1%	5.7%	10.7%
10-Year ARM	0.5%	4.8%	11.0%
Occupancy Status			
Owner Occupied	91.7%	78.0%	87.9%
Investor	5.9%	14.8%	1.5%
2nd Home	2.4%	7.2%	10.6%
Documentation			
Full Doc	48.5%	18.1%	46.6%
Low Doc	51.1%	78.2%	49.3%
No Doc	0.3%	3.6%	4.1%
N/A	0.0%	0.1%	0.0%
Piggyback Second Mortgage Loans			
With Piggybacks	55.4%	57.0%	29.4%
Without Piggybacks	44.7%	43.1%	70.6%

TABLE 2.1   What Is a Subprime Mortgage? Characteristics of Securitized Mortgage Purchase Loans, 2006

	Subprime	Alt-A	Jumbo
Property Type			
Single-Family	67.7%	53.4%	66.4%
Condo/Coop	8.7%	13.5%	13.5%
2–4 Units	7.8%	7.0%	1.5%
Other	15.8%	26.1%	18.6%
40-Year Mortgage			
40-Year FRM	0.2%	0.2%	0.0%
40-Year ARM	2.9%	6.1%	0.1%
Not a 40-Year Mortgage	96.6%	93.7%	99.9%

Subprime lending took off everywhere across the country, but ground zero was in California and Florida. More than one-third of the loans made in 2006 in the Central Valley of California and throughout south Florida were subprime (see Figure 2.1).[4] The border areas of Texas and those around Detroit were also hotbeds of such lending. Subprime was less prevalent in areas where credit scores were higher, such as New England and much of the farm belt. The lowest average credit scores in the country are along the Texas–Mexican border; Wisconsin households have the highest credit scores in the nation.[5]

Fixed Versus Adjustable

Subprime borrowers' financial woes were worsened by the fact that most took out adjustable-rate mortgages (ARMs). ARMs have existed for a quarter-century, but lenders historically have offered them only to home buyers with good credit, bigger down payments, and stable incomes. This changed quickly during the housing boom; 90% of subprime loans made in 2006 carried adjustable rates.

The fixed-rate mortgage loan, in which monthly mortgage payments never change, no matter what happens to interest rates or financial markets, is a uniquely American financial instrument. It is

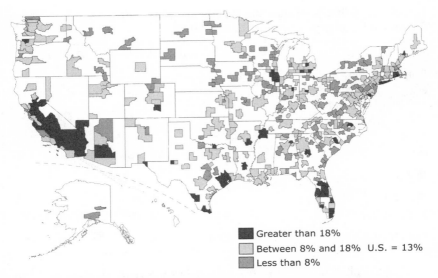

Greater than 18%
Between 8% and 18% U.S. = 13%
Less than 8%

Figure 2.1 Where is subprime? Subprime share of mortgage debt outstanding, 2007q4.

the predominant type of mortgage, accounting for three-fourths of mortgage debt outstanding. Thirty-year, fixed-rate loans were born in the wake of the Great Depression and fostered by the federal government, via the FHA and Fannie Mae, as a way to promote home ownership.

Fixed-rate mortgages have succeeded in putting and keeping households in their homes. Households with fixed mortgages can accurately budget their housing costs, making payment problems unusual. When long-term interest rates decline (fixed mortgage rates are commonly pegged to the rates on ten-year U.S. Treasury bonds), borrowers can easily and cheaply refinance at the lower rate.

Fixed-rate loans have obvious advantages for borrowers, but they can be unaffordable when inflation and interest rates are high. ARMs were developed in the early 1980s, a period of double-digit inflation and interest rates, to help with these affordability problems. Lenders can offer borrowers lower rates to start, pegging the interest rate to short-term market rates, which are generally lower than long-term rates. Borrowers don't know for sure what their future mortgage payments will be, but they accept the greater uncertainty in exchange for an initially more affordable mortgage.

Policymakers have also encouraged the use of ARMs over the years. During the 1980s, regulators viewed ARMs as a way for lending institutions to reduce some of the interest-rate risk they continually struggle with. The savings and loan crisis of the early 1990s grew out of the mismatch between the fluctuating interest rates savings depositors demanded and the fixed interest payments S&Ls received on the mortgages they held. Regulators believed ARMs would help solve lenders' problems matching their borrowing costs with their interest income on their loans.

Federal Reserve Chairman Alan Greenspan <$IGreenspan, Alan>was still singing the praises of ARM loans as recently as this decade. Greenspan argued that most people remain in their homes less than ten years, so why should they pay the added interest expense associated with a fixed-rate loan based on a ten-year bond? ARM loans that adjusted after three, five, or even seven years would be cheaper and fit better with American families' lifestyles.

Yet ARM loans also shift substantial risk to borrowers when rates fluctuate. Falling short-term rates are not a problem for borrowers, but rising rates can quickly create a major financial headache. Indeed, homeowners with ARM loans are much more likely to have credit problems than those with fixed-rate loans. Even in the best of times, the delinquency rate on ARM loans is 50% greater than on fixed-rate loans.[6]

The fact that most subprime and alt-A loans made in the housing boom were ARMs is disconcerting. ARMs account for a fourth of total mortgage debt outstanding, but they make up three-quarters of subprime loans and almost two-thirds of alt-A loans. Most subprime ARM loans are designed to "reset" after two years. That is, their interest rates remain fixed for the first 24 months; after that, the monthly payment is tied to a benchmark index. Payments generally adjust every six months. The bulk of subprime loans made in 2006 began to reset in early 2008.

The size of a reset depends on prevailing interest rates. Home-owners who took out ARMs in 2005 saw their payments soar in 2007 because short-term rates were very high early that year. Most sub-prime loans have an adjustment cap of 2 percentage points, meaning that the rate can't reset by more than that. In early 2007, many ARM loans hit the cap. Monthly payments on these loans jumped by an average of $350, taking the average homeowner's monthly payment from $1,200 to $1,550.

In a quest to improve affordability, lenders heavily marketed ARM loans with features that shifted even more interest-rate risk to borrowers. One such feature was the "teaser" rate, an extraordinarily low initial rate designed to enable borrowers to qualify for a loan. At times, teasers were offered at rates of only 1% or 2%. Borrowers qualified for loans based on the monthly payments implied by the low teasers, even though the payments would rise substantially when the ARM began to reset. That was a problem for another day.

"Interest-only" and "option" ARMs also became popular ways to arrange low initial monthly payments. Interest-only ARMs allow bor-rowers to forgo principal payments. Option ARMs give borrowers a choice; they can make standard interest and principal payments, pay only the interest, or pay only a minimum amount that doesn't even cover the interest due. Interest not paid is added back into the loan principal. This is known as negative amortization, a reverse of the way most mortgage loans behave. Most loans self-amortize over their life, typically 30 years. Not surprisingly, most borrowers who take out option ARMs use the negative-amortization payment option.

Interest-only and option ARMs are very effective ways to signifi-cantly lower monthly payments early on, but they impose much higher borrowing costs in the future. The larger the amount of negative amortization and the longer the period over which it occurs, the larger the increase in the payment needed later to fully amortize the loan.

In the teeth of the housing boom, teaser rates on subprime loans were common. Interest-only loans grew in use. Option ARM loans had not yet become common for subprime borrowers, although lenders were beginning to consider them. Yet the housing and mortgage markets unraveled before they had a chance.

Risk Layering

With so many borrowers with sketchy credit getting increasingly complex ARMs, a growing number faced difficulty staying current on their loans. Yet for millions to actually begin losing their homes, something else had to be at work. Credit risk managers call that something else "risk layering." This was the combination of subprime borrowers and their unmanageable ARMs with little or no down payment, unverified and thus unreliable incomes, and already burdensome debt loads.

Down payments were the first traditional lending standard to crumble. For many potential borrowers, the principal impediment to purchasing a home was saving that initial stake. Typically at least 20% of the purchase price, the down payment represented the owners' equity, their stake in the home. The down payment was large enough to convince lenders that a new owner was truly committed and would not risk losing the investment. This standard steadily eroded. Down payments shrank to 10% and then 5%; in the midst of the housing boom, many subprime borrowers were putting down little, if anything.

To compensate for a low down payment, borrowers in the past had been required to purchase mortgage insurance. Without much of a financial stake in the home, a borrower was more likely to default; insurance was necessary to cover the lender and pay any associated costs in a foreclosure. This insurance was costly, however, so creative lenders came up with an alternative: Take out two loans. Buyers could obtain a first mortgage equal to 80% of the home's purchase price, and a second mortgage that covered the remaining 20%. These so-called "piggyback" second loans, which usually took the form of home equity lines of credit, were cheap, particularly when the Federal Reserve Board was easing monetary policy. Rates on most home equity lines were linked to short-term lending rates, as opposed to longer-term (and usually higher) rates that governed standard home mortgages.

Putting a piggyback loan on top of a standard mortgage was a very sweet deal for a home buyer. To have a house of your own, you needed little or no money; all you had to do was sign some papers. Essentially all the money paid to the seller of a house was borrowed. For lenders, however, this was an exceptionally risky proposition. Before the housing bubble, the average American homeowner's mortgage debt equaled 40% of the home's purchase price. Excluding families that already had paid off their mortgages, the average U.S. mortgage still equaled only 65% of a home's market price. But by 2006, the average subprime borrower had mortgage debt equal to 95% of the home's purchase price. That was a recipe for disaster: If home prices fell, many of those homeowners would owe more on their loans than their homes were worth. That's exactly what happened.

Most homeowners will work to make good on their mortgage even in tough circumstances. If they also have to struggle with a substantial increase in their mortgage payment or a disruption to their income, however, they will find it all but impossible to keep the house. If, in addition, their own equity stake in the house is gone—because the amount they owe on their mortgages exceeds the market value of the home, putting it "under water," in the parlance of the trade—they might easily lose hope and simply decide to walk away.

Not only did lenders stop asking for down payments, but they also stopped asking for proof of income. Asking for a W-2 form or a tax return had always been a standard part of making a loan. In some cases, a self-employed borrower didn't have the necessary documentation, but they were uncommon, and lenders had enough other information to feel comfortable that the borrower could support the loan. This changed during the boom. Lenders stopped asking for proof of income altogether. By 2006, well over half of subprime loans were so-called "stated income" loans; the borrower simply stated the income, and the lender accepted that number. Some borrowers lied outright, and many more stretched the truth to stretch into a mortgage.

In most cases, the mortgage they stretched into put a heavy burden on their stated income, even at the teaser ARM rate. The average recipient of a subprime mortgage in 2006 was committing more than 40% of her income to mortgage payments. Of course, most borrowers had liabilities beyond their mortgages. Staying current on credit cards, auto loans, student loans, and other debts required more than half these borrowers' incomes.

Alt-A and jumbo borrowers weren't quite as layered up, but they weren't far behind. In 2006, for example, nearly 15% of alt-A borrowers were investors; they bought a house not to live in, but to sell quickly at a profit. These buyers were much more likely to walk away from a bad mortgage deal.

To Securitize or Not to Securitize

To fully understand a subprime mortgage, you need to know how it is financed. Fundamentally, loans either are financed directly by financial institutions such as commercial banks and thrift institutions, or are repackaged as bonds (that is, securitized) and sold to investors, who keep or trade them in global financial markets. The overwhelming majority of subprime loans have been securitized.

A quarter-century ago, most mortgage loans were funded the old-fashioned way: Commercial banks or savings and loans loaned the money they had received from depositors. Only a tenth of mortgage loans were securitized, and the securities market was dominated entirely by the government-related agencies Fannie Mae, Freddie Mac, and Ginnie Mae, the agency that insures mortgage securities backed by FHA and VA loans (see Figure 2.2).

Figure 2.2   Securitization flourishes: share of mortgage debt that is securitized.

This all changed during the 1980s and 1990s. Securitization flourished, partly because the S&L industry had all but collapsed. That collapse, in turn, can be traced to how S&Ls had mismanaged the fixed-rate mortgage loans they originated. Meanwhile, Fannie and Freddie were flourishing. Both had become publicly traded companies in the late 1980s; the move unfettered them from the government but did not take away the advantage they enjoyed as "government-sponsored enterprises." Both were able to raise money cheaply from investors who assumed they were safer than other banks. As a result, both grew rapidly in size and scope. By the mid-1990s, more than half of all mortgage loans had been securitized.

The securities market also underwent a substantial transformation beginning in the 1990s, when private financial institutions (mainly investment banks) became substantial players. Fannie and Freddie were barred from making subprime, alt-A, and jumbo loan business, so these other institutions moved in, expanding these markets as well. At the peak of activity, just before the subprime shock, these private-label securities financed one-fifth of all mortgage loans.

The benefits of securitization appeared substantial. For institutions that originated loans (commercial banks, but also nonbank mortgage lenders and others), securitization reduced their risk and freed up cash for additional lending. For global investors, it provided an opportunity to invest in a much broader array of assets and to precisely calibrate the amount of risk in their portfolios. Wall Street loved the hefty fees involved in packaging and selling the securities. Policymakers also liked securitization because it appeared to spread risk broadly among global investors.

By mid-2008, as the effects of the subprime shock spread, mortgage lending seemed to have gone full circle. Private-label securitization had collapsed, and banks, S&Ls, and the agencies were trying to fill the void. The volume of mortgage securities issued by Fannie, Freddie, and Ginnie Mae was slowly reviving. And while banks and thrifts weren't making subprime and alt-A loans, they were beginning to make prime jumbo loans.[7] How this trend developed became critical in determining when and how quickly the U.S. housing market revived.

Sizing Subprime

The home sales and mortgage lending craze lasted from spring 2004 to fall 2007. Throughout this period, the market was flooded with the riskiest varieties of subprime, alt-A, and jumbo ARM loans, the types of loans lenders would have been too nervous to make even a few years before.

The frenzied lending hit an apex in 2006. Of the $3 trillion in loans extended to all mortgage borrowers that year, $615 billion were subprime, $475 billion were alt-A, and $395 billion were jumbo ARMs. An incredible $250 billion in the riskiest stated-income, no-down-payment subprime ARM loans were originated.

In truth, barely anyone expected these loans to be around very long. The expectation was not that they would default, but that they would be refinanced before trouble hit. The thinking was that house prices would continue to rise strongly, creating new wealth in the form of housing equity for even borrowers who had put down no money. This equity would be enough to convince future lenders to replace the existing loan with a new one, with possibly even better terms for the borrower.

House prices peaked just as lending was at its most crazed, in spring 2006, and then began to fall. By early 2009, they were back to levels that had prevailed in mid-2003. That left most subprime borrowers who had received loans with little or no down payment during the boom in a dangerous situation, owing much more than their properties were worth. Refinancing was no longer an option because a new loan could not be enough to pay off the old one.

Fourteen million American homeowners, more than one-fourth of all mortgage holders, are now in this untenable financial situation. The face value of their mortgages is a whopping $2.5 trillion, equal to nearly a quarter of all mortgage debt outstanding. Most of this, some $2 trillion, consists of subprime, alt-A, and jumbo ARM debt; the remaining $500 billion is among prime conforming borrowers (see Figure 2.3).

$ Billions

Figure 2.3   Lots of subprime: mortgage debt outstanding.

Given the millions of homeowners and trillions of dollars involved, it was perhaps inevitable that the global financial system would react. But what happened next was bigger than anyone had foreseen.

3

Everyone Should Own a Home

The roots of the subprime financial shock begin in the American psyche and run through the typical household's balance sheet. Most of us define financial success by the size and quality of our home. The pecuniary and psychological benefits we attach to home ownership are unique; no other country values hearth and home more highly. Most of us spend far more on housing than we do on anything else, and American wealth is critically linked to the home—a house is the typical family's largest asset, and the mortgage is the largest liability.

Most economic policies since the Great Depression have been designed to help people acquire homes. Nothing receives more tax breaks than a house, from the ability to deduct mortgage interest and property taxes, to the low tax rate on the profits from a home sale. A host of government agencies and related institutions, such as the Federal Housing Administration (FHA), Fannie Mae, and Freddie Mac, exist to ensure that almost anyone who wants a home can own one.

The national obsession with home ownership reached a crescendo in this decade's housing boom. Home sales, housing construction, and house prices surged nearly everywhere. Most of us understood that home prices wouldn't go straight up forever, but many accepted the notion that they would never fall. At the height of the frenzy, we were all investing aggressively in our homes. We expected this to pay off big—certainly bigger than any other investment opportunities. We were all speculating.

Renters in places such as Los Angeles and Boston, who thought they'd never be able to own a home, were finally able to get in the door. Soaring house prices were no longer an impediment; a first-time home buyer could obtain a mortgage with little money down and a (just barely) low enough monthly payment. The loan might have been complicated and hard to understand, but lenders seemed sure it was affordable.

The market also brought trade-up buyers, people who had purchased their first home a few years earlier and now wanted something bigger. Others wanted to upgrade their current house, adding a bigger deck, a swimming pool, or a built-out basement. And why not? With real estate prices rising quickly and cheap credit readily available, didn't it make financial sense to aggressively invest in your home? And with 9/11 just a recent memory, spending more time at home—in a bigger, better home—seemed the prudent thing to do.

Older people, especially higher-income baby boomers, were thinking ahead to their retirements. If they didn't move quickly, that second home on the golf course or near the beach might soar out of reach. And with stocks gyrating in the wake of the tech bust, and CDs and money markets paying rock-bottom rates, where better to put your savings than in real estate?

On the far end of the market were so-called "flippers," who bought and sold houses quickly for profit. They were pure speculators who cared nothing about home values beyond a few months into the future. No investment had offered better returns since the collapse of the Internet bubble, and all that easy credit meant you were putting someone else's money at risk.

By summer 2005, the housing boom was at its apex. Nearly everyone believed there was no place like home. The housing market had come unhinged from the underlying forces that determine sales, construction, and house prices. The subprime financial shock, or something similar to it, was inevitable.

Hearth and Home

Outside of employment, nothing determines the economic well-being of most American households more than a house. Most of us spend as much on our home as our incomes and wealth allow. Substantial financial incentives—the most obvious being the tax code—enable this, although our preoccupation with houses is more deep-seated. Owning a home is a basic theme of nearly everyone's American dream.

Perhaps the best measure of the nation's economic success is the home ownership rate—the percentage of households who own their homes. From a historical perspective, we've done well. From just before World War II to 2005, the home ownership rate rose a stunning 25 percentage points.[1] It rose even faster for groups with historically lower rates of home ownership, such as younger, African-American and Hispanic households.

After World War II, returning GIs took advantage of the period's low borrowing costs and new, no-down-payment mortgages backed by the Veterans Administration (VA).[2] Home ownership surged, rising from 44% of households in 1940 to 55% by 1950 (see Figure 3.1). The rate rose more slowly after that but still increased another 10 percentage points during the next quarter-century. A key factor was the expansion of the interstate highway system in the 1960s and 1970s, which helped turn millions of urban renters into suburban homeowners.

Housing struggled during the 1980s and early 1990s. Double-digit borrowing costs and unemployment weighed heavily on home ownership early in the period. Then the savings and loan crisis and resulting credit crunch in California and the Northeast caused housing prices to fall sharply in these areas. The home ownership rate in 1995 was not much higher than in 1965.

In the late 1990s, however, falling mortgage rates, low housing prices, and rapidly increasing access to mortgage credit brought housing back to life. As the market grew increasingly frenzied after

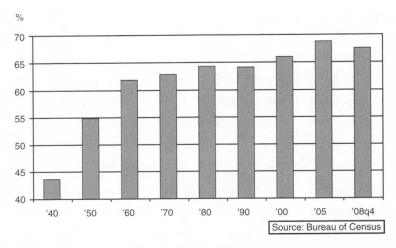

%

Figure 3.1   Steadily rising homeownership: the % of households that own their own homes.

2000, the home ownership rate rocketed higher. From 1995 to 2005, the home ownership rate jumped 5 percentage points to an all-time high of 69%.

No Place Like Home

A home is the largest budget item for most American households. From the mortgage payment and property taxes, to heating oil and furniture, the average family devotes a third of its spending to the house.[3] Nothing else comes close, even cars. Most households own at least two vehicles, and purchase, operations, maintenance, and all other transportation-related costs account for only one-seventh of the average household budget. Food, including restaurant dining, accounts for one-tenth.

Spending on homes makes Americans unique. By comparison, households in New Zealand devote about a fourth of their budgets to housing. For French households, it's a fifth, and only a seventh for the Japanese and Koreans.

Housing is equally important to rich and poor Americans. Spending on houses increases lockstep with incomes; the highest-earning homeowners devote as large a slice of their budgets to housing as do middle- and lower-income households. We spend as much on our homes as our incomes, wealth, and mortgage lenders will allow.

A home is most households' largest asset. Collectively, homeowners owned $22 trillion in residential real estate at the peak of the housing boom in 2006.[4] This was two and a half times the amount a decade earlier. Most of us finance our homes with mortgage loans, although a surprising one-fourth of homeowners owe nothing on their homes. Collectively, homeowners are on the hook for more than $10 trillion in mortgage debt. Homeowners' equity—the value of all homes minus the mortgage debt owed on them—totaled about $12 trillion.

The average homeowner's equity was $110,000 at the peak.[5] Housing wealth is distributed relatively evenly; it's not that a few wealthy homeowners own most of the equity. More than three-fourths of homeowners had equity worth more than $30,000. Housing wealth does vary substantially across the country. On the Monterey Peninsula in California, the average homeowner had more than $400,000 in equity, although homeowners in Indianapolis had only $25,000.

Although we seem to spend more time thinking about stocks, most of us shouldn't. No more than half of all households own any stock, and the value of all U.S. stock holdings, held directly or through pension funds, now amounts to less than $12 trillion. Stock ownership is distributed very unevenly; only about half of all investors' portfolios exceed $25,000. Except during the height of the Internet bubble at the turn of this century, housing has always been the most important asset owned by households (see Figure 3.2).

Incentives to Own

Buying a home is a goal for most Americans, and government policies provide big incentives to do so. Ever since the Great Depression cost millions of people their homes, promoting home ownership has been a central objective of public policy. Home ownership is

$ Trillions

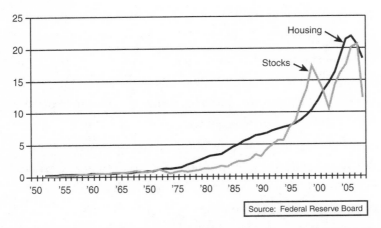

Figure 3.2   Households' most prized asset: households' holdings.

believed to be good for communities because homeowners are expected to care more about their neighborhoods. Policymakers have also long believed that it was good macroeconomic policy, as housing plays such a fundamental role in the economy's growth prospects.

The government most clearly promotes housing through the tax code. The U.S. Treasury gives up $150 billion each year in revenue, thanks to the tax breaks housing enjoys. The biggest tax break is the mortgage interest deduction. Part of the income tax code since its inception in 1913, the mortgage deduction wasn't initially designed to promote home ownership. Only 1% of the population earned enough money to pay income tax a century ago, and very few homeowners even had a mortgage. The interest deduction was instead aimed at businesses paying taxes on their profits. For tax purposes, profits were defined as revenues minus expenses, and interest payments were defined as an expense. The same formula was extended to individuals; taxable income was defined to exclude interest. Later amendments took the privilege away from nonmortgage debt, so taxpayers cannot deduct credit card or auto loan interest. But mortgage interest is still deductible. And today nearly 40 million taxpayers take advantage of this unintended consequence of the original tax code.

Other key tax breaks include deductions for state and local property tax payments and the treatment of capital gains on home sales.[6] Capital gains taxes on sales of a primary residence were significantly reduced a decade ago; profits of less than $250,000 ($500,000 for a married couple) are not taxed. Even before this addition, homeowners could take a once-in-a-lifetime exclusion on all the profit earned from selling a home. Sellers also received a big break early in the decade when President George W. Bush lowered the tax rate on capital gains.

Taken together, tax benefits on housing lower the effective mortgage rate to borrowers by nearly a full percentage point. If you buy a home today, putting down 10% and taking out a prime, fixed-rate mortgage of $225,000, the tax code saves you $150 per month, lowering your monthly payment from $1,425 to $1,275.[7] Importantly, the full benefits of these tax breaks go to only those who itemize deductions on a tax return; therefore, higher-income households tend to be the biggest winners.

The government also boosts housing by providing a reliable source of cheap mortgage credit. This isn't particularly important in good times, but in tough times it's vital. During the Great Depression, commercial banks and savings institutions, the traditional sources of mortgage loans, found themselves losing depositors; without deposits, they couldn't make loans. The Federal Home Loan Bank (FHLB) system was established to fill this breach. As a government-backed entity, it could raise funds cheaply from investors and loan money at low interest rates to member banks, which then made loans to households and businesses. The FHA and Fannie Mae were also set up during this period to provide funds to the distressed housing market.[8]

We have recently learned about the importance of these institutions. When the private mortgage lending industry fell into disarray and funding sources dried up, lenders turned in near desperation to the FHLB system. FHLB lending then ballooned. FHA lending, which mortgage lenders had all but forgotten about during the housing boom, has soared and has been a critical part of the policy response to solving the housing crisis. Policymakers have also turned to Fannie Mae and Freddie Mac. Now that they are part of the government, they are getting more financial resources to insure bigger mortgage loans, to purchase more mortgage securities, and to refinance loans that they own or insure, but without the historically requisite 20% down payment.

Even the Federal Reserve Board (the Fed) has been drafted to support the flow of mortgage credit. The U.S. central bank started a lending program in late 2007 to aid cash-strapped financial institutions, taking mortgage security holdings as collateral for loans. The Fed hoped to stabilize the value of those assets, shore up the mortgage securities market, and keep the credit crunch from getting worse. More recently, it has even begun to purchase the debt-issued by Fannie and Freddie and the mortgage securities that they insure, in an effort to bring down mortgage rates, with some success.

First-Timers

Of course, obtaining credit was not a problem during the housing boom, and no one seemed to benefit more from free-flowing mortgage loans than the first-time home buyer. First-timers enjoyed a once-in-a-lifetime opportunity: All the traditional hurdles to home ownership—including credit scores, down payments, and high monthly mortgage bills—crumbled in the home-lending frenzy.

In many places across the country, first-timers had found it nearly impossible to afford the American dream. This was true even early in the decade, when mortgage rates were as low as they had been in a generation and before housing prices had taken off. Before subprime lending became widespread, a first-timer with good credit who was earning the median household income and able to put down 10% still didn't have enough income to purchase the median-priced starter home. Things had been even tougher in the early 1980s, when mortgage rates were at their highest and affordability at its lowest; a median household income was only about half of the amount needed to afford a median-priced home. ("Median" means that half of all houses would be priced higher and half would be priced lower.)

This all changed with the subprime lending explosion. As if by magic, the average first-timer now had just enough income to afford to purchase a median-priced starter home. How could that be? Incomes weren't higher; the median household had barely seen any real gains in earnings. And housing prices weren't lower; indeed, prices had soared in many areas of the country. The difference was that no-down-payment, subprime, teaser-rate adjustable-rate mortgage (ARM) loans were ubiquitous. And despite higher mortgage rates and much higher housing prices, the initial rate on a subprime loan was low enough to enable first-time buyers to squeeze into a typical home.

This affordability math was even more compelling for potential first-timers in the nation's priciest housing markets. In Los Angeles and Miami early in this decade, when mortgage rates were low but subprime loans were still uncommon, a first-timer with a median income had only about 60% of what was needed to buy the median-priced starter home. By early 2006, when the most aggressive subprime loans were readily available, the same Los Angeles and Miami home buyers had 85% of the income needed to buy a median-priced home, even though that house had nearly doubled in price from a few years earlier. And with a bit of financial sleight of hand, such as a no-documentation loan, a first-timer could close the deal and move into that home.

All this was too much for many first-timers to pass up. Many saw it as a rare opportunity. With mortgage rates on the rise and housing prices appreciating rapidly, if they didn't walk through the proverbial door now, wouldn't they be locked out for good?

It's clear now that many first-timers who walked through the door with a teaser-rate, subprime ARM did not understand that their mortgage payments would rise sharply a couple years later. The Fed conducted borrower surveys and found a substantial amount of misunderstanding regarding all ARM loans.[9] Some borrowers did not know their mortgage payments would ever rise, and others were confused about how much and when. Lower-income people, less educated people, and members of minority groups were much less likely to understand the terms of their ARM loans (see Table 3.1).

TABLE 3.1   Percent of Homeowners Who Don't Understand Various Features of Their ARM Loan

	Per-Period Cap	Lifetime Cap	Index
All ARM Borrowers	35	41	28
Age of Mortgage Borrower			
25–44	33	37	33
45–64	33	41	19
Income of Mortgage Borrower			
Less than $50k	40	53	40
$50k–$150k	35	34	23
More than $150k	13	21	8
Education			
College education	27	34	14
Less than college	42	47	43
Race or Ethnicity			
White, non-Hispanic	26	37	24
Nonwhite or Hispanic	59	52	38
Subprime			
Yes	37	42	25
No	23	36	45
Mortgage Debt Service Ratio			
15% or less	32	40	26
15–28%	35	35	27
Greater than 28%	41	51	36

Source: Federal Reserve Board—Based on Survey of Consumer Finances conducted by the Federal Reserve—*Subprime* is defined as having a mortgage rate more than 3 percentage points above the annual rate on comparable 30-year Treasury.

However, many other first-timers understood the financial implications of their mortgage, particularly in the high-priced markets. Yes, lenders likely told them they could refinance into a new loan before their mortgage payment rose. And, yes, they might not have known that refinancing would be exorbitant, given the prepayment penalties on their loans, but they also knew they were taking a gamble. It seemed like a good one at the time.

Trade-Up Buyers

With a flood of first-time home buyers coming into the market, it seemed to be an opportune time for others to trade up. First-timers are generally in their 30s, and trade-up buyers are dominated by 40-somethings. In 2005, the population count was more than 45 million American 40-somethings—people born at the peak of the post–World War II baby boom (see Figure 3.3). More 45-year-olds lived in the United States that year than any other single age group. Many had children in school and housing needs that had grown beyond the size of their starter homes.

Millions

Figure 3.3   How many home buyers?

Interestingly, the number of American 30-year-olds—the prime demographic base of first-time home buyers—was much smaller during the housing boom. Most of the baby boomers celebrated their thirtieth birthdays in the mid-1990s, and the number of 30-year-old

Americans has been steadily shrinking since. Yet despite this substantial demographic drag, first-time home buyers fueled the housing boom—proof that the subprime loan was the catalyst for the explosion.

Terrorism also provided a substantial lift to home buying. As with nearly everything else, fallout from the World Trade Center attack on September 11, 2001, significantly shaped the housing market. This is clearest among trade-up buyers, who had the financial means to travel but largely stopped doing so out of fear that more attacks would come. Air travel was particularly nerve-wracking, and going overseas seemed downright foolhardy. Instead of traveling, households stayed home. As this nesting took hold, household spending on bigger and better homes surged.

Home builders became particularly reliant on trade-up buyers. They were building homes for first-timers, but the real money was in putting up larger homes for the more affluent trade-up market. The average size of a new home ballooned to nearly 2,500 square feet, 25% bigger than a decade before and twice the size of homes built in the 1950s.[10] Nesting 40-somethings were trading up to big, brand-new homes.

But by 2008, the trade-up buyer was fading fast as a source of housing demand. Terrorism fears had abated, and although travel still included numerous hassles—a falling U.S. dollar, rising gasoline prices, airport delays, and security screening—the nesting impulse had cooled. Demographics were changing as well. More boomers were reaching their 50s and beginning to consider life without children at home. These empty nesters would soon be trading down.

Investors

Most home buyers are normally motivated simply by the need for shelter. This changed during the housing boom. For many, the house was not just to live in; it was also a great investment. At the peak of the boom, Americans invested aggressively in their homes, effectively shifting money out of other financial investments such as stocks and bonds.

It's easy to see why investment in housing took off early in the decade. Housing brought much bigger returns than stocks, bonds, or cash. The stock market was especially unattractive after the dotcom bust in 2000. Stock prices peaked soon after Y2K; three years later, the major stock indices had been sliced nearly in half. Some $7 trillion in household wealth evaporated in the collapse, and the market has yet to fully recover. Needless to say, most households were not interested in making a major commitment to stocks during this period.

Holding cash also made little sense. The Fed had slashed short-term interest rates following the stock market crash, 9/11, and the invasion of Iraq. Soon after U.S. troops occupied Baghdad, the federal funds rate was at 1%, a rate not seen since just after World War II. Most money market accounts and CDs didn't pay enough to even match the period's low rate of inflation.

Long-term bonds offered better returns, but not significantly better; yields were historically very low. A ten-year Treasury bond in summer 2003 offered less than 3.5%, historically a rock-bottom rate. High-grade corporate and mortgage-backed bonds carried slightly higher yields, but most households had few easy ways to directly invest in them.

A house looked like a no-lose proposition by comparison. National housing prices were rising each year, posting high single-digit gains, and many parts of the country saw prices rising far faster. Even without rising housing prices, investors early in the decade found they could earn double-digit returns simply by buying a home and renting it out. This compares with 7% on an investment in an office building, 5% on a long-term Treasury bond, and 3% on an investment in the S&P 500 (see Figure 3.4).

Cash Yield

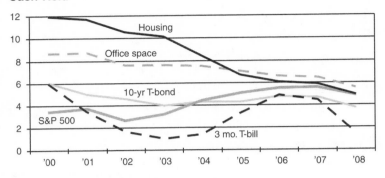

Figure 3.4   Housing loses its investment luster.

Investment returns on housing were even more attractive because the typical home was highly leveraged—most of the investment consisted of borrowed money. Leverage multiplies investment gains: For example, if you buy a house with 10% down and the value increases a mere 5% the following year, you've made a whopping 50% return on your investment. Even for someone carrying a mortgage balance equal to 50% of the home's value, a 5% increase in the house price generates a 10% return on investment. That's not bad, either.

You didn't even need to buy a new house to take advantage of this investment math. Many people invested in the homes they already lived in, simply by borrowing against them and using the cash to finance an improvement project or addition. Home equity borrowing surged, as did cash-out refinancing. This occurred when a homeowner took out a larger mortgage, paid off the previous one, and pocketed the difference. With mortgage rates low and falling, homeowners could increase the size of a loan without increasing the monthly payment. Millions of homeowners jumped on this bandwagon, withdrawing nearly $1 trillion a year in equity from their houses collectively at the peak of the boom. Approximately one-third of this went back into homes as additional investment.[11]

Older, wealthier households also invested in housing by purchasing second and vacation homes. The number of second-home purchases rose from a couple hundred thousand a year to nearly half a million at the height of the boom. The typical second-home buyer did not expect a quick profit; a second house could be used occasionally, rented out, or both. Meanwhile, the value would rise, producing a healthy investment gain for the future.

Flippers

It didn't take long for such long-term housing investors to be overwhelmed by flippers, speculators who aim to buy and sell properties quickly for a profit. Such speculation is rarely based on investment fundamentals such as long-term supply and demand. Instead, it is "forecasting with a ruler"—leaping to the assumption that because prices have been rising quickly, they will continue to do so.

Speculation is not uncommon in financial markets, but it had been rare in housing. It might have happened in South Florida and Texas in the late 1970s, and in California and New England in the late 1980s, but this is difficult to document. Buying and selling houses involves transaction costs—fees, interest, and so on—which normally make it hard to turn a quick profit this way. But not during the recent housing boom. At the height of the frenzy, flippers flooded large parts of the housing market, and their own speculation helped drive the price boom they were betting on. As flippers bid up prices, it raised the appraised values on neighboring properties, which induced still more flipping and even higher prices.

The worst flipping occurred in California, coastal areas of the East, Florida, and much of the Mountain West. Not surprisingly, flippers were aggressive users of loans with low or no down payments; the high leverage of those loans juiced their returns. Here's how it worked: A flipper might purchase a new condominium for $200,000 and put down $10,000, only to sell it three months later for $225,000. Even after expenses of $5,000, the flipper would end up $10,000 richer. The annualized return on such a transaction is an incredible 400%—that is a $20,000 profit on a $10,000 investment in only three months.

The lure of such windfalls made flipping surge. The share of mortgages issued to investors, as opposed to people buying homes to live in, doubled between 2001 and 2005, going from 8% to 16%.[12] And this statistic certainly understates the increase because many flippers fudged their intentions when they applied for loans, to obtain the better credit terms given for owner-occupied houses.

Flippers were most active in the hottest markets. In Miami, Florida; Myrtle Beach, South Carolina; Phoenix, Arizona; and Las Vegas, Nevada, the reported investor share of mortgage originations and house sales topped out at more than one-third (see Figure 3.5). But flipping occurred even in relatively staid places such as the condo market in downtown Philadelphia, and even in homes by a lake in Lansing, Michigan.

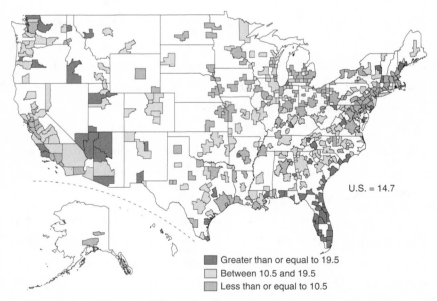

Figure 3.5   Where was the flipper? Investor share of home purchase originations, % of $, 2006.

Flippers operated in a gray area of the housing market. Many home builders, particularly the large national firms, publicly disapproved of flipping and instituted policies to stop it. But this had little effect. In some cases, the policies weren't strictly enforced; in others, the builders knowingly looked the other way; and in still others, flippers devised clever ways to avoid detection. In hindsight, it became clear that entire tracts of new homes were built and bought by speculators who never intended to live there. Those developments stood vacant long after the boom subsided.

At the Peak

It's fair to say that, by the middle of the decade, a vast number of Americans had become housing speculators of some kind. Flippers were the most overt, but millions of others also believed that home prices would stay high permanently. Not that annual double-digit gains would go on forever, but prices would surely not fall—at least, not for very long, and certainly not very far.

This belief persuaded first-time home buyers that it was okay to stretch their finances to achieve home ownership. Trade-up buyers used the power of positive thinking to dream big, particularly because they planned to spend more of their leisure time at home. Even homeowners who didn't plan to move accepted the idea of housing as a good investment, especially compared with stocks and bonds. Others thought it was a perfect time to buy a second home. The flipper took this faith to the extreme. Lenders might have empowered us to act on our impulses, and regulators might have failed to adequately warn us of the dangers. But at the peak of the boom, we were all believers.

4

Chairman Greenspan Counts on Housing

For most Americans, owning a home is a deep-seated and long-standing desire. The quest for home ownership has arguably motivated households' financial decision making since the nation's founding. Yet why, in the middle of the century's first decade, did so many of us decide to buy houses all at once? During the peak of the housing boom in 2005, an astounding proportion—more than one-tenth—of the nation's homes were bought and sold.

Many factors drove this home-buying binge, but the biggest was easy credit—more specifically, the period's record-low mortgage rates. In a normal year, more than three-fourths of all home sales require a mortgage loan, and, on average, about three-fourths of a home's purchase price is paid for with borrowed money. The cost of borrowing money is critical for home sales; nothing else we buy as consumers depends so much on it.

Houses seemed a once-in-a-lifetime buy at the start of this decade. A fixed-rate loan to a prime borrower carried an interest rate of slightly more than 5%; rates on adjustable mortgage loans were well below 4%. Fixed-rate loans had not been so cheap since just after World War II, and ARM rates had never been lower. These rates were even more enticing because, only a few years earlier, fixed-loan rates were above 8% and ARM rates more than 7%.

Behind the bargain-basement interest rates was a Federal Reserve on high alert. An unending string of calamities, beginning with the bursting of the Internet stock bubble and extending through

9/11 and the invasions of Afghanistan and Iraq, weighed heavily on the economy. Even the massive Bush tax cuts weren't providing much of an economic boost. China's rapid emergence on the global scene was also creating an economic upheaval. Thanks to China's ultra-low-cost production, prices for manufactured goods were falling all around the world. The Fed's overriding concern quickly became not inflation, but deflation—the kind of broad price decline that the United States hadn't seen since the Great Depression.

Fed Chairman Alan Greenspan responded with an unprecedented reduction in interest rates. Greenspan had refused to use the powers of the Fed to prick the tech-stock bubble of the late 1990s, arguing that it wasn't the central bank's place to second-guess investors. But he believed the Fed had a duty to step in aggressively *after* bubbles burst if their fallout threatened the real, outside-of-Wall-Street economy. And if the economy was at risk of falling into a deflationary trap, the Fed had to ride to its rescue.

Greenspan believed that if interest rates were quickly brought low enough, they would ignite a surge in housing activity. He was correct; home sales, construction, and housing prices all took off. The housing boom had begun. As people noticed their neighbors' house prices rising, they began to feel wealthier themselves. They also discovered that lenders were eager to help them take some of that wealth out of their homes, via refinancing, home equity loans, and other newly popular financial schemes. In effect, homes were being turned into cash machines, helping fuel a consumer buying binge.

Some saw danger in this; Greenspan did not. The Fed chairman believed that although stocks and other financial assets might be prone to bubbles, housing was immune. He argued that the costs involved in buying and selling homes were too high for speculation to take root. Moreover, even if some local housing markets became overheated, the danger to the wider economy was limited because housing was inherently a local market, not a national one.

Greenspan was partly correct; the housing boom lifted the economy out of its post–9/11 malaise. But he was dead wrong about the impact of a housing bubble. When it burst, it set off the subprime financial shock.

Lower Rates, Bigger Homes

Nothing matters more to a potential home buyer than the prevailing mortgage rate. This rate determines how large a home, if any, a household can afford. Other things matter, too—such as employment, credit history, and whether the buyer can come up with a down payment—but the principal hurdle between a household and a home is the mortgage rate.

During the past quarter-century, this hurdle has grown steadily smaller, and it all but disappeared in the housing boom. It was hard to even remember how high mortgage rates had once been. In the early 1980s, annual interest on a 30-year fixed mortgage exceeded 18%. A decade later, it had fallen to a more manageable 10%, and by 2000, it was even lower, at 8%. As recession and deflation fears took hold after 9/11 and during the invasion of Iraq, fixed rates briefly touched 5.25%. They moved higher during the decade but rarely stayed much higher than 6% for long (see Figure 4.1).

Figure 4.1   Steadily falling mortgage rates.

The decline in rates translated into much smaller monthly mortgage payments. The average home buyer in 2000 took out a $150,000 mortgage. At the 18% mortgage rates of two decades earlier, such a loan would have required a $2,400 monthly payment,[1] half the average household's after-tax income. At 8%, the payment is $1,250; at 6%, the cost drops to a very manageable $1,050 per month.

You can best see the difference between the housing market of the early 1980s compared to the market early this decade through the experience of a first-time home buyer. A first-timer 25 years ago couldn't afford to purchase the home he grew up in—the home his parents had bought when they were about the same age. In contrast, a first-timer early in this decade, just before the housing boom, could not only buy the home he grew up in, but also afford to add a pool or another bedroom.

A Call to ARMs

A quarter-century of falling interest rates helped make housing much more affordable to more Americans. The rise of the adjustable-rate mortgage (ARM) further magnified this process. ARMs had been around since the late 1960s in a few California communities, but they went nationwide during the period of high and volatile interest rates in the early 1980s.[2] Lenders liked ARMs not because they were cheaper for borrowers—although that was a plus for marketing—but because they reduced the lenders' own interest-rate risk. Banks make a profit only when the rates they charge for loans exceed the rates they pay to depositors. When mortgage rates are fixed for 30 years, banks run a risk that deposit rates might rise in the interim and wipe out their earnings. This happened in the early 1990s; thousands of savings and loan institutions became insolvent as a result.[3]

Enter the adjustable-rate mortgage. Because ARM rates move periodically, lenders can more easily match ARM rates with the rates they pay depositors. The initial rate on an ARM is much lower than that on a fixed-rate loan, largely because the borrower is taking on the interest-rate risk the lender wants to avoid. If deposit rates rise—which they generally do if rates in money markets or for securities such as Treasury bills rise—borrowers' ARM payments rise soon thereafter. But a borrower who is willing to take this risk can start out with a much cheaper mortgage. During the past quarter-century, ARM rates have averaged almost 2 percentage points below rates on fixed-rate loans. For a $200,000 loan—about the average size of a mortgage in 2008—this translates into a monthly saving of $275, a large difference for a household stretching its budget to buy a home.

Many homeowners who don't plan to stay put for long also find ARM loans attractive. The average American moves at least once every seven years; for these people, the industry invented a hybrid version of the ARM in which the initial interest rate can remain fixed for up to seven years before adjusting. Such loans are less costly than fixed-rate mortgages because the ARMs are linked to short- and intermediate-term interest rates, which typically are lower than the long-term rates that govern fixed-interest mortgages.

Shifting interest-rate risk from lenders to borrowers was thought to be a win-win proposition: The chance of another S&L-style debacle would diminish, and home buyers would have new choices, potentially saving them money if they chose wisely. Even Fed Chairman Alan Greenspan was an avid fan of ARMs. In a speech to a credit union trade group in early 2004, Greenspan argued, "Recent research within the Federal Reserve suggests that many homeowners might have saved tens of thousands of dollars had they held adjustable-rate mortgages rather than fixed-rate mortgages during the past decade, though this would not have been the case, of course, had interest rates trended sharply upward."[4]

Greenspan urged mortgage lenders to provide "greater mortgage product alternatives to the traditional fixed-rate mortgage. To the degree that households are driven by fears of payment shocks but are willing to manage their own interest rate risks, the traditional fixed-rate mortgage may be an expensive method of financing a home."

Lenders responded to Greenspan's "call to ARMs" aggressively, developing a new, wider array of adjustable loans. Originally, ARMs had been designed relatively simply, with rates that adjusted based on the one-year Treasury note or an S&L's cost of funds—mostly short-term deposits.[5] Perhaps it was just coincidence, but soon after Greenspan's speech, lenders began aggressively marketing a plethora of ARM products, ranging from the hybrid ARM, to the option ARM, to the teaser-rate subprime ARM.

The steady decline in interest rates and smorgasbord of loan products provided a lift to housing that became magnified several times over during the housing boom. Most households hunting for a home begin by meeting with a real estate agent. Realtors are adept at quickly sizing up the prospective buyer's financial circumstances. Based on those, the agent determines the lowest mortgage rate available and, therefore, just how much the buyer can spend on a house. Often the first home shown is priced just above what the agent has determined the buyer can afford. For all but the most disciplined buyers—and there weren't many in the housing boom—you psychologically can't go back. Buyers are primed to buy as much home as they can possibly afford.

Home sellers can sense this, of course, and as agents and buyers show up at the door more frequently, asking prices begin to rise. It doesn't take long for lower mortgage rates to result in higher house prices. Rising prices don't necessarily dissuade prospective buyers—at least, they didn't during the housing boom—as buyers begin to factor future house-price gains into their decision making. The higher the expected future profit, the more willing a buyer will be to buy a bigger home and take on a bigger mortgage. Moreover, if the value of a home appreciates faster than the interest rate on its mortgage, then the bigger the mortgage, the bigger the gains for the homeowner.

Under such conditions, it makes sense to buy as much house as a lender will allow.[6]

Greenspan's "Put"

Interest rates fell steadily through the 1980s and 1990s, but they plunged in the early 2000s to lows rarely experienced, igniting the housing boom and setting the stage for the subprime financial shock. Driving interest rates lower was the Greenspan-led Federal Reserve Board. Between New Year's Day 2001 and Memorial Day 2003, the Fed engineered a dramatic decline in the benchmark lending rate for banks, taking it from 6.5% all the way to 1%. Not since John F. Kennedy was president had the Fed funds rate been so low.[7]

The Fed drove rates down as the collapse of Silicon Valley's tech-stock bubble in early 2001 began to ripple through the economy far beyond California. Stock prices had surged nearly five-fold during the 1990s, and prices for the shares of technology companies—particularly those exploiting the amazing new Internet—had skyrocketed by some ten times, as measured on the NASDAQ exchange (see Figure 4.2). Speculation fueled this bubble; investors bought stock assuming that because their prices had been rising rapidly, they would continue to do so, using borrowed money—leverage—to multiply their bets. Margin debt—money borrowed from stockbrokers and used to purchase extra shares—piled up in record amounts.[8]

Source: NASDAQ

Figure 4.2   The technology stock bubble: NASDAQ Stock Index.

The bubble began to burst only days after stock prices hit their peak, in the weeks just after the turn of the decade. By the end of 2000, investors were completely panicked. The value of the NAS-DAQ was slashed in half. Other, broader measures of stock prices held up better, at least for a while, but more than $2 trillion in household stock wealth eventually disappeared. The economic fallout was substantial. By Christmas 2000, consumer confidence was plunging, hiring had come to a standstill, and businesses were cutting back on investment spending, even for new high-tech equipment. The economy was heading fast into the 2001 recession.

The Fed began to aggressively lower interest rates. This was precisely how Chairman Greenspan said the Fed should respond to a bursting investment bubble. Greenspan had laid out his position in a June 1999 appearance before Congress's Joint Economic Committee. He argued that policymakers could not accurately identify bubbles until after they had burst and, thus, should not try in advance to deflate them: "Bubbles generally are perceptible only after the fact. To spot a bubble in advance requires a judgment that hundreds of thousands of informed investors have it all wrong. Betting against markets is usually precarious at best."

Greenspan believed the Fed should respond aggressively after the fact, lowering rates only when a bursting bubble appears to threaten the economy. "While bubbles that burst are scarcely benign, the consequences need not be catastrophic," Greenspan said. Japan's bubble economy burst in the late 1980s, but that country's failure to react promptly, not the bubble itself, caused the decade-long recession that followed. Similarly, the Great Depression of the 1930s arose not from the stock market crash of 1929, but from the government's failure to manage the aftermath.

Greenspan argued that his decision to lower rates aggressively in the wake of the October 1987 stock market crash had kept that financial crisis from ending the economic expansion of the 1980s. Similarly, dramatic rate cuts in 1998 seemed to have successfully limited the fallout from the collapse of hedge fund Long-Term Capital Management. These experiences had shaped his thinking about how to handle the tech-stock bust.

These words and actions strongly suggested to Wall Street that the Fed would stop any future market mishap from becoming a complete financial meltdown—that, in effect, the chairman had their proverbial financial backsides covered. Commentators called this notion "the Greenspan put,"[9] using a term from the options market. A "put" option gives its owner the right to sell a stock or bond at a preset price, offering protection against future drops in the market. Greenspan's "put" was an implied promise that if things ever went badly awry for Wall Street, the Fed would step in and cut rates enough to cushion the fall. It wasn't a guarantee that investors couldn't lose money, but it did suggest that they wouldn't lose their shirts.

Greenspan's conviction that the Fed should not prick bubbles, but rather should wait to clean up the economic mess after they burst, contributed significantly to the subprime financial shock. So did his belief that housing markets, unlike stock markets, were largely bubble proof. He spelled this out in a March 2003 speech:[10]

> It is, of course, possible for home prices to fall as they did in a couple of quarters in 1990. But any analogy to stock market pricing behavior and bubbles is a rather large stretch. First, to sell a home, one almost invariably must move out and in the process confront the substantial transaction costs in the form of brokerage fees and taxes. These transaction costs greatly discourage the type of buying and selling frenzy that often characterizes bubbles in financial markets. Second, there is no national housing market in the United States. Local conditions dominate, even though mortgage interest rates are similar throughout the country. Home prices in Portland, Maine, do not arbitrage those in Portland, Oregon. Thus, any bubbles that might emerge would tend to be local, not national, in scope.

Deflation Fears

Greenspan's position on house price bubbles was not simply an academic debate; it was part of the intellectual foundation of his strategy for handling the apparent trend toward deflation in the wake of 9/11. The turmoil that followed 9/11 gave the Fed no option but to lower rates aggressively. Yet despite this aggressive response and the massive Bush tax cuts, the economy continued to sputter. As American forces were preparing to invade Iraq in spring 2003, deflation was Greenspan's predominant worry.

He described the economic pain of deflation in a late 2002 speech before the Economic Club of New York.[11] Deflation, he feared, would undermine incomes and profits, making household and business debt loads financially overwhelming. The resulting credit problems and bankruptcies would feed further deflation, launching a vicious cycle. The Fed chairman calculated that the economy's only chance of avoiding such a deflationary trap was an unprecedented 1% funds rate.[12] This, he reasoned, would ignite a housing boom without creating a housing bubble.

Greenspan's strategy worked. As interest rates fell, the housing market took off and lifted the economy into a self-sustaining economic expansion. By 2004, home sales, housing starts, and housing prices were surging. Thousands of jobs were being created in housing-related industries, and other industries were adding to payrolls as well. Deflation quickly faded from the economic lexicon.

The irony is that deflation wasn't the grave threat Greenspan feared. His worries were based on data from surveys that are subject to revisions—sometimes large revisions. It turned out that inflation did slow during this period, but as the revised data later showed, it slowed not nearly as much as Greenspan and others thought (see Figure 4.3).[13] Perhaps it is just as difficult to know how the economy and inflation are performing as it is to know if a bubble is forming. Equally ironic is that Greenspan thought dispelling deflation was necessary to ensure that debt loads wouldn't crush overextended households and businesses. As it turned out, the borrowing boom that Greenspan ignited created its own, perhaps equally damaging, credit debacle.

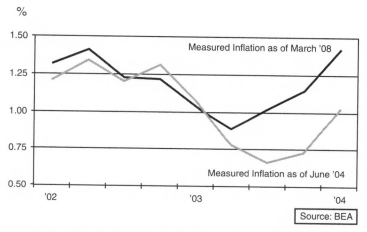

%

Figure 4.3 **Deflation wasn't the threat feared: inflation, % change a year ago, core personal consumption expenditure deflator.**

Households on a Buying Binge

Greenspan was counting not only on an interest-rate-juiced housing market to pull the economy out of its post–9/11 malaise, but also on the hedonism of the American consumer. With housing prices and housing wealth rising quickly, and homeowners able to cheaply tap that wealth for ready cash, his expectations turned out to be well founded.

A well-established economic theory known as "the wealth effect" states that as your wealth increases, you will spend more and save less. The more your assets—a house, a retirement fund, a child's college fund—appreciate in value, the more willing and able you will be to spend your current income. Not only does the theory make intuitive sense, but it also has proved true in practice. And once again in the 2000s, as housing prices and housing wealth soared, homeowners became more avid spenders.

Although economists accept that the wealth effect exists, they do debate its size. How much does increased housing wealth add to spending? Estimates vary, but given more than $8 trillion in increased housing wealth during the boom, even a very small wealth effect implies a lot more spending.[14] Suppose that for every $1 increase in housing wealth, consumer spending subsequently increased by only a nickel—a conservative estimate of the effect. The housing boom then added more than $75 billion a year to consumer spending—enough to raise the economy's overall rate of growth by half a percentage point every year.

It's actually likely that the housing wealth effect was measurably greater than 5¢ per dollar and that the traditional pattern was supercharged as homeowners withdrew massive amounts of cash from their homes. For many, their house became another ATM. Greenspan thought the topic was so important that he personally conducted research published in Federal Reserve working papers.[15]

Homeowner cash withdrawals began to rise early in the decade via an unprecedented wave of mortgage refinancing. As fixed mortgage rates plunged from more than 8% to less than 6%, nearly anyone with a mortgage could profitably refinance it; they could quickly make up the transaction costs of the refinancing by saving the interest on the new mortgage.[16] These transaction costs were also falling fast, thanks to roaring competition among mortgage lenders and the spreading use of the Internet to reduce loan processing costs. In 2000, the value of all U.S. home-refinancing deals totaled less than $300 billion; as the refinance (refi) boom peaked three years later, the annual pace of such deals topped $4 trillion (see Figure 4.4).

The cost saving to homeowners was enormous. On the mortgage loans refinanced in 2003 alone, homeowners were cutting their interest expenses by more than $50 billion a year. Homeowners were also using their refis to raise cash. In a cash-out refi, the homeowner takes a new and bigger loan, pays off the original mortgage, and gets a check for the difference. Because mortgage interest rates were falling, the new, larger mortgage didn't necessarily require a larger

$ Billions

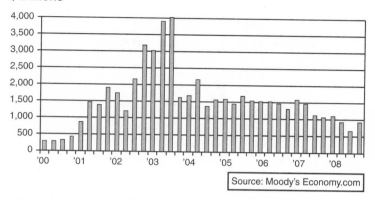

Figure 4.4   Mortgage refinancing boom: value of mortgage refinancings.

monthly payment. Homeowners cashed out an estimated $100 billion in the 2003 refi boom. This was a bonanza for consumers, who used some of the cash to pay down higher-cost credit card debt and finance other investments, but spent most of it on home improvements, cars, or anything else they could shop for.

Homeowners also raised hundreds of billions via increased home equity borrowing. With interest rates low, homeowners could cheaply borrow against the value of their homes, either taking a lump-sum check with a second mortgage or setting up a home equity line of credit up to a set amount—the average was $20,000.[17] The amount of home equity debt surged four-fold during the first half of the decade, from $200 billion to $800 billion, with homeowners tapping their houses for cash as they did through cash-out refinancing (see Figure 4.5).[18]

The housing boom also prompted many homeowners to cash out by trading down—selling their homes at a high price and buying smaller places or even renting. Empty nesters, in particular, saw this as an opportune time to take a capital gain. In resort communities, some homeowners seized the opportunity to sell their properties to developers or investors for large profits. Some long-term residents of New Jersey beach towns, for example, moved to less expensive homes

$ Billions

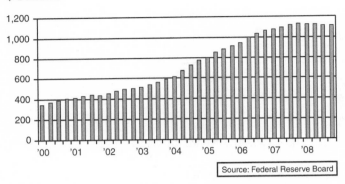

Source: Federal Reserve Board

Figure 4.5   Home equity borrowing soars: home equity loans outstanding.

inland. They reinvested much of the resulting profits, creating comfortable family nest eggs—but they also spent some.

The Federal Reserve's dramatic interest-rate cuts had worked. Instead of remaining in a slump after 9/11 and the Afghan and Iraq invasions, the U.S. economy recovered. But that growth was built on a housing boom—a boom that ultimately became a bubble. Chairman Greenspan had expected the boom, but he had not counted on the bubble—and he certainly hadn't expected what came afterward.

To this day, former Chairman Greenspan rejects the notion that his aggressive lowering of interest rates earlier in the decade helped contribute to the subprime financial crisis. Indeed, it is reasonable to argue that based on the apparent threat of deflation at the time, it was necessary for the Federal Reserve to act forcefully. It is even understandable why Greenspan felt that the most efficacious way to lift the broader economy was through a booming housing market. But it is wrong to argue that these policies did not contribute to the crisis that subsequently ensued. They did.

5

Global Money Men Want a Piece

The Greenspan-led Federal Reserve wasn't the only source of easy money powering the housing boom and inflating the bubble. A flood of capital also poured in from around the world. Global investors thought U.S. housing was a great investment. Their funds drove mortgage rates lower and empowered lenders to offer increasingly aggressive—and, ultimately, unmanageable—mortgage loans.

International investors were flush with dollars that the swollen U.S. trade deficit generated. Hundreds of billions of dollars flowed overseas each year in exchange for the imported goods Americans craved.

U.S. consumers had been on a buying binge, fueled by the Federal Reserve's rate cuts, the massive Bush tax cuts, and all the credit they needed. Imports, in particular, were bargains, thanks to an explosion of low-cost Chinese production and the high-flying U.S. dollar. Surging prices for oil and other commodities, driven in part by booming Chinese demand, also added to the import bill. As a result, investors in places from China and India to Russia and Brazil were collecting huge pools of dollars.

For these newly flush global money men (and women), the bonds and other credit market securities Wall Street devised seemed to be perfect investments. Global investors could match the amount of risk they were willing to take with an instrument tailored to provide it— or, at least, that's what they thought. And the U.S. bond market was huge, liquid, and historically safe. Liquidity showered U.S. credit markets, pushing interest rates lower.[1]

It didn't take long for global investors to become especially enamored with mortgage-backed bonds. Foreigners had historically been buyers of risk-free U.S. Treasuries, and the bonds government-tied institutions such as Fannie Mae and Freddie Mac issued and insured were only a small step removed. It wasn't much of a leap to invest in mortgage securities whose ties were to Wall Street instead of to the U.S. government.

A self-reinforcing cycle developed: American consumers were eager to buy and the rest of the world was happy to sell, producing the goods Americans wanted and collecting their dollars. But those dollars didn't stay overseas; they reentered the U.S. economy as investments in a broad array of financial securities—none more popular than mortgage-backed bonds. As foreign investors bid up the prices of those bonds, they pushed interest rates lower, following the rule of all debt securities that price and yield move in opposite directions. The lower interest rates were passed along to mortgage borrowers, and competition among lenders led to easier lending terms as well. Cheap and easy credit spurred more home purchases and still more borrowing and spending. The cycle was complete.

The easy-money policies of most central banks also revved up the global cash engine. Most economies had struggled in the wake of 9/11 and the U.S. invasion of Afghanistan and Iraq, and their manufacturers were withering under the onslaught of Chinese competition. With inflation giving way to deflation, they had a green light to slash interest rates. The Japanese were particularly panicked after more than ten years of economic malaise; they pushed their interest rates literally to zero. Cash was everywhere.

At first, investors were skittish about the U.S. stock market after the technology-stock bust. They also had qualms about investing in emerging economies, remembering the late-1990s Asian financial crisis and Russian bond default. But these concerns quickly faded. By the mid-2000s, investors acted as if the stock, bond, and real estate markets were full of screaming buys. The enthusiasm was even greater if they could be bought with borrowed money.

By early summer 2007, risk taking in global financial markets had reached unprecedented levels. Global investors were taking huge gambles and paying premiums for the privilege. All the preconditions for a major financial upheaval were in place.

China Muscles In

Where did all this global capital come from, and why did so much of it end up in the U.S. housing market? The answer begins in China at the turn of the millennium, just as the new Chinese economy was bursting onto the global stage.

The catalyst for China's stunning economic ascent was its entry into the World Trade Organization (WTO). Membership in the international organization that sets the rule for trade among its members conferred economic advantages of lowering barriers and opening doors. It also signaled that a country mattered—that it had a seat at the table of global commerce. The Chinese leadership had long lobbied to join the WTO, and it finally happened in 2001.

Entry into the WTO significantly opened up global markets for China's goods. For increasingly footloose global manufacturers, it meant new or expanded opportunities to hire hundreds of millions of Chinese workers on better terms than could be obtained anywhere else on the planet. Combined with a fixed and increasingly undervalued currency, the yuan, this made China the lowest-cost location to produce goods for the rest of the world.[2]

China's manufacturers received another big lift in 2005, when the 20-year-old multifiber trade agreement expired. This trade treaty had limited the exports of textiles and other garments from developing economies such as China to the United States and other developed economies. With its expiration, shipments from low-cost Chinese producers surged.[3]

In the mid-1990s, China was a small player in the global economy, but within ten years, it was producing more than one-tenth of
the globe's manufactured goods (see Figure 5.1). China's gains came
at the expense of manufacturers everywhere else: Apparel, textile,
and furniture producers in the Southeastern United States were hit
hard, as were lower-end producers in Mexico and Central America.
Even Italian producers of fine consumer goods struggled. Because
manufacturing is so important to most global economies, China's
rapid grab of global market share caused wrenching adjustments in
many places around the world.

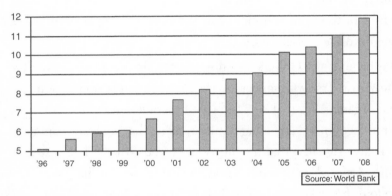

**Figure 5.1   China blows onto the economic scene: Chinese share of
global manufacturing.**

Outside of China, the principal beneficiaries of the country's
ascent were American consumers. No other nation produced more
items for U.S. store shelves than China; by 2008, more than one-tenth
of America's imported consumer goods were crossing the Pacific and
through the ports of Los Angeles or Seattle.[4] Big U.S. retailers—most
notably Wal-Mart—showed themselves extraordinarily adept at setting up efficient supply chains: from Chinese factories, to container
ships, to U.S. shopping malls or Internet catalog sites. Prices plunged.
The cost of Chinese-made products, from sweaters to computers,
plunged by 20% during the first half of the decade, enabling U.S.

retailers to actually lower the prices on the goods they sold to consumers. Inflation had given way to deflation—outright declining prices—in most stores.

These bargains were too good to pass up. As consumers scarfed up the deals, the nation's import bill and trade deficit ballooned. The red ink in U.S. trade with China was $50 billion when 2000 began; by 2008, it totaled a whopping $250 billion. Trade with China alone now accounts for almost one-third of the total U.S. trade imbalance.

The Chinese were initially unsure of what to do with their new riches. Investment had been anathema under Mao, and few mainland residents, even among the government elite, had any idea how to go about it. The easiest and most obvious place to put U.S. dollars was in U.S. Treasury bonds. They were safe and liquid, and didn't require much financial sophistication to understand. The Chinese were similar to any young person earning a salary for the first time; they wanted to make sure they had cash socked away for a rainy day. In a sense, U.S. Treasury bonds became China's certificates of deposit. And before long, China had a lot of them—almost $500 billion, or about a tenth of all the Treasury bonds in circulation, by mid-decade.[5] Only the Japanese owned more, although that has since changed: The Chinese stake has continued to rise, while the Japanese are no longer adding to theirs (see Table 5.1).[6]

TABLE 5.1   Foreign Holdings of U.S. Treasury Securities (Billions $)

Country	Dec 2008	Dec 2006	Dec 2004	Dec 2000
China, Mainland	727	397	223	60
Japan	626	623	690	318
Caribbean Banking Centers	198	72	51	37
Oil Exporters	186	110	62	48
Brazil	142	52	15	—
United Kingdom	131	92	96	50
Luxembourg	97	60	41	—

TABLE 5.1   Foreign Holdings of U.S. Treasury Securities (Billions $)

Country	Dec 2008	Dec 2006	Dec 2004	Dec 2000
Hong Kong	72	54	45	39
Ireland	72	12	—	—
Switzerland	62	34	42	16
Germany	56	46	50	49
Taiwan	39	59	68	33
Singapore	38	31	30	28
Russia	35	8	—	—
Mexico	35	35	33	15
Thailand	32	17	13	14
Korea	31	67	55	30
Turkey	31	23	12	—
India	29	15	—	—
Norway	23	32	—	—
Israel	19	—	—	—
Total	**3,077**	**2,115**	**1,814**	**1,021**

Source: U.S. Treasury Department

As China's nest egg grew larger, its financial expertise and infrastructure grew, enabling it to make bigger and bolder investments. A ten-year Treasury bond yielding 4% is fine when all you want is safety, but a 4% return looks paltry when you are rolling in cash and your own economy is growing at more than twice that pace. The Chinese began to expand their portfolios to include U.S. agency bonds—debt issued by Fannie Mae, Freddie Mac, and the Federal Housing Finance Board—to fund their own purchases of U.S. mortgage loans and securities. Although the U.S. government did not officially back these bonds, they were all but guaranteed. However, the return on agency bonds soon began to look lame to the Chinese. They began to pay attention when Wall Street's emissaries came calling to pitch other investments: corporate bonds, residential mortgage securities, and eventually even exotic derivatives such as collateralized debt obligations.

When it came to residential mortgage securities and their derivatives, Wall Street's story line was particularly convincing to the Chinese: Trillions in dollars of residential mortgage loans had been made to U.S. homeowners during the previous half-century, and the losses on those loans could be counted in basis points—in hundredths of a percentage point. Yes, home prices had declined in some parts of the country, but only briefly and temporarily; since the Great Depression, nationwide price declines had never existed. And the securities the Chinese were buying had been structured so that they would always get their money back, according to the rating agencies so revered by international investors.

Emerging Investors

The Chinese weren't the only global investors piling into U.S. credit markets. Other emerging economies—nations whose populations were still poor but whose living standards were rising fast—were also suddenly flush. Globalization had been good to them; about half of global production was now coming from emerging economies such as Brazil, India, Poland, and Russia.[7]

Soaring prices for the oil and other commodities they produced also lifted these economies.[8] The average cost of crude soared from $20 per barrel at the start of the 2000s to an all-time peak of over $150 in summer 2008; other raw-materials prices, from copper to soybeans, also jumped. This was due to booming Chinese demand; China needed commodities to drive its factories and feed its expanding middle class. Because international buying and selling of commodities was mostly done in U.S. dollars, emerging economies were showered with greenbacks, and as with the Chinese, they thought a U.S. bond was a great investment.

The sums earned in trade were massive. The U.S. trade deficit with emerging economies swelled from $150 billion a year in 2000 to more than $350 billion in 2008. Half this increase was with OPEC nations—the big oil-exporting countries upon which the globe relies for much of its energy—whose Treasury bond purchases increased in lockstep with the dollars they raked in as the price of oil rose. The other half was with oil and natural gas producers such as Russia, copper producers such as Chile, coffee exporters such as Columbia, plywood producers such as Indonesia, and so on.

Developed economies weren't left out of the action; they, too, were taking in large amounts of dollars in trade with the United States. Only a few years earlier, the dollar had been trading near record highs against the euro, the British pound, the Canadian looney, and the Japanese yen. The lopsided exchange rate had made these nations a bargain for U.S. tourists and U.S. importers alike. Dollars flew from American pockets to British, Canadian, and Japanese cash registers; the U.S. trade deficit with these economies doubled to $200 billion annually during the first half of the decade. Investors in London, Frankfurt, and Tokyo are wealthy and experienced, and they were more interested in investments offering high returns than safe investments. Treasury bonds wouldn't suffice; their yields were much too low. More complicated U.S. credit instruments, such as mortgage-backed bonds and their derivatives, filled the bill.

If we add up the hundreds of billions of dollars that flowed out of the United States in trade and then back in as investments in U.S. credit markets, we can clearly see the magnitude of global investors' contribution to the housing bubble. The U.S. trade imbalance was without historical comparison; the deficits doubled during the first half of the decade, reaching a record $800 billion in 2006. All those billions flowing overseas each year financed a three-fold surge in the foreign holdings of bonds, to an astonishing $6 trillion (see Figure 5.2). Overseas investors' Treasury holdings more than doubled and were on pace to become the majority owner of all publicly traded

U.S. Treasury debt. The foreign appetite for mortgage-backed bonds was even larger; overseas holdings of agency-related debt and Wall Street–issued mortgage securities swelled. At the peak of the housing boom in 2006, international investors owned nearly one-third of all U.S. mortgages.

$ Billions

Figure 5.2   International investor holdings soar: credit market instruments held by foreigners.

Central Banks Pump It Up

The extraordinary easy-money policies pursued by most of the globe's central banks also helped pump up the U.S. credit and housing market. Fallout from 9/11 and the U.S. invasions of Afghanistan and Iraq had hit the global economy hard early in the decade. Europeans were still absorbing the formerly Communist states of the East into their economic community and adjusting to their newly adopted currency, the euro. Much of Central and South America had recently reformed those national economies, and Southeast Asia was still recovering from its late-1990s financial crisis.

China's rapid economic ascent created new challenges for nearly everyone. Although the burgeoning mainland economy lowered prices for global consumers, it also destroyed the profits and jobs of its competitors. Not only were higher-cost developed economies such as the U.S. and Germany losing market share to China, but so were developing economies such as Mexico or Poland, where production costs were low—but not as low as in China.

Central bankers tried to ease the pain of all these adjustments by cutting rates. With a flood of cheap Chinese goods helping to lower inflation, policymakers had the latitude to reduce borrowing costs dramatically. The U.S. Federal Reserve led the way, but most other central banks soon followed. The Bank of England, the fledgling European Central Bank, the Mexican Central Bank, and the Bank of Canada all lowered rates. The average global central bank target interest rate declined from a peak of 5% in late 2000 to a low of 1.5% in 2003, where it stayed throughout much of 2004 (see Figure 5.3).[9] Even more telling was the negative *real* central bank target rate—the difference between the stated rate and inflation. (If the benchmark interest rate is 1.5% but inflation is 2.5%, the real rate is –1%—a condition at least theoretically attractive to borrowers.) Central bankers have historically reserved negative real rates for times of economic crisis or recession. The global real rate went negative in 2002, and it didn't turn positive again until well into 2006.

No central bank was pumping out more cash than the Bank of Japan. China's success rocked the Japanese economy. Japan had been the global export powerhouse in the 1970s and 1980s, but its bigger problems stemmed from the collapse of Japan's real estate and stock markets. A speculative bubble had developed in Japanese asset markets in the 1980s; as it unraveled during the 1990s, bad loans piled up in the country's banks. The banks took years to recognize their mistakes, refusing to write off their bad loans and tying up what capital they had. A long, painful credit crunch ensued, making it hard for even healthy businesses to expand their operations or for households to spend. With the Japanese economy moving sideways and deflation a persistent fact of life, the Bank of Japan steadily lowered rates. By the early 2000s, the rate targeted by the Japanese central bank was

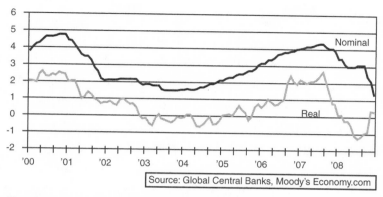

Figure 5.3   Global central banks pump it up: average central bank target rate.

nearly zero—0.10%, to be more precise—and Japanese policymakers insisted it would stay that way for as long as it took to revive their economy and rid themselves of deflation.[10]

Global investors quickly devised a way to take advantage of Japan's zero-interest-rate policy: They borrowed yen in Japan and then traded the yen for dollars, euros, or Australian dollars—any other currency that seemed safe and offered better returns when invested. This became known as the yen carry trade. The trade was profitable as long as the yen stayed weak; investors could trade their higher-yielding dollars or euros back into yen, repay their loans, and pocket the difference. The Bank of Japan's steadfast promise not to change its monetary policy made a weak yen a safe bet. Trillions of yen poured out of Japan and into investments across the globe; U.S. credit markets and housing received a fair share.

A Global Sea of Liquidity

By mid-decade, a sea of cash was washing over global asset markets. Investors couldn't get enough of whatever was for sale, wherever it was. Stocks, bonds, and real estate in Moscow, Beijing, or Los

Angeles all seemed to offer buying opportunities, and prices rose sharply.

Even the professional investors who managed global pension funds, insurance companies, and hedge funds were swept up in the excitement. Initially, skeptics argued that markets were becoming overpriced, and for a time they were heeded; the financial pain of the tech-stock bust and the Asian financial crisis had not been forgotten, and most of the signals used to value investments were flashing red. However, as asset prices continued to march higher, those arguing that something was askew in global asset markets steadily lost credibility. Eventually, they either changed their minds—skepticism could be bad for your career—or their views were dismissed as simplistic and impractical.

A few academics and policymakers—mostly at central banks—continued to warn that investors were taking on too much risk and that global markets were overheating. But the realities of the investment world dictated: If a manager is given money to deploy, he must deploy it or the money will go elsewhere. Managers are evaluated based on the returns they bring relative to their peers, not over several years or even over a single year, but over the space of a quarter—three short months. Life can get very lonely for a cautious investment manager in a runaway market.

Some hand wringing at investor conferences about rising global asset prices and aggressive risk taking did occur. Professional investors had a general sense that someday a market correction would bring asset prices back down modestly. But as time went on, those discussions grew increasingly theoretical and less relevant to the actual investment decisions being made.

A mounting intellectual defense of lofty global asset prices existed among managers searching to make sense of their investment decisions. This time it was different—or so the argument went. Never before had the global economy been this stable or this open. In the new economic world, business cycles might be milder and briefer than they had been historically. Ups and downs in employment and income, corporate profits, landlords' rents—conditions that determined the value of mortgage-backed bonds, corporate shares, or the price of an office tower—were growing progressively less volatile.

What some called the Great Moderation was driven by a shift in economic activity to more stable industries, such as information and health services, and away from businesses that suffer bigger swings, such as manufacturing. Better and timelier business decisions, resulting from the use of new information technologies, made it less likely that firms would misjudge their sales and get stuck with excess inventories, forcing production and job cuts. A more globally integrated economy ensured that countries suffering an economic setback could sell their wares to stronger ones, thereby cushioning their problems. Public policy was also smarter; governments and planners were better at managing their economies. As an example, most central banks had been granted enough political independence to pursue what could be unpopular efforts to achieve the explicit inflation targets they had adopted.

Global investors also took comfort in the cornucopia of new investments now available—collateralized debt obligations, collateralized loan obligations, leveraged loans, credit default swaps, auction-rate securities, and so on. These Wall Street concoctions were thought to more finely parse the risks of investing than a plain-vanilla stock, bond, or parcel of real estate could do. Risk could be more easily hedged, matched with other investments that would rise or fall in value in roughly the opposite direction. Hedging could limit gains on an investment, but it would also limit losses—or so money managers thought. Investors believed they could sign up for precisely as much risk as they wanted—no less and, importantly, no more.

Investors were emboldened. A more stable global economy meant more stable returns, and the new designer investments enabled them to fit their needs with precision. Feeling secure, their inclination was to magnify their returns through leverage—they borrowed money to buy even more of whatever they were investing in. Leverage can generate extraordinary returns if the bet works out, but it can be financially devastating if it doesn't.

The typical money manager acted similar to the owner of an over-sized SUV with a five-star safety rating. He felt safe not only driving fast, but also chatting on his cell phone at the same time. More crashes might occur, yet the SUV driver will suffer no more bodily injury than if he had driven more carefully in a smaller car with only a three-star rating. For other drivers, however, the damage would be substantially worse.

The liquidity sea also filled with new money—savings that had been locked away in different corners of the world and only now was finding its way into the global financial system. Similar to others, the owners of these funds were attracted by rising asset prices, the stable economy, and the risk matching afforded by designer investments. Many nations also began to remove the limits on their citizens' ability to invest outside their borders. For the first time, a Japanese or Finish saver could invest in Irish stock or a Fannie Mae bond.[11]

Euphoria in global asset markets reached an apex in the weeks leading up to the subprime financial shock in summer 2007. In most countries, stock prices, commercial property values, and prices for most bonds had risen to record highs. Investors had never been willing to pay so much to get so little. The tie between stock prices and corporate earnings—called the price-earnings (PE) ratio—went skyward in most emerging economies.[12] The ratio of rental income to commercial real estate prices—called the capitalization rate—hit record lows in most developed economies. The yields on most bonds compared with yields on risk-free Treasuries—known as the yield spread or the risk premium—was wafer thin, particularly in the United States (see Figure 5.4).

Figure 5.4   Investors asked for little compensation: yield spread between junk corporate bonds and treasuries.

By the time the financial shock hit, global asset markets were awash, even drowning, in a sea of liquidity. Investors had driven up prices for all assets, had taken on leverage, and were still desperate for something to invest in that would generate a sufficient return. U.S. credit markets—in particular, securities backed by residential mortgages—were attracting more than their share of investors. All the preconditions for a financial shock were in place, with American homeowners in the middle.

6

Bad Lenders Drive Out the Good

Residential mortgage lending was previously a very staid business. Lenders meticulously considered the merits of making loans: They obtained careful appraisals, required sizable down payments, and made sure each borrower had a stable job and reliable income. Lenders knew their institutions would take substantial financial hits if borrowers failed to make good on their loans. They also knew regulators were watching, checking to make sure each loan was sound.

Staid was the last thing you could call mortgage lending during the housing boom. *Frenzied* might be a better term—and as the boom became a bubble, *out of control* would be even more appropriate. The mortgage business had been completely transformed. Lenders now made their money solely on volume; the more loans they originated, the greater their profits. Whether borrowers would be reliable payers was, at best, a secondary concern; Wall Street was buying the loans and, it was thought, using its financial alchemy to ensure that everyone made out. Regulators still cared, but they took comfort in the fact that the lenders they oversaw weren't on the hook if things turned out badly. The institutions most exposed were unregulated private mortgage lenders and investment banks, ranging from New Century Financial to Bear Stearns. And although they were growing in size and number, they weren't the regulators' responsibility.

Wall Street drove the changes in the mortgage-lending business. Making a loan and maintaining ownership of it was no longer as profitable as making the loan and selling it to an investment bank. The investment banks had connections to yield-hungry investors all over the world who were willing to pay fat premiums for anything lenders could originate.

Lenders obliged en masse. They had been making subprime loans for some time, but these originally required large down payments and careful scrutiny of subprime borrowers' income and savings. Lenders also demanded compensation for the extra risk of making a subprime loan; under the so-called "risk-based pricing" model, the greater the chance of default, the higher the interest rate and the bigger the fees a borrower would need to pay. However, as the market heated up, down payment requirements shrank and documenting a borrower's income slid from a requirement to a recommendation. Risks were rising, but in the hypercompetitive environment, interest rates and fees could not.

Lenders let their standards slip because if they didn't make a loan, their competitors would. No industry had more avidly embraced the Internet than mortgage lending, and the effect had been intoxicating for both consumers and lenders. Borrowers previously had few choices; if they needed a loan to buy a house, they could apply at their neighborhood bank branch. Now a horde of eager prospective lenders was only a mouse click or two away. The Internet was a boon for lenders as well, offering any storefront or basement-based operation access to customers across the country, and dramatically cutting the overhead costs involved in making loans. But the net effect was a competitive frenzy, with lenders furiously undercutting each other to gain customers. Everyone, it seemed, was in the mortgage business. Alongside traditional banks and thrifts were largely unregulated real estate investment trusts, Wall Street investment banks, and even home builders trying to move their unsold units. In this atmosphere, a lender demanding strict, old-fashioned credit standards would soon be out of business.

A few old-time mortgage lenders worried that the tried-and-true rules were being abandoned, but most were swept up in the hubris of the time. The housing boom was built on a solid foundation, or so they reasoned. Loans with no down payment were a problem only if housing prices weren't rising, and prices were rising rapidly. Certainly, they would eventually slow down and level off, but no one expected prices to actually decline. And the lenders' math-whiz consultants had devised new, sophisticated models of borrower behavior. Applying their algorithms and formulas to past performance, they were confident they could separate the good borrowers from the deadbeats.

As the housing bubble expanded, mortgage lending moved from merely aggressive to increasingly reckless and, in some cases, disingenuous and predatory. On TV, over the Internet, and through the mail, lenders hawked an array of loans with questionable-sounding names: "stated-income," "piggy-back," "interest-only," "pay-option," and "negative amortization" loans. All were designed to squeeze borrowers with sketchy incomes and no down payment money into homes they couldn't afford, except under the very best of circumstances. Much of this seemed obvious in retrospect: For example, the ubiquitous so-called "2-28" subprime ARM loan was financially tenable only if a borrower could count on refinancing before the two-year fixed-rate term of the loan expired and the monthly payments shot up. And even if they could refinance in time, borrowers were nailed with a hefty penalty for paying off the loan early.

Mortgage Monkey Business

Given the financial stakes involved, getting a mortgage was surprisingly easy. During the mid-2000s, all it took was a visit to the local bank branch or mortgage broker, either of which a borrower could find in the nearest strip mall. The process took only a short time—the loan officer did a few calculations, pulled a credit report, and requested some additional financial information. When the deal closed, the borrower needed to sign a handful of documents, and the money and property title were transferred.

All this is a breeze when times are good and credit is easy, but even when things tighten up, such as in the current period, the mortgage-lending business is very efficient. It has to be; profit margins are paper thin and volume is necessary to make any kind of money. With thousands of brokers working on commission, they needed to make a lot of loans to earn a good living.

For a home buyer seeking a loan, the most important contact was often either a mortgage banker or a mortgage broker. These professionals' jobs involve examining the borrower's financial situation, working out the math to determine the appropriate size and type of loan, collecting the relevant documents, and securing the funds necessary to make the loan. Similar to independent insurance agents, who provide a broader distribution channel for the large insurance carriers, mortgage bankers and brokers provide a service for the big financial institutions with the cash to originate loans.

Mortgage banks and brokerages are generally small businesses; at the peak of the housing boom, 75,000 of them were scattered across the country, employing 350,000 workers (see Figure 6.1). They are low-cost operations that often appear and disappear quickly, depending on origination volumes and business conditions in a particular region. Their competitive advantage is choice; they offer borrowers a variety of potential deals, from government-backed loans to those offered by major depository institutions.[1]

Mortgage bankers and brokers had historically been lightly regulated; states set the rules that applied to them, which varied substantially across the country.[2] This enabled these originators to become major players in subprime lending; during the housing boom, they accounted for more than half of subprime lending. But after a mortgage deal closed, the broker's role ended. Only if homeowners came back to refinance or buy another home would they ever encounter a broker twice—assuming that the same broker was still in business.

Thousands

Figure 6.1 **Mortgage banking booms: employment in mortgage banking/brokerage.**

Most borrowers never meet the other professionals involved in making and managing their loans. These include appraisers, inspectors, and title agents—people who are supposed to make sure the house being purchased is worth its agreed-upon price. Mortgage underwriters evaluate the lender's risk in making a loan. The underwriters' models compare information about a borrower to details about others in similar circumstances, to determine the chance that a loan will be paid back regularly and on time. Mortgage insurers provide a backup in case the models are wrong and the borrower defaults. Mortgage servicers collect monthly payments and pass along the proceeds to the owners of a mortgage, and they are also responsible for working with borrowers who are struggling to make their payments.

The financial institutions that put up the funds for home buyers—banks or primarily unregulated financial companies—are very large. During the peak of the housing boom in 2005, the nation's 30 largest institutions accounted for half of all the loans originated (see Table 6.1). Countrywide topped the list, originating more than one million loans worth almost a quarter-trillion dollars that year.[3]

TABLE 6.1   Top Mortgage Lenders at the Peak of the Housing Boom in 2005

Mortgage Originations	#	% of Market	$ Volume	% of Market	Current Status
Countrywide FC	1,017,752	6.5	222,860,047	7.9	*Acquired by Bank of America.*
Wells Fargo & Co.	914,234	5.9	197,138,611	7.0	—
Washington Mutual BK FA	403,285	2.6	118,285,145	4.2	*Capital infusion by private equity firm TPG.*
Bank of America Corp.	419,120	2.7	85,789,951	3.0	—
Chase Manhattan Mortgage Corp.	367,831	2.4	72,545,438	2.6	—
National City Corp.	423,668	2.7	72,223,807	2.6	*Capital infusion: senior notes issued to shore up Tier 1 capital ratio.*
Citigroup	305,809	2.0	51,248,743	1.8	—
World SVG BK FSB	171,198	1.1	49,554,657	1.8	*Acquired by Wachovia.*
GMAC Mortgage Corp.	255,861	1.6	43,863,220	1.6	*ResCap unit supported by parent GMAC. Cerberus owns GMAC, but the private equity firm has not injected fresh outside capital yet.*

TABLE 6.1   Top Mortgage Lenders at the Peak of the Housing Boom in 2005

Mortgage Originations	#	% of Market	$ Volume	% of Market	Current Status
Argent Mortgage Company LLC	254,398	1.6	43,701,933	1.6	*Wholesale lender bought by Citi during the summer of 2007 from ACC Capital Holdings.*
American Home Mortgage Corp.	207,427	1.3	42,044,067	1.5	*Bankrupt. Wilbur Ross bought it in bankruptcy.*
New Century Mortgage Corp.	221,829	1.4	40,838,123	1.4	*Bankrupt.*
Suntrust BK	214,472	1.4	38,287,405	1.4	—
Fremont INV & LOAN	193,564	1.2	36,144,403	1.3	*Bankrupt.*
Option One Mortgage Corp.	203,279	1.3	35,883,131	1.3	*Wilbur Ross bought it from H&R Block.*
First Horizon Home Loan Corp.	195,121	1.3	34,567,932	1.2	—
Greenpoint Mortgage Funding	118,098	0.8	33,399,038	1.2	*Does not originate any new loans; Capital One owns it.*
ABN Amro Mortgage Group, Inc.	176,504	1.1	33,295,165	1.2	—
Indymac BK FSB	126,119	0.8	31,895,022	1.1	—
HSBC Holdings Plc.	267,355	1.7	30,601,979	1.1	—
Washington Mutual BK FSB	171,896	1.1	28,410,818	1.0	*Capital infusion by private equity investors led by TPG.*

TABLE 6.1 Top Mortgage Lenders at the Peak of the Housing Boom in 2005

Mortgage Originations	#	% of Market	$ Volume	% of Market	Current Status
Ameriquest Mortgage Co.	161,472	1.0	27,456,887	1.0	*Shut down after Citi bought Argent from ACC Capital Holdings. ACC owned both Ameriquest and Argent; the former is a retail lender and the latter is a wholesale lender.*
WMC Mortgage Corp.	142,201	0.9	27,300,288	1.0	*GE sold it in summer 2007.*
Wachovia Corp.	174,429	1.1	25,802,339	0.9	—
Flagstar BK FSB	149,366	1.0	24,922,760	0.9	—
First Magnus Financial	133,567	0.9	23,085,302	0.8	*Bankrupt.*
Corp. Ohio SVB BK	109,352	0.7	21,440,298	0.8	—
MortgageIT, Inc.	90,910	0.6	20,439,166	0.7	—
PHH Mortgage Corp.	111,079	0.7	19,948,314	0.7	—
Wachovia Mortgage	89,725	0.6	18,831,044	0.7	—
All other lenders	7,785,931	50	1,265,547,260	44.9	
Total	**15,576,852**	**100**	**2,817,352,293**	**100**	

Sources: Mortgage Bankers' Association, Moody's Economy.com

These institutions aren't necessarily the ultimate owners of the mortgage loan. Owners include depositories—a commercial bank or savings and loan—or an investor who bought an interest in the loan via a mortgage-backed security. Investors can reside anywhere in the world and might be an individual or an institution—a pension fund, hedge fund, investment bank, or any of the other players in the global capital markets. Depositories own about half of all residential mortgage loans, and investors own the other half. Whoever or whatever they are, mortgage owners are often far removed from the mortgage-making process. They've never met the brokers who originated the loans they own, and they will meet the loan servicer only if a loan goes bad and the party at the other end of the chain—the borrower—stops making monthly payments.

The housing boom was a heady time for the mortgage business. The entire industry—from brokers to servicers—was humming, with many mortgage professionals working long hours, nights, and weekends. The volumes were astounding; between 2004 and 2006, more than $9 trillion in loans was originated, accounting for half of all U.S. first mortgages in effect in 2008 (see Figure 6.2).

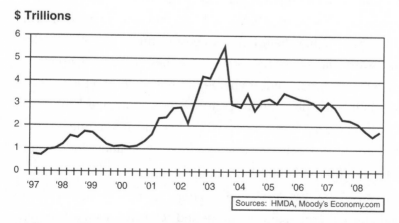

$ Trillions

Sources: HMDA, Moody's Economy.com

Figure 6.2 Mortgage lending soars: mortgage originations.

With soaring volumes came soaring profits, but the mortgage business remained fiercely competitive and margins remained thin. Lenders were driven to keep volumes up and the cash coming in—and they became increasingly creative in finding ways to put households with shaky finances into homes.

Gresham's Law at Work

Starting a mortgage brokerage firm in the early 2000s was easy; there were few barriers to entry and even fewer to shutting down and leaving the business. Brokerages appeared quickly whenever home buying picked up, and they vanished just as quickly when activity cooled. Costs were low: office rent, a few desks and computers, and some commissioned agents. Relationships with real estate agents and home builders helped but weren't necessary for success. The key was offering the best interest rate, the lowest origination fees, and—particularly during the housing boom—the easiest loan terms.

But gaining a competitive edge just by offering low interest rates and origination fees grew difficult early in the decade. Rates were already about as low as they had ever been, and lenders were offering rates not much higher than their own cost of funds—in effect, offering borrowers the wholesale price of money. Fees and points on mortgage loans—what lenders charge for their costs and their time—had also fallen sharply. The average fee on a mortgage loan in the midst of the housing boom was 0.35% of the loan amount—a rock-bottom rate.[4] Only a decade earlier, such fees had amounted to more than a percentage point (see Figure 6.3).

The mortgage industry's quick adoption of the Internet also pumped up competition during this period. The Web seemed custom-built for a business that had been drowning in documents—simply managing it all had required a substantial back-office bureaucracy to review, organize, and file. With the Internet, obtaining needed

Figure 6.3   Mortgage fees plunge: average fees and points on a mortgage loan.

information from a credit bureau, appraiser, or title company required only a few clicks.

The Internet also empowered consumers; home buyers could now shop for the best or cheapest mortgages. The local neighborhood bank was no longer the only effective choice. Lenders saw an enormous opportunity to reach borrowers in far-flung places; beginning in the late 1990s, lenders poured resources into developing Web sites and other Internet-based marketing tools. As it happened, Congress had just recently given lenders the legal go-ahead to seek customers nationwide.[5] With the growth of online marketing, borrowers could immediately match up offers from lenders across the country and see how tweaking their own financial information—the size of their down payment, the credit score, and so on—affected the interest rates and terms available.

Borrowers were becoming much savvier loan shoppers for other reasons. Tens of millions of homeowners had refinanced their loans at least once to take advantage of the period's falling interest rates, and they had gained an understanding of the lending process.[6] They were much more willing to challenge lenders' origination fees and to move on to the next lender if they weren't satisfied.

Barriers to competition were also being ripped down as cheap (low-interest-rate) money became available to lenders of all stripes. Previously, depositors in commercial banks and savings and loans provided the only source of funds to make mortgage loans. However, as Wall Street figured out how to securitize loans, funds began coming in from all corners of the globe, and having deposits was no longer an advantage. Moreover, the investment bankers who sliced, packaged, and sold mortgage loans to investors wanted a full pipeline; the more lenders were out there signing up borrowers, the more there was to securitize. In fact, some investment banks grew frustrated that they couldn't get enough and began setting up their own mortgage-lending subsidiaries. Bear Stearns, Lehman Brothers, Credit Suisse, and others quickly became among the industry's most aggressive lenders.

Competition was also taking new forms. Mortgage-lending companies were being set up not as traditional depositories or brokers, but as real estate investment trusts (REITs). In the 1990s, REITs became the favored corporate form for developers as a way of avoiding corporate income taxes. Technically, all REIT profits were paid out to shareholders, who then paid personal taxes on them.[7] But REITs also avoided the watchful eyes of bank regulators; because they were publicly traded, they fell under the umbrella of the Securities and Exchange Commission (SEC). The SEC regulates the stock market, with its main focus on issues such as insider trading and corporate transparency—not the ins and outs of mortgage lending. Mortgage-lending REITs fell through the regulatory cracks, and their sponsors took full advantage of the status. Some of the most egregious, aggressive, and ultimately failed players in the housing bubble were REITs, including American Home Mortgage, New Century Financial, and NovaStar.

As the Federal Reserve slowly raised interest rates between summer 2004 and summer 2006, competition among lenders boiled over. To keep generating new mortgages, even as higher rates made homes less affordable, lenders had to lower their underwriting standards. The REITs and investment banks led the way. A form of

Gresham's law took hold, in which the most aggressive lenders forced the rest—even the more cautious among them—to either lower their standards or lose their market share.[8] Lenders could keep going only by making loans on terms they would have considered unimaginable only a few months earlier. The bad lenders were driving out the good ones, as even well-established, conservative lenders gave in to the pressure.

Policymakers Change the Rules

The nation's financial policymakers encouraged both the burgeoning competition in the mortgage industry and the rapid expansion in lending that resulted. Officials' motivations ranged from altruistic to crassly political. For both ideological and partisan reasons, the Bush Administration had long disdained government-supported mortgage lenders such as the FHA, Fannie Mae, and Freddie Mac. These institutions had been plagued by management problems and accounting irregularities. In the case of Fannie and Freddie, even the Federal Reserve Board thought they were too large and insufficiently capitalized. The administration believed that the private market could provide all the mortgages Americans needed, more efficiently and at less cost than government-sponsored lenders.

With administration support, regulators began putting fetters on the government-related lenders just as they were easing up on private lenders—at precisely the moment when regulatory oversight was most needed. Even under normal circumstances, regulators have a difficult time encouraging lenders to be prudent. When times are flush and borrowers are paying on their loans, lenders resist any suggestion that they might be overdoing it—extending too much credit and not properly accounting for the risks. But this is precisely when lenders tend to make mistakes and, therefore, when regulators need to be most vigilant. But cracking down wasn't a politically popular idea during the housing boom; many legislators and the White House were looking for less oversight, not more.

Model Hubris

If mortgage lenders were nervous about their falling loan standards, they could always take confidence in their models. Lenders believed deeply that, whatever their guts told them, their statistically based, computer-driven models could reliably determine whom they should lend to, what kinds of loans they could offer, and how much interest they should charge. The models were brilliant; using the available information on the borrower and the property, they would forecast the odds of the borrower paying regularly and on time. Fannie Mae and Freddie Mac had long been champions of these so-called automated underwriting (AU) models, and now other lenders became converts as well.[9] Lenders felt sure that their AU models could accurately judge a borrower's creditworthiness.[10]

One essential input into every lender's model is a borrower's credit score.[11] This is a number, typically ranging from 300 to 850, indicating the risk that a borrower will eventually face a credit problem. The lower the score, the more problem-prone the borrower is. A score below 620 generally marks a borrower as subprime. Scores are constructed from credit files—information that lenders report regularly to credit bureaus. Scores reflect not only past payment history, but also how a person uses credit. For example, the more credit cards in your wallet and the closer you are to your credit limits, the greater the risk is of lending you more money and, therefore, the lower your score.

Another essential input into all mortgage-lender models is the value of the house being purchased. Lenders use old-fashioned appraisals, but they also rely on so-called automated valuation models (AVMs) for this. An AVM is automated because it doesn't require an actual human being to look at the property; instead, it uses statistics and computing power to estimate a home's value: recent sales of comparable homes, tax assessments, other characteristics of the property, and price trends in the immediate area. AVMs are much less costly than human appraisals and require no waiting for an appraiser to visit a home.

Lenders had little choice but to believe in their models during the housing boom. Loan applications were coming thick and fast; without models that could spit out answers instantaneously, the applications couldn't be processed quickly enough to meet the competition among lenders. Automated underwriting models, credit scores, and AVM-produced house values are, in most circumstances, effective and promising tools, but lenders were much too comfortable with the results and had come to totally rely on them.

Models are only as good as the information that goes into them, and by 2007, the information going into many models was increasingly suspect. Borrowers had figured out how to manipulate their own credit scores, not by improving their habits, but by making a few simple adjustments in how they managed their debts. For instance, some borrowers paid a fee to be added as an "authorized user" on the credit card accounts of people with higher scores. The positive payment information from the good cardholder improved the additional user's credit score. Such transplanting of credit DNA wasn't widespread, but it shows how borrowers were able to game the system and affect lenders' models.[12]

Another serious problem with AVMs was that they could fall significantly behind market conditions, particularly at times when those conditions were changing rapidly. For months after housing prices began to bust, AVMs were still showing values that reflected a much stronger market. Lenders were making decisions as if the good times were still rolling, long after they had ended. AVMs also had trouble capturing the real prices being paid for homes at a time when sellers were offering back-door discounts in the form of seller financing or other nonprice concessions. Such off-the-books discounting became common as housing markets weakened; sellers were offering to fix decks or repave driveways to close a sale instead of dropping their official prices. (In fact, a weakness of automated valuations is that they can't quantify all the small and intangible characteristics that determine a home's market value. A model might capture the price of a pool or built-out basement, but not the value of the view from the front porch or a troublesome neighbor.)

Lenders' models depend fundamentally on the premise that history is an accurate guide to the future. Most times this is a reasonable assumption and models will predict the behavior of borrowers reasonably accurately. But at times—such as during the housing boom—conditions don't match anything experienced historically, and then the models no longer work. In the housing boom, lenders failed to recognize this. Their belief in the predictive prowess of their models emboldened many of them to throw aside philosophical concerns and make what proved to be colossally bad decisions.

The quality of lenders' underwriting inexorably eroded. At its most crazed point at the apex of the housing bubble, disingenuous, predatory, and even fraudulent lending corrupted significant parts of the mortgage market. The mortgage industry's dramatic transformation from a staid business to a financial Wild West created the fodder for the subprime financial shock.

7

Financial Engineers and Their Creations

The Italians make designer sunglasses, the Japanese manufacture precision vehicles, Russian vodka has no comparison, and until the subprime financial shock, everyone wanted some of America's financial ingenuity. It was thought to be our comparative advantage. The efficiency of the U.S. financial system was the envy of the world; it could take the nation's paltry savings and direct it to financing investments that reaped big returns. Why save 50% of your income—as they do in China—or even 10%, as the Germans do, if you could put aside close to nothing and get the same returns or better simply by making the right kind of investments? The U.S. financial system was better at this than anyone; the wizardry of America's financial engineers seemed unparalleled.

Despite the complexity of the American financial system, its basic function is quite simple: Lend what we save to others who can do something productive with it. In times past, this was done entirely by banks.[1] Making a loan was very straightforward. A bank took cash from depositors and lent it to a household or business. The bank paid the depositor some interest and made a profit by charging a little more in interest from the borrower. The bank owned the loan until it was repaid and took the loss if the borrower fell into unhappy circumstances and defaulted. Because the banks' deposits were insured by the government, regulators required them to hold some cash—capital—aside in case too many borrowers defaulted. Regulators also monitored the banks' lending to make sure it was prudent; if a bank made too many bad loans, it could fail, putting the government on the hook to repay depositors' money.

The banks lost their tight grip on the financial system beginning in the 1970s and 1980s. These were tough times for banking; volatile inflation and high interest rates made it difficult to make a profit.[2] The high rates crimped lending and sent deposits fleeing to newly established money market funds, which offered higher returns to savers. Many banks also stumbled badly in the early 1980s by lending too aggressively to Latin American nations who mismanaged their debts and ultimately defaulted on billions.[3] The collapse of the savings and loan (S&L) industry was even more devastating, with more than 1,000 institutions failing between the mid-1980s and early 1990s. The massive financial debacle left regulators to sort out hundreds of billions of dollars of loans from the defunct S&Ls.

The vicissitudes of financial markets and the financial chicanery of unscrupulous S&L owners created the S&L mess, and eventually high finance resolved it. The Resolution Trust Corporation (RTC), established by policymakers to dispose of the S&L's assets, gracefully employed a financial technique known as securitization. In a securitization, loans are combined or pooled, and their collective interest and principal payments are used to back a tradable security that is sold to investors. As a group, the investors become owners of the loans and are entitled to receive its interest and principal payments. The RTC securitized everything from auto loans to commercial mortgages, sold them to investors, and resolved the S&L crisis at a surprisingly low cost to taxpayers.[4]

Securitization wasn't born at the RTC—that honor goes to mortgage lenders Fannie Mae, Freddie Mac, and the FHA in the 1970s—but the RTC demonstrated that the technique could be used commercially for all types of loans. The RTC also helped create the legal and accounting rules necessary for securitization to work, as well as the trading infrastructure needed for investors to buy and sell the securities. As the RTC wound down its operations in the mid-1990s, Wall Street happily took the wheel of the securitization machine.

Investment bankers first applied securitization to the mass market via credit cards. Using borrowers' credit scores and targeted direct-marketing techniques, banks had already figured out how to put cards in the hands of millions of average-income or even low-income households. The only limit on the banks' growth in this area came from their own balance sheets—banks lacked sufficient deposits or capital to grow freely. Securitization lifted both constraints. When a credit card was securitized, banks didn't need deposits; the investors buying the credit card–backed securities provided the money. Capital wasn't an issue, either, because the investors—not the card-issuing banks—owned the loans. Credit card lending soared, with receivables doubling in the mid-1990s.

Securitization also powered a boom in home equity and manufactured housing lending. Second-mortgage loans had received a big lift in the late 1980s, when Congress eliminated the tax deductibility of interest payments on nonmortgage debt.[5] Interest on a home equity line of credit was still deductible, however, giving homeowners a cheap and easy way of borrowing against their houses. Manufactured homes took off as house prices rose, making it harder for prospective first-time home buyers to come up with down payments on traditional dwellings. Creative marketing also made manufactured homes seem attractive alternatives to apartment living. The number of outstanding home-equity and manufactured-home loans almost tripled during the mid-1990s.

Many of the most active credit card, home equity, and manufactured-housing lenders were not banks at all, but finance companies. These institutions didn't collect deposits—they didn't need to because the loans they originated were securitized. And since they didn't collect deposits, finance companies weren't subject to the same regulatory oversight as banks. Taxpayers weren't on the hook if they went belly up—only their shareholders and other creditors were.

Finance companies thus had little to discourage them from growing as aggressively as possible, even if that meant lowering or winking at traditional lending standards.

The banks' long-standing "originate-to-hold" model of lending, in which they kept the loans they made on their own balance sheets, was rapidly giving way to a new "originate-to-distribute" model, in which loans were securitized and sold to a wide array of investors. This change in the banking business model was roundly endorsed by regulators. Because banks didn't own the loans, they didn't bear the risk, diminishing the odds of another S&L-type crisis. Regulators felt anything banks could get off their balance sheet was fine by them. Of course, the risk involved in making these loans didn't go away; it simply shifted to investors and, by extension, to the broader financial system.

What happened next should have sounded an alarm about the limitations of securitization. Delinquencies, defaults, and personal bankruptcies ballooned, as households that shouldn't have gotten a credit card or home equity line in the first place ran into trouble. The securities backed by these loans were also hit hard and contributed to the global financial crises of 1997–98. That episode began among the indebted economies of Southeast Asia, extended to Russia (which defaulted on its debt), and ended with the collapse of hedge fund Long Term Capital Management. Less remembered is the freezing up of the asset-backed securities market, in which credit card, home equity, and manufactured-housing securities were traded. For several days during the fall of 1998, no trading at all took place in these markets. The panic was quickly quelled when the Federal Reserve slashed interest rates and Fannie and Freddie stepped in to buy a lot of mortgage securities, providing much-needed liquidity to the markets. But it wasn't enough for many finance companies, which either failed or were acquired—in many cases, by banks. The dollar amounts involved in that crisis were dwarfed a decade later by the subprime financial shock, but much of what happened later seemed all too familiar.

Securitization Dissected

At bottom, securitization is not very complicated. The interest and principal payments paid on the pooled loans are paid to investors in a specific order, which is spelled out by the securities' *tranches*— French for "slices." Those investors who are particularly averse to risk buy the tranches viewed as most secure by the credit-rating agencies. Investors in these senior tranches get paid first, before all other investors. To add more protection, a pot of money from the loan payments is set aside just in case a large number of borrowers default.[6] The tradeoff for all this protection is a lower return—investors in senior tranches receive lower rates of interest on their investment. Senior tranches make up the bulk of most securitizations; in the average residential mortgage-backed security (RMBS), for example, senior tranches account for 80% of the face value—also called the capital structure—of the security (see Figure 7.1).

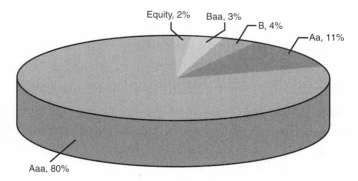

Equity, 2%   Baa, 3%   B, 4%   Aa, 11%   Aaa, 80%

Figure 7.1   Most mortgage securities are mostly Aaa: capital structure of a typical mortgage security.

After senior investors get their money, investors in the middle-rated or mezzanine tranches receive theirs. Investors in these tranches are assured of payment under most circumstances, but if the economy suffers a recession or housing experiences a cyclical downturn, things could get dicey, and mezzanine investors might not get all their money back. Mezzanine tranches account for 18% of the average security's capital structure.

The remaining 2% is the riskiest slice of the security, known as the equity tranche. This portion isn't even rated by the credit-rating agencies. Investors in the equity tranche are the last to be paid, and thus may not get all their money back if too many borrowers default. Because of the obviously high risks, the returns can be large if all goes well.

Wall Street's securitization machine went into overdrive during the housing boom, producing a frenzy in the mortgage securities market. At its peak in 2005, more than $1.1 trillion in RMBS was issued and sold to investors. Another $1 trillion was sold in 2006. In the first half of 2007, leading up to the subprime financial shock of that summer, RMBS sales came in not far off the $1 trillion mark.

For any securitization to succeed, investors must be willing to buy each of the tranches. Banks themselves were first in line, picking up most of the senior-rated segments. Returns on these were low, but greater than the banks were paying to their own depositors. Just as important, regulators required banks to hold very little capital in reserve against the chance these high-rated securities would default. The high rating meant there was very little risk—or so regulators thought. Insurance companies and various types of asset managers bought the bulk of the mezzanine tranches. These firms were searching for higher returns than the senior tranches offered, and they didn't have the same regulatory constraints as the banks. Besides, the mezzanine pieces were still A-rated securities, and the chance of default was thought to be relatively low. The biggest buyers of the equity tranches were hedge funds. The managers of these investment pools knew they were taking bigger risks, but their clients demanded extraordinary returns, which are tough to generate without substantial risk and lots of leverage (borrowed money).

Financial Alphabet Soup

Securitization didn't stop with plain-vanilla RMBS. Instead, it evolved into a dizzying, mind-numbing alphabet soup of financial products. The most notorious was called a collateralized debt obligation (CDO). This was essentially just a mutual fund for bonds and loans. Like a stock mutual fund, which holds stocks from many different companies, a CDO buys bonds; these can be straight-up corporate bonds, or securitizations backed by mortgage loans, credit cards, auto loans, and so on. One key benefit of stock mutual funds is diversification; they enable investors to avoid the risk of keeping too many eggs in one basket. In theory, the same benefit applies to a CDO. If the CDO invests in a wide enough variety of bonds, it should be less risky.[7]

The CDO's lineage can be traced back to the late 1980s, but it came into its own in the early 2000s.[8] CDOs were backed initially by investment-grade corporate loans and bonds and were particularly attractive in the wake of the tech-stock bust, when businesses had to offer high interest rates to attract nervous investors to buy their debt. CDO managers could make good money by simply collecting these interest and principal payments, passing most of it along to CDO investors and keeping a cut for themselves.

But this simple scheme became increasingly difficult as the economy improved; financial pressure on firms receded, as did bankruptcies, and corporate bond yields declined. CDO originators—mostly investment banks—quickly focused their attention on higher-yielding credit card– and auto loan–backed securities, and ultimately on mortgage securities, including those backed by subprime loans. The product they created was referred to as an ABS CDO (because "asset-backed security collateralized debt obligation" was quite a mouthful), and it exploded onto financial markets. ABS CDO issuance soared from virtually nothing in at the start of the 2000s to nearly $300 billion at its peak in 2006 (see Figure 7.2).

Billions $

Figure 7.2   CDO issuance soars in housing boom: ABS CDO issuance.

ABS CDOs were overwhelmingly popular; they seemed to offer a win-win proposition for everyone. Investors liked CDOs for their high returns, apparent diversification benefits, and capability to precisely calibrate the risk they were taking on. CDOs have the same tranching structure as traditional securitization, with payments going first to senior tranches and then mezzanine tranches, and an equity tranche that shouldered the most risk. CDO managers collected fat fees that were especially attractive if the CDO allowed for active management of the securities in the CDO. Managers could buy and sell securities out of the CDO to enhance its return or lower its risk. CDO originators also earned lucrative fees and solved one of their biggest problems in putting together a securitization: finding enough investors for all the tranches. At times, depending on market conditions, investors weren't quite as interested in one of the tranches. Mezzanine tranches, in particular, could be a tough sell. Most investors wanted either the safety of a senior tranche or the high return of the equity tranche, not the stuff in the middle. So-called mezzanine CDOs were created from the mezzanine tranches of traditional securitizations, tranching them up further and creating more of the better-liked senior and equity tranches, but now within a CDO.

If that wasn't confusing enough, it became even more tangled. CDOs were created from tranches of other CDOs. These were called "CDOs-squared" or "CDOs of CDOs." And as the securitization machine spun out of control just prior to the subprime shock, CDOs-of-CDOs-of-CDOs—or "CDOs-cubed"—were being manufactured. There were also synthetic CDOs, as opposed to "real" ones. With most asset-backed securities, including subprime mortgage securities already accounted for in CDOs, originators needed to cook up something else, lest the market cool off. A synthetic CDO did not buy tranches of securitized loans or even tranches of other CDOs; it bought credit default swaps (CDS).[9] A CDS is an insurance contract on a bond or loan in which one party pays the other an insurance premium and expects to be compensated in return if there is a default. Most credit default swaps are written on corporate bonds, but plenty of CDS are also written on residential mortgage securities. With the notional value of CDS—the face value of the bonds being insured—totaling in the tens of trillions of dollars, there seemed to be no limit to what the securitization machine could produce.

Shadow Banking System

By the time the subprime financial shock hit in summer 2007, the machine was tranching and distributing trillions of dollars in securities to investors across the globe. Securitization's financial web was expanding exponentially, as was its dizzying complexity. Yet policymakers thought this was precisely securitization's most significant strength. The risks involved in making a loan were no longer concentrated within any one financial institution; rather, they were spread across the entire global financial system. Loan defaults were less likely to jeopardize the viability of any particular institution, as their financial pain would be diffused widely among many investors and institutions.

Global banking regulators encouraged banks to securitize their loans, pushing the risks off their balance sheets. This attitude was codified in a series of agreements known as the Basel Accords, named for the Swiss city in which they were first hammered out.[10] The most recent of these agreements, called Basel II, imposes global rules on banks regarding the amount of capital they must hold in reserve to cover loan or investment losses. These capital requirements vary based on the expected risk of the investment—if a bank holds relatively safe government bonds, for example, it is required to hold less capital to guard against loss. This is called risk-weighting, and it makes sense as long as the rules reflect the true risks of a particular asset or investment. For years, highly rated residential mortgage-backed securities, collateralized debt obligations, and similar securities were assigned relatively low-risk weights, and regulators thought they were safe.

Banks thus had a strong incentive to avoid making and keeping mortgages and other loans, and to hold mortgage-backed securities instead. Banks were happy to originate loans—processing borrowers and accepting origination fees—but less interested in actually funding the loans, which required them to hold more capital in reserve. Funding for loans thus came increasingly from nonbank institutions. These institutions were a mixed bag; they included investment banks, hedge funds, money market funds, and finance companies, as well as newly invented entities called "asset-backed conduits" and "structured investment vehicles" (see Figure 7.3). Together they formed a shadow banking system, which was subject to little regulatory oversight and also not required to publicly disclose much, if anything, about itself. By the second quarter of 2007, just prior to the financial shock, the shadow banking system provided an astounding $6 trillion in credit and was rapidly closing in on that provided by traditional banks.

It was clear that the banks had off-loaded a substantial amount of risk to the shadow banking system, but it was not at all clear which institutions in this opaque galaxy were bearing those risks—or exactly how large those risks were. Policymakers took comfort in the notion that risk seemed to be spread widely around the globe and thought

Figure 7.3   The global financial system.

that any problem in the shadow banking system wasn't theirs to worry about. Unfortunately, the system didn't work the way they thought.

Liquidity Evaporates

Take the structured investment vehicles (SIVs), for example. Many big global banks established these to make big bets on securitized loans. At their peak in mid-2007, SIVs held $1.4 trillion in subprime RMBS and CDOs (see Figure 7.4). Banks generated handsome profits from their SIVs, earning fees for creating and managing them. Making them particularly attractive, SIVs could be structured so that their investments didn't sit on the banks' balance sheets; thus, banks faced no requirement to hold capital to protect against the SIVs' risks.

SIVs took substantial risks, starting with their habit of selling short-term commercial paper—IOUs that came due within a few days or weeks—to finance investments that would mature over much longer periods of time. In banker-speak, they were borrowing short and lending long, much like those doomed S&Ls of the 1980s that were taking deposits on which they had to pay prevailing market rates

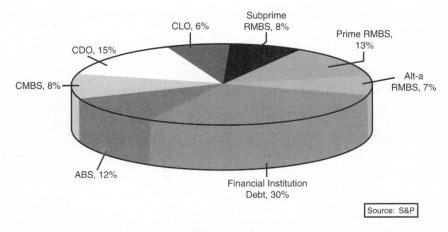

Figure 7.4 What SIVs invest in: SIV share of investments, October 2007.

or risk losing them to finance 30-year mortgage loans. It was a profitable practice as long as money market funds and others were willing to buy the SIVs' commercial paper. It quickly unraveled when the subprime financial shock caused the SIVs' investments to go sour. Money markets began shunning SIVs' commercial paper, fearing they would never be paid back. In response, the SIVs turned back to the banks that had created them. Most SIVs had credit lines with their parent organizations, set up to tide them over any short-term need for cash. The banks had been happy to set these up, using them to collect additional fees, and had never thought they would really be needed. Now the SIVs were desperate for cash.

At one point in late 2007, it seemed that nearly all SIVs were about to fail, creating a huge forced fire sale of their investments. Such a sale would have meant plunging prices and a much bigger financial shock. Alarmed, the U.S. Treasury Department intervened, brokering a deal among major banks to try to keep this from happening.[11] The deal was never implemented; the SIV-owning big banks chose to resolve their problems individually. Yet as the SIVs' investments flowed back onto the banks' own balance sheets, it became clear that the shadow banking system hadn't spread risk as widely as had been thought. The regulators, moreover, were still on the hook if something went wrong.

Similar short-term funding issues also threatened the asset-backed conduits. Like SIVs, these financial vehicles had been created by big global banks to hold loans that the banks had originated for securitization. The conduits were like warehouses, where loans could reside until they were pooled into securities. Because the banks never technically owned the loans, they were not required to hold any capital against them. In early 2007, some $400 billion worth of loans sat in such warehouses. Like the SIVs, these were funded with short-term commercial paper—and like the SIVs, by summer 2007, the conduits could no longer sell their commercial paper because the money funds and other investors feared they would never be repaid. As the conduits were forced out of business, the securitization machine ground to a halt.

Leverage Kills

The shadow banking system also amplified risk through leverage. Hedge fund managers were particularly aggressive about investing with borrowed money, even when their investments included the riskiest equity tranches of securitizations. At the peak of the financial frenzy in 2005–2006, many hedge funds were leveraging such investments as much as 15 times—that is, for every dollar of their own money they invested, they borrowed $15. The hedge funds had promised to deliver supersized returns, and these could only be generated by taking large risks with lots of leverage.

Leverage can indeed turbocharge returns when investors bet right, but it can be financially cataclysmic if they bet wrong. Take the case of a hedge fund buying a subprime mortgage security worth $100. The fund puts down $10 of its own money and $90 that it borrowed. If the price of the security rises 10%, the fund's return is 100%—it has doubled its original $10. But if the security's price falls 10%, the fund's equity is wiped out. At that point, either it can put up more of its own money, replenishing its equity, or it will lose the investment to whoever loaned it the $90—just like a homeowner who gets foreclosed.

Unlike many ordinary homeowners, however, hedge funds were supposed to be sophisticated about risk. They hedged—hence the name—which made them bolder about taking on risk and leverage. They hedged against the risk that an investment's value would fall by making another investment they thought would rise in value in such a circumstance. One popular hedging technique was to balance investments in subprime mortgage securities by short-selling the ABX index.[12] Shorting is a bet that the value of what is being shorted will fall. Like the Dow Jones Industrial Average or the NASDAQ, the ABX index condenses a lot of market trading into a single number; the trading it tracks reflects the price of credit-default swaps—sophisticated insurance contracts—on subprime securities. When worries about mortgage defaults rise, the cost of insuring against a default on these securities rises and the ABX falls. Long before the subprime financial shock hit, it was evident that conditions were deteriorating because the ABX was falling. Those who shorted the ABX—thus betting it would fall—were making money even as prices for subprime securities were also falling. If, like the hedge funds, they were also buying subprime securities, they were thus at least partially covering their own losses.

Yet investing with leverage can be lethal, even when combined with hedges. This was demonstrated by the implosion of two prominent Bear Stearns hedge funds in July 2007,[13] arguably the proximate catalyst for the subprime financial shock. The hedge funds had invested in CDOs of Aaa-rated subprime mortgage securities. Their investments had been highly leveraged, but to hedge at least some of the risk, the funds used the ABX index. It seemed like a winning formula: Factoring in interest received on the CDOs with the cost of the debt to purchase them and the cost of the credit insurance to hedge them, the funds ended up with a hefty positive rate of return—"positive carry," in hedge fund lingo. Yet it all went badly awry as surging mortgage delinquencies rapidly undermined the price of the funds' subprime securities. The fund managers had not hedged enough to cover their leverage-enlarged losses. The banks that had loaned money to the funds grew nervous as their collateral—the subprime bonds—evaporated. The banks demanded the Bear funds put up more collateral, forcing them to sell their bonds to raise cash. That selling made prices for subprime bonds fall even faster, making the banks even more nervous and sparking more demands for collateral, which caused more selling. It didn't take long before the Bear hedge funds were wiped out.

Diversification Disintegrates

Regulators were much too confident that diversification would protect the new-fangled securitizations being distributed throughout the shadow banking system. CDOs, in particular, were supposed to benefit from diversification, by combining securities that weren't alike. If one of the securities in a CDO performed poorly, it would be offset by another, better-performing component in the CDO soup.[14] CDO managers were paid handsomely for their presumed ability to mix securities just right and produce a well-diversified CDO.

CDOs of corporate bonds were able to achieve diversity by including bonds from companies in different industries. Combining bonds from Delta Airlines with ExxonMobil, for instance, was one way to protect a CDO from the impact of big spikes in oil prices. As Delta is hurt by surging fuel costs, Exxon's bonds are soaring for the same reason. Similarly, combining bonds from a home builder with those of a healthcare provider helps cushion investors in a downturn; as builders struggle to raise cash, healthcare remains largely unaffected.

CDOs of mortgage securities were supposed to achieve diversity by mixing mortgage securities from different parts of the country. In the past, housing downturns were relatively concentrated; house prices can fall in Los Angeles, Houston, or Boston, but never in too many places all at once (the Great Depression aside). Because a CDO effectively combined mortgages from all over the country, it seemed a good, safe way to invest in housing.

CDO issuers, managers, and investors largely dismissed the idea that a downturn could affect more than a few overvalued local markets; they failed to recognize that they were in a national housing bubble. When prices started falling and homeowners stopped paying on their mortgages nearly everywhere, it quickly became clear that the CDO had not diversified risk at all—it had concentrated risk in a highly leveraged investment.

Who's Responsible?

Of all the places you can point the finger for the housing bubble and subprime financial shock, perhaps the most deserving is the removal of responsibility from the financial system. Lost in the rapid, wholesale rush to securitization and the shadow banking system was the notion that someone—anyone—should ensure that individual loans are made responsibly, to responsible borrowers. A bank that makes and holds a loan has a clear incentive to be responsible and guard against excess because its own bottom line will suffer if it isn't repaid. Government regulators also have a responsibility to make sure that banks are lending prudently because taxpayers will pay if they don't.

Securitization undermined this incentive for responsibility. No one had enough financial skin in the performance of any single loan to care whether it was good. A shaky mortgage would be combined with others, diluting its problems in the larger pool. At every stage along the long securitization chain, there was a belief that someone— someone else—would catch mistakes and preserve the integrity of the process. The mortgage lender counted on the Wall Street investment banker, who counted on the CDO manager, who counted on the ratings analyst or perhaps the regulator.

In the period leading up to the subprime financial shock, America's financial ingenuity seemed without parallel. Our best financial minds appeared to have devised a machine to channel the world's savings into productive uses more efficiently and with less risk than ever before. The machine's engineers were reaping unimaginable benefits—billions of dollars a year in compensation were going to just a few thousand individuals. There were a few complaints, but they were faint; households with no prospects for homeownership just a few years earlier were now becoming homeowners.

Yet it turned out the machine was running amok, as all along the chain, everybody assumed someone else was in control.

8

Home Builders Run Aground

Home building is a cyclical business. Few other industries experience the same roller-coaster ride in demand and price. As clear as this seems in retrospect, it was far from conventional wisdom during the housing boom. For an unprecedented 15 years, beginning in the early 1990s and lasting until the boom's peak in 2005, home building posted steady annual growth in activity, sales, and profits. Even during the 2001 recession, the industry's ascent was interrupted only briefly.

The home-building industry seemed to have gotten its act together in the 1990s. From a fragmented collection of small, privately held and essentially local builders, each putting up a few dozen homes a year, the industry had transformed itself, becoming dominated by a dozen publicly traded national firms that built thousands of homes annually. In 1990, fewer than one in ten U.S. homes was built by a publicly held firm; by 2005, the proportion was nearly one in three.

The industry's consolidation had been driven by the cost savings that came with scale. Everything from lumber to dry wall was cheaper in bulk. More important than materials, however, was the big builders' ability to acquire large tracts of the most attractive land in the nation's most lucrative housing markets. Because of their heft, large firms were better able to navigate the labyrinth of zoning and permitting restrictions thrown up in many places to thwart development. Builders with large national operations were also more likely to withstand the kinds of regional economic downturns that had done in many of their smaller competitors.

In theory, publicly traded builders' advantages included more and better information about their customers and markets. They had the resources to precisely gauge the demand for their product and what the competition was up to; therefore, they were less likely to make a serious business misstep. Small builders knew their communities, but they had little understanding of the broader economic and demographic forces shaping demand and supply for homes—a vital tool for success in such a sensitive business.

Shareholders and the global capital markets were also expected to impose discipline on the large construction firms, improving their performance. The smart money, it was believed, would ensure that egotistical builders didn't get carried away and put up more homes than the market could absorb. In the past, many smaller home builders had gotten into trouble erecting homes "on spec"—that is, with no bona fide buyer, only a local banker willing to put up the funds in anticipation of a sale. This sort of trouble wasn't going to happen again, or so it was thought.

The optimism was misplaced, however. On the contrary, publicly traded builders' access to freely flowing capital enabled them to put up homes long after housing demand had begun to wane. In the end, builders and their shareholders turned out to be about as good at gauging demand as Silicon Valley's tech gurus had been during the dotcom craze of the late 1990s. Like tech-company executives, builders had become intoxicated, as well as hugely wealthy, by their own lofty stock prices. Such prices could be justified and sustained only by building and selling more homes at higher prices.

The builders quickly forgot the pain their colleagues in the manufactured housing industry had experienced just a few years earlier. Mobile homes had gone upscale in the mid-1990s; the industry thought it had found a foolproof way to turn lower-income renters into homeowners while attracting older empty-nesters as well. At one point, manufactured housing accounted for an astounding 20% of all residential construction. But those soaring sales did not stem from genuine growth in demand or better product design—they were simply the result of very easy credit. Loans to buy mobile homes were being securitized and sold into global capital markets. Households were happy to borrow the nearly free money—they just weren't able to repay it. When global investors figured this out, the lending stopped. Without credit, unsold manufactured homes piled up on dealer lots, and the industry has never recovered. It was a sobering tale the home builders knew well; they just figured it didn't apply to them.

During the decade's housing boom, builders put up far too many single-family homes and apartments. At its worst, millions of empty units flooded the housing market. Builders were choking on unsold inventory, and investors who had purchased homes couldn't sell or rent them. There just weren't enough American households to fill all the vacant homes. And unlike past periods of regional overbuilding, such as in Texas in the mid-1980s, these unsold homes weren't stick-like structures that could as easily be torn down as sold; they were large and well-appointed residences.

Builders had swallowed their own marketing hype. The industry's most vocal CEOs argued that demand for new homes would rise strongly ad infinitum, powered by a steady increase in foreign immigrants seeking a first home and aging baby boomers looking for a second one. Builders also had faith that Americans would rather own than rent, and that with low mortgage rates and ample credit, the national rate of homeownership could climb steadily higher. But their logic and arithmetic didn't add up. Home builders' enduring optimism, so instrumental in driving past housing cycles, had completely pervaded this one.

As the number of vacant homes mounted through 2006, 2007, and 2008, builders had no choice but to slash construction and house prices. It quickly became a matter of survival, and many builders didn't make it; bankruptcies and liquidations mounted. The home-building cycle, which had powered the broader economy during the boom, cost it dearly in the bust. During the first half of the 2000s, rising home construction alone accounted for as much as one-third of the economy's growth; when construction collapsed in the subsequent bust, it became the major cause of the 2008 recession.

Booms and Busts

Veteran home builders are much like wizened commercial fisherman—they have weathered many storms. Indeed, making it through the housing market's ups and downs had been as tricky for builders as navigating an Atlantic nor'easter could be for a sailor. Over the years, rough economic weather had claimed as many builders as the ocean storms had claimed ships at sea.

A housing storm could be extraordinarily severe. In nine housing busts since World War II, residential investment—the dollar value of all new housing construction and remodeling by existing homeowners—had dropped nearly 25% on average.[1] Housing's booms have been equally impressive, with average investment rising well over 50% during periods of growth. Home building's swings dwarf those of the broader economy, which rarely deviates from its long-term growth trend by more than a few percentage points (see Figure 8.1).

Figure 8.1   Homebuilding is a very cyclical business.

Housing busts through the early 1980s were particularly harsh, exacerbated by credit crunch conditions—no loans available for anyone, no matter how good their finances. The problem: Only a banker could make a mortgage loan, and the banker could lend only as much as his depositors gave him. But depositors were fleeing traditional banks, which were barred by a Depression-era rule called Regulation Q from paying interest on checking accounts. As the Federal Reserve raised short-term interest rates to double-digit levels to quell the raging inflation of the 1970s, depositors moved their funds to money market accounts and Treasury bills, where rates were then far higher than in traditional bank accounts. As money flew out of the banks, mortgage credit for housing shut down.

Builders understood the dynamics of mortgage finance; they knew that when credit was ample, they had to take advantage of it, putting homes up to market as quickly as possible. Economic rebounds produced plenty of pent-up housing demand, from people who had put off home ownership during the lean times for lack of a loan.[2] Builders worked hard to make money during a boom so that they could survive the inevitable bust.

Housing booms didn't simply end after pent-up demand had been satisfied. Builders kept building as long as their bankers provided necessary up-front money to purchase cement and lumber, and hire masons and electricians. Even if builders wanted to plan around the market, it was hard to gauge the strength of housing demand or know how fast their competitors were adding to supply. Typically, builders misjudged and overdid it, constructing more homes than there were potential buyers. This set the stage for the next downturn.

The home building industry was largely a collection of small, privately held firms, each one focused on just a few neighborhoods. It was difficult for a home builder to venture far because his source of funding was a local banker, and banks were legally barred from crossing state lines to make a loan. If a builder wanted to expand to another state, he needed to find another banker. Local housing markets also tended to be idiosyncratic; building styles and desired amenities varied substantially from place to place. Knowing how to build center-hall colonials in New England suburbs wasn't much use for constructing Spanish-style homes in the desert Southwest. Most builders stayed close to home.

Publics Ascend

Housing's storms have moderated over the decades, the recent downturn notwithstanding. Regulation Q was phased out during the 1980s, and mortgage securitization came into its own, funneling capital from global financial markets to local U.S. mortgage and housing markets.[3] By the mid-1990s, mortgage loans were almost always available; it was a question of the interest rate, which was generally falling, and the loan terms, which were easing.

By the mid-1990s, the fragmented housing industry was ripe for consolidation. Many of the nation's smaller builders had failed or been severely hobbled by the late-1980s real estate bust and savings and loan crisis. Throughout Arizona, California, and the Northeast, it seemed as if the entire real-estate industry was in some stage of bankruptcy or liquidation. A nationwide home-buying market was also being created by the strong migration flows of households from the Northeast and Midwest to the South and West, and from California to the rest of the western U.S. Demographically speaking, Florida had become more like New York and Seattle more like San Francisco. The stock market was beginning its 1990s' bull run, and investors were eager to finance the roll-up of small builders into large, publicly traded businesses. Those builders who were already publicly held had stock that was rising in value and could be offered to smaller builders to entice them to sell out.

Home building acquisitions multiplied. A handful of major deals were made during the first half of the 1990s, but more than 50 were done during the decade's second half. The merger wave spilled over into the first half of the 2000s, with such mega-mergers as Lennar's purchase of U.S. Homes in 2000, Pulte's 2001 purchase of Del Webb, and Beazer's acquisition of Crossman in 2002. In 1990, public builders accounted for fewer than one in ten new home sales nationwide and generated no more than $10 billion in annual revenue. By 2000, their share of the market had surged to one new home sale in four, and at the peak of the boom in 2006, it had grown to nearly one in three, with sales of some $100 billion (see Figure 8.2).

%

Figure 8.2   Public builders grab market share of new home sales.

As the publicly traded builders grew larger and their earnings seemed more predictable, their access to credit opened up, accelerating their expansion and tightening their grip on the industry. Construction and land-development loans—the money provided by bankers to finance home building—expanded three-fold during the first half of the 2000s to nearly half a trillion dollars. Major home builders could also tap the corporate bond market for cash; those borrowings soared from effectively nothing in the mid-1990s to well over $30 billion at the height of the housing boom.

The big builders concentrated on the nation's most lucrative and fastest-growing housing markets. Some two-thirds of their construction was in half a dozen states, including Arizona, California, Florida, Nevada, North Carolina, and Texas. The big firms completely dominate building in these markets; they account for nearly all home building in places such as Orlando, Florida; Fresno, California; and Las Vegas, Nevada; and more than three-quarters of house construction in San Diego, California; Miami, Florida; and Phoenix, Arizona (see Figure 8.3).

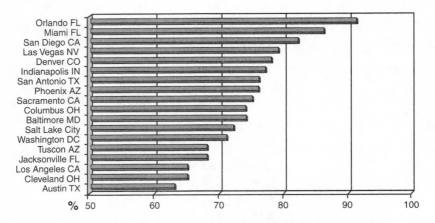

Figure 8.3   Where public builders build: share of home sales, 2007.

Not coincidentally, these are the areas where the housing boom turned into a bubble and where the subsequent bust was especially severe. Here the public builders were particularly aggressive about seeking to control developable land; this significantly pushed up prices for both land and houses because, in many areas, a home's price is largely the cost of the land it occupies.[4] Builders either bought vacant lots outright or took out options to buy them in the future. Options were preferred because little cash was needed to effectively gain control. In 2000, public builders owned or had options to buy 700,000 lots. By 2005, this had soared to 2.2 million lots, with nearly two-thirds optioned. Builders meant to construct as many homes as they could on this land, and that's exactly what they did.

Optimism Overflows

As the housing boom gained momentum, builders felt they could do no wrong. Sales volumes and house prices were hitting new records, builders' stocks tripled and then quadrupled in value, and there was plenty of cheap capital to finance more acquisitions and build out more communities. Builders were still like those fishermen, but now they were guiding large vessels equipped with satellite weather technology, and this made them certain they could avoid most storms and power through the rest. Some builders even seemed to believe that with their new financial tools and management acumen, they could make the housing storms go away permanently. It was certainly much easier to find a home buyer than a school of tuna.

Builders' optimism resembled what technology entrepreneurs had felt during the Internet bubble a few years earlier. Many newly minted dotcom firms had never generated a profit, but as long as Internet traffic and advertising were booming, shareholders were convinced payday would come eventually. Dotcom stock prices had soared; the value of Internet-related tech companies went from close to nothing in the early 1990s to nearly $1 trillion before the bubble burst.

Tech executives had woven compelling stories. "E-tailers" would sell everything from pet supplies to industrial equipment; virtual stores would overwhelm bricks-and-mortar retailers; advertisers would abandon newspapers and television for the Internet; and professionals of all types would work from home over the Web instead of in nondescript office parks. All these predictions rang true—and, indeed, all have come to pass, to some extent—but not necessarily as scripted in the 1990s.

Investors eventually grew tired of hearing the stories; they wanted the Internet to start producing profits. As the decade ended, demand was turning soft; new customers were harder to come by, and existing customers had already purchased as much technology as they could digest. The tech companies didn't give up without a fight, however. Some firms borrowed a trick from Detroit's automakers: They started providing their customers with financing to buy their products. This worked for a while, but even easy money couldn't keep increasingly stretched customers from cutting back forever. Some of those loans weren't being repaid, moreover. The Internet bubble burst.

On the face of it, home builders seem to be the antithesis of the tech companies. There's nothing virtual about a 3,000-square-foot home, and builders made plenty of money during the housing boom. Yet like the techs, the new publicly traded home builders became captivated by their own quickly rising stock prices. During the early 2000s, the stock market value of all publicly traded home builders surged four-fold to $150 billion. While not in the same league as the tech boom, this was financially intoxicating for the builders. They realized the only way to hold on to their newfound wealth was to demonstrate that their firms could consistently generate strong annual growth—if not at the pace of the 1990s dotcoms, then something close to it.

The builders developed some appealing stories to tell investors. Strong foreign immigration was a favorite. More than a million immigrants come to the U.S. every year—legal and illegal—and builders pointed out that all these people would need places to live.[5] Given the period's low mortgage rates and ample mortgage credit, new immigrants would likely gravitate toward single-family homes. Then there were the aging and affluent baby boomers, all of whom, builders asserted, were looking either to trade up to new, larger homes or to purchase vacation homes. Florida and South Carolina golf courses; condo towers in downtown Boston or Washington, DC; and mountain resorts in Idaho and Colorado were especially popular.

The builders weren't wrong—these were indeed important sources of new housing demand—but they significantly overstated the case. The attacks of 9/11 crimped immigration more than they knew or let on, and many more boomers were worried about surviving in retirement than about finding the ninth tee.

As the home builders' stories bumped up against the reality of a peaking housing market, the builders did what the techs had done: They became their customers' bankers. Most builders had established mortgage-lending units earlier, but now they ramped up these activities to ensure a steady flow of credit to their increasingly pressed buyers. The largest builders, such as Pulte Homes and Centex, financed nearly all the homes they sold during the height of the housing boom. It was one-stop shopping for home buyers: a new home and the mortgage loan from the same place. The builders were glad to book profits from what was then a very lucrative lending business—but more important, they wanted to make sure sales weren't deterred for lack of mortgage credit.

Awash in Homes

Builders had been aggressively constructing homes early in the 2000s, but in the 2003 summer building season, they really let loose. The initial angst over the Iraq invasion had passed, fallout from 9/11 and the 2001 recession was fading, mortgage rates had fallen to new lows, and subprime lending was coming into its own. The number of new homes added to the market—including completed single-family houses, condominium and apartment units, and pre-fab manufactured homes—jumped to well over two million a year.

You can argue endlessly about what constitutes overbuilding, but two million units were clearly too many. At that pace, supply was growing substantially faster than demand. Fundamentally, housing demand equals the sum of all new households being formed, second or vacation homes, and homes being torn down for structural or economic reasons. This makes intuitive as well as mathematical sense: New households of whatever type—new college graduates, the newly married, or the newly divorced—must live somewhere. People who own second or vacation homes might not live there year-round, but they have no immediate plans to sell. A torn-down home or one blown away in a hurricane adds to housing demand as well; whoever lived there now needs a new home. Throughout the early 2000s, total fundamental housing demand consistently ran near 1.8 million units a year (see Figure 8.4).[6] What had been a manageable gap between housing supply and demand early in the decade became an overwhelming gulf by the spring 2006 home-building season, when housing construction hit its all-time peak.[7]

Thousands

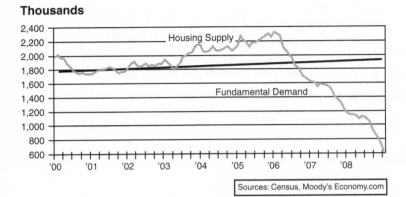

Sources: Census, Moody's Economy.com

Figure 8.4   Housing supply and demand: housing starts and manufactured housing.

Single-family home builders may have been initially fooled into thinking that the market could support a faster pace of building, because the effect of the early overbuilding had been felt mainly in rising vacancy rates for apartment rentals. The nationwide rental vacancy rate rose from 8% at the end of the 1990s to more than 10%, an all-time high, by the spring of 2004. The period's low mortgage rates and easy credit were prompting tens of thousands of apartment dwellers to become homeowners.

Overbuilding in the single-family market was also disguised by the arrival of housing flippers, people who buy homes as an investment without intending to live in them. As the market heated up, these opportunistic buyers purchased several homes in a new community, intending to sell them quickly at a profit. It seemed like easy money; builders were eager to show prospective buyers that prices in their developments were rising, to spur prospective buyers to act quickly. Flippers, however, took this as vindication of their own investment strategy. Builders quickly grasped the risks this posed for them; as more flippers started showing up, builders began demanding that buyers declare their intention to actually live in the home they were purchasing. Some builders also attempted to restrict quick resales in their contracts with buyers. But these efforts were no match for crafty investors, who continued to gather up properties. Builders' sales agents were also conflicted: Because their compensation was determined by sales volume, they had an incentive not to try too hard to weed out flippers. Better to make the deal, collect the commission, and move on.

The enormous magnitude of overbuilding in the United States thus did not become clear until the housing bust. Only after flippers stopped buying—and were only selling—and only after foreclosures began to mount did the number of vacant homes for sale balloon. Even a well-functioning housing market has some unsold inventory, but a healthy level of inventory in today's housing market would amount to no more than 1.25 million homes, roughly the level seen during the first half of the 2000s. By early 2008, inventories had surged to more than 2.25 million homes and were still climbing (see Figure 8.5). Compared with the total number of homes nationwide, inventories have never reached anything close to this level.[8]

Thousands

Source: Census

Figure 8.5   Awash in homes: number of vacant homes for sale.

No one is more motivated to sell than a homeowner, banker, or builder trying to move an empty home. The property is generating no rental cash; meanwhile, there are property taxes and maintenance costs to pay, not to mention legal fees and a mortgage payment. Banks that take possession of homes dumped by flippers and hapless homeowners in foreclosure are exceptionally eager to sell. Homes sold in foreclosure generally go for about half their previous sale price. The financial pressure on home builders awash in unsold homes isn't quite as intense, but they also tend to aggressively cut prices or offer large noncash incentives, such as built-in appliances, to try to move their vacant units. One large publicly traded builder, Hovnanian, drew special attention in late 2007 for its "fire sale" offer of six-figure discounts for homes in some high-end communities. Other builders offered up new cars or even college tuition payments to make their homes more attractive.

This was a housing nor'easter as severe as any that ever had roiled the home-building industry. The large public builders had not only failed to tame the economic weather, but they also had helped create a storm so large that it threatened to run nearly all of them aground.

9

As the Regulatory Cycle Turns

No part of the nation's economic life has more legal and regulatory oversight than housing and mortgages. Federal and state government agencies have a say in nearly every stage of mortgage lending, from determining whether a loan is appropriate to deciding how to foreclose on a defaulting homeowner. Yet regulatory supervision all but disappeared during the housing boom. Where were the regulators?

It wasn't as if regulators didn't understand subprime lending's risks. They had dealt with the issue in the mid- and late 1990s, when home equity lenders—that period's subprime pioneers—were aggressively making loans. Many of those home equity loans defaulted, and many of those lenders went belly-up by the end of the decade. Regulators responded in 1999 and again in early 2001 by "issuing guidance"—sending an official warning to lenders about the perils of such lending. The regulators told lenders to be sure they set aside adequate reserves to cover the potential losses on risky subprime loans and also warned lenders to avoid predatory lending.

Regulators carefully defined a "predatory" loan as one made without regard to the borrowers' ability to make timely payments.[1] Lenders had to do more than make sure the borrower's house was worth more than the amount of the mortgage; they also had to determine that borrowers had enough income to stay current on the loan. Loans that appeared designed mainly to generate fees for the lender were also declared predatory. A refinancing deal that did not lower the borrower's monthly payment or allow the borrower to take cash out of the house fell into the category of predatory practices, as did lying or withholding relevant information to make a loan to unsophisticated borrowers.

Yet as the subprime market heated up not long after the 2001 guidance was issued, predatory lending practices spread. Lenders appeared to be violating the rules' spirit, if not the letter. The nation's mortgage regulators largely went silent. They might slap the hand of a small lender for something particularly egregious; a few tweaks were made to the rules regarding property appraisals and mortgage fraud. But regulators had little of consequence to say during the housing bubble of the mid-2000s.

Not until late 2006, well after the bubble had begun to burst, did regulators issue their first formal guidance on what they called "nontraditional mortgage products."[2] Regulators had debated what to say in the guidance for more than a year, and what they finally agreed to still didn't directly address most subprime lending. Lenders limited their own definition of "nontraditional" mortgages to interest-only and negative-amortization loans, in which borrowers were allowed to pay less each month than the actual interest due, with the difference added to the principal amount of the loan. Most such deals were, in fact, prime—not subprime—loans.

The late 2006 guidance was much needed, but it was clearly too little and too late. It included some instructions that might have been considered common sense: For instance, lenders should not qualify borrowers for a loan based on low introductory "teaser" rates, but rather should ask whether a borrower had enough income to pay the higher rates that would kick in down the road. The guidance warned against making loans with no verification of income and savings, and it demanded that lenders disclose whether a loan included a large prepayment penalty (as most loans did). The guidance was fashioned by federal regulators, but it quickly became national policy as mortgage-industry regulators at all levels of government adopted it. It was a laudable step; unfortunately, the mortgages whose defaults would precipitate the subprime financial shock had already been made.

Federal and state regulators finally addressed subprime lending formally in June 2007, just weeks before the financial shock hit.[3] In this guidance, regulators told subprime lenders to qualify borrowers assuming a loan's full monthly cost, not just at the low initial teaser interest rate. Borrowers hit with large hikes in their mortgage payments would also need to have at least 60 days to refinance into a more favorable loan before they could be charged a prepayment penalty. By the time this guidance went out, however, subprime lending was already evaporating; the new rules applied to a type of lending that was speeding toward extinction.

Too Many Cooks

One reason mortgage regulation is not more effective is simply the mishmash of regulators, all overseeing different aspects or regions of the market. Their sheer numbers muddied the response to the frenzy leading up to the subprime financial shock. Some regulators recognized that increasingly easy lending standards would soon be a problem; a few publicly warned of the risks. But with so many diverse groups involved, it was difficult to get a working quorum for decision making.[4] At a time when oversight was most desperately needed on mortgages, half the nation's lenders were regulated at the federal level and half by the states (see Table 9.1).

TABLE 9.1   Mortgage Lending Regulators

Regulator	Who It Regulates	Examples of Lending Institutions
Federal Reserve	Financial holding companies, bank holding companies, member state banks	Citigroup, JPMorgan Chase, KeyCorp, SunTrust Bank, Wachovia Corporation

TABLE 9.1 Mortgage Lending Regulators

Regulator	Who It Regulates	Examples of Lending Institutions
Office of the Comptroller of the Currency (OCC)	Nationally chartered banks	Citibank, National Association; Mellon Bank, N.A.; PNC Bank National Association; Wells Fargo Bank, National Association
Federal Deposit Insurance Company (FDIC)°	State-chartered banks that are not members of the Federal Reserve System	BancorpSouth Bank, Bank of the West, Branch Banking and Trust Company, GMAC Bank
Office of Thrift Supervision (OTS)	Savings and loans associations (thrifts)	Countrywide Bank, FSB; Washington Mutual Bank; World Savings Bank, FSB
National Credit Union Administration	Federal credit unions	BECU (formerly Boeing Employees' Credit Union), Navy Federal Credit Union, Pentagon Federal Credit Union
State regulators°	State-chartered banks, mortgage brokers, nondepository lenders	New Century Financial

°Banks regulated by the FDIC can also be regulated by the state they are located in.

The Federal Reserve Board is by far the nation's most important banking regulator. It is responsible for keeping an eye on the largest banks and financial holding companies (FHCs), which historically account for about one-fourth of all mortgage lending. Another fourth comes from a hodgepodge of depository institutions, including commercial banks, savings and loans, and credit unions. The federal Office of Comptroller of the Currency (OCC), the Federal Deposit Insurance Corporation (FDIC), the Office of Thrift Supervision (OTS), and the National Credit Union Association (NCUA) oversee these lenders.

Federally regulated lenders are not generally subject to state laws, but the states have more than their share of regulatory responsibility.[5] States are charged with monitoring the most aggressive mortgage brokers and nonbank lenders, including mortgage finance companies and real estate investment trusts, that accounted for the remaining half of mortgage lending during the boom.[6] Most states also require mortgage brokers to be licensed and registered; many, although not all, require the same for individual loan officers. Some loose coordination occurs among the states via umbrella organizations, such as the Conference of State Bank Supervisors and the American Association of Residential Mortgage Regulators.

Other government agencies also have a voice in guiding the mortgage market. The Federal Trade Commission monitors mortgage lenders and brokers' compliance with antidiscrimination statutes and other federal laws. The Securities and Exchange Commission (SEC) oversees publicly traded companies, and the Federal Housing Finance Agency (FHFA) regulates Fannie Mae and Freddie Mac.

In some cases, more than one regulator is involved in overseeing a lender's activities. Wells Fargo & Company, one of the nation's largest mortgage lenders, is an example. The Federal Reserve watches over the bank's holding company, whereas the OCC monitors its lending subsidiary. In other cases, lenders receive very little scrutiny. New Century Financial, which made some of the most questionable subprime loans before it went bust, fell under California's state regulators and the SEC, neither of which had expertise or interest in evaluating the company's mortgage-lending policies.

Clear cracks exist in the regulatory patchwork that oversees mortgage lending, and the most aggressive mortgage lenders exploited them during the housing boom. Understaffed state regulators lacked resources to monitor a rapidly growing and increasingly sophisticated mortgage industry; they were the most vulnerable to the most aggressive and least scrupulous lenders, who were also among the biggest casualties when the boom went bust (see Table 9.2).

TABLE 9.2   Regulators of Bankrupt Mortgage Lenders

Lender	Primary Regulator
Central Pacific Mortgage	California Department of Corporations
Eagle First Mortgage	Arizona Department of Financial Institutions
Mortgage Lenders Network USA	Connecticut Department of Banking
New Century Financial	California Department of Corporations
Ameriquest	California Department of Corporations
CoreStar Financial Group	State of Illinois Department of Financial and Professional Regulation
First Horizon	Tennessee Department of Financial Institutions
Homefield Financial	California Department of Corporations
Innovative Mortgage Capital	California Department of Corporations
Mortgage Tree Lending	California Department of Corporations
Columbia Home Loans	New York State Banking Department
No Red Tape Mortgage	California Department of Corporations
Heritage Plaza Mortgage	California Department of Corporations
Right Away Mortgage	California Department of Corporations
Oak Street Mortgage	Indiana Department of Financial Institutions
First Street Financial	California Department of Corporations
Alliance Mortgage Banking Corp.	New York State Banking Department
Heartwell Mortgage	Michigan Office of Financial and Insurance Services
ACT Mortgage	Office of Financial Regulation, State of Florida
Altivus Financial	New Jersey Department of Banking and Insurance
Bridge Capital Corporation	California Department of Corporations
Steward Financial	California Department of Corporations
Freestand Financial	Arizona Department of Financial Institutions
Unlimited Loan Resources	Ohio Department of Financial Institutions
Starpointe Mortgage	Michigan Office of Financial and Insurance Services
Entrust Mortgage	Colorado Department of Regulatory Agencies, Division of Banking

TABLE 9.2   Regulators of Bankrupt Mortgage Lenders

Lender	Primary Regulator
American Home Mortgage	New York State Banking Department
Winstar Mortgage	Minnesota Department of Finance
Aegis	Texas Department of Banking
Mylor Financial	California Department of Corporations
Express Capital Lending	California Department of Corporations
Kirkwood Financial Corporation	Arizona Department of Financial Institutions
Lexington Lending	California Department of Corporations
Golden Empire Mortgage	California Department of Corporations
Spectrum Financial Group	Arizona Department of Financial Institutions
First Magnus	Arizona Department of Financial Institutions
Novastar	Missouri Division of Finance
First National Bank of Arizona	Arizona Department of Financial Institutions
Amstar Mortgage Corporation	Texas Department of Banking
Quality Home Loans	California Department of Corporations

Why wasn't lending better regulated? Beneath the muddle of agencies and authorities was the nation's long-standing distrust of centralized government authority. The system might have worked well enough in an earlier time, when banking and mortgages were primarily local or at most regional businesses. Regulators knew the lenders in their jurisdiction intimately. As regional barriers to lending came down, the nation's Byzantine regulatory structure did not change, making its oversight of lenders increasingly unwieldy and ineffective.

Home Ownership Politics

Regulators' efforts to cool the lending frenzy were also fettered by America's fierce and long-running devotion to the ideal of home ownership for all. Since the Great Depression, politicians had viewed the percentage of American families who owned their dwellings as a key benchmark of economic success. Regulators were given an open-ended mandate to help drive that number higher. Any agency or administrator who did not actively pursue this vision was roundly criticized.

The pursuit of higher home ownership went into high gear beginning in the 1970s, as it also became a test of the nation's success in promoting civil rights. The 1977 Community Reinvestment Act had outlawed "redlining," historically the practice by bankers of defining neighborhoods—literally outlined on maps in red—where they would not make mortgage loans. Such neighborhoods were usually poor and most often home to minorities or out-of-favor ethnic groups. The Community Reinvestment Act (CRA) was meant to actively reverse the effects of such discrimination by offering banks both carrots and sticks to encourage lending in underserved areas. The CRA was given more teeth during the Clinton Administration in the mid-1990s: Regulators could then require banks to explicitly target disadvantaged neighborhoods for both business and home-mortgage lending.

About this time, the Federal Reserve also unveiled new statistical methods for detecting discrimination in mortgage lending.[7] Marrying data from mortgage loan applications and approvals (as required under the 1975 Home Mortgage Disclosure Act) with sophisticated econometric techniques, researchers at the Fed felt they could tell whether lenders were racially discriminating.[8] A bank tagged by the Fed's models could be denied permission to acquire or merge with another bank.[9] This was a period of active consolidation in the banking industry, and any institution that could not be a shark quickly became a minnow. Only a handful of banks actually failed the Fed's test, but they were soon acquired, reinforcing the message from regulators to lenders to push home ownership aggressively.[10]

The Clinton Administration was especially proud of the rise in home ownership during the 1990s, particularly among lower-income and minority groups. While home ownership rose 7% among white households during the decade, it increased 13% among African-American households and 18% among Hispanic households. This could not have happened without the regulators' blessing and encouragement.

President Bush readily took up the homeownership baton at the start of his administration in 2001. Owning a home became one pillar of his "ownership society," a vision in which everyone would possess a stake in the American economy. For millions, this meant owning their own home. In summer 2002, Bush challenged lenders to add 5.5 million new minority homeowners by the end of the decade; in 2003, he signed the American Dream Downpayment Act, a program offering money to lower-income households to help with down payments and closing costs on a first home. Lenders gladly accepted Bush's challenge.

To reinforce this effort, the Bush Administration put substantial pressure on Fannie Mae and Freddie Mac to increase their funding of mortgage loans to lower-income groups. Both Fannie and Freddie had been shown to have substantial problems during the corporate accounting scandals in the early 2000s, and both were willing to go along with any request from the administration. OFHEO, their regulator at the time, set aggressive goals for the two giant institutions, which they met in part by purchasing subprime and alt-A mortgage securities. By the time of the subprime financial shock, both had become sizable buyers of the Aaa tranches of these securities.

Democrats in Congress were worried about increasing evidence of predatory lending. Some noted that the 2001 rule prohibiting such lending applied only to federally regulated lenders. North Carolina had passed a law banning predatory practices in 1999, and the Democrats wanted a federal equivalent that would cover all lenders nationwide. The Bush Administration and most Republicans in

Congress were opposed, believing legislation would overly restrict lending and thus slow the march of home ownership; moreover, the Republicans argued, existing regulations were adequate to discourage the worst excesses. The last attempt to pass anti–predatory lending legislation occurred in 2005, but it was also stymied. It was thus up to regulators to strike the appropriate balance between promoting home ownership and ensuring prudent lending. All too obviously, they failed to strike that balance.

Greenspan's Regulatory Failure

The Federal Reserve not only sets monetary policy, but it also plays a central role in guiding the nation's banking regulatory infrastructure. Without the Fed's leadership, other regulators could not take an effective stand against the frenzied mortgage lending of the early 2000s. But the Greenspan-led Fed was not eager to use its considerable authority to significantly curtail mortgage lending.

The Fed's regulatory stature stems from its intimate relationship with the largest financial institutions, established as part of its monetary policy responsibilities. Given the importance of these institutions to the entire financial system, policies set by the Fed quickly radiate throughout the system. The Fed's leadership also stems from its enormous financial and intellectual resources; more economists work in the Fed system than in any other institution in the world. Most important, the Fed is largely independent: Although it is not completely outside the political process, it is more able than any other regulator to adopt policies and positions without regard to what the president or Congress think.

Chairman Greenspan's reluctance to flex the Fed's regulatory muscles stemmed from his own oft-voiced skepticism about regulation. Greenspan believed a well-functioning market with the appropriate incentives could police itself more effectively than could government bureaucrats. Mortgage lending qualifies as such a market,

Greenspan thought. Lenders ultimately had to answer to smart and self-interested global investors, who surely saw no lasting profit in making bad mortgage loans.

Greenspan wasn't the only policymaker who held such views; the 1980s and 1990s had been marked by a steady march toward deregulation. The trend climaxed in 1999 with Congressional passage of the Gramm–Leach–Bliley bill, which overturned Depression-era banking laws barring banks from merging with securities dealers and insurance firms. The resulting financial holding companies were put under the regulatory domain of the Federal Reserve. The Basel II rules on banks' capital reserve requirements were being fashioned at about the same time. These rules rely heavily on market forces. How much capital banks need, and, therefore, how aggressive they can be in their lending, is determined mainly by the market value of their holdings. The fashion in banking circles was to let the market—not old-fashioned regulators—determine what was appropriate.

Some notable dissent on this came from within the Federal Reserve itself. Fed governor Edward Gramlich, a well-respected former economics professor from the University of Michigan, was notably vocal early in the lending boom. Gramlich, who was responsible for consumer affairs at the Fed, felt that the central bank should take the lead in weeding out predatory lending by examining both the federally regulated banks, which were under the Fed's auspices, and their mortgage affiliates, which were not.[11] These proposals went nowhere. Chairman Greenspan argued that Gramlich's proposed examinations would not have stopped shady lending and that they might inadvertently bestow on shady lenders the ability to claim the Fed's seal of approval.[12]

At various times, Congress also exhorted the Fed to address nagging concerns about excesses in the mortgage market. In 1994, the House and Senate passed the Home Ownership and Equity Protection Act (HOEPA), which authorized the Fed to prohibit unfair or deceptive mortgage lending.[13] Under HOEPA, the Fed has the authority to prohibit predatory lending practices by any lender, no matter who regulates it. The Fed used these powers only sparingly, arguing against the need for blanket rules on unfairness or deception. Each case is different, Fed officials claimed.

Almost a decade later, Congressional Democrats pushed the Fed to use its authority under the Federal Trade Act to write rules on unfair and deceptive lending practices. Again, it was to no avail. Greenspan tossed the ball back to Congress, saying the legislature was better suited to define the practices it wanted to bar and make whatever laws were necessary. In other words, if there was improper lending going on, Congress would have to deal with it—not the Fed, and not, by extension, the nation's bank regulators.

Don't Worry, Be Happy

Although Greenspan ultimately acknowledged that he had erred in thinking that the market would discipline lenders, his doubts about banking regulation were not without merit. Among other problems, it is hard for regulators to avoid getting caught up in the same euphoria that envelops lenders during good times. Instead of restraining overly aggressive lenders in such periods, regulators may encourage them.

The housing boom period illustrates the point. Mortgage credit conditions couldn't have seemed better in those years. By 2005, with unemployment declining and house prices surging, delinquencies and defaults had dropped to record lows. Hardly a borrower in San Diego or Miami was even late with a payment. Regulators would have had great difficulty making the case to lenders that their lending standards were out of whack: The regulators had no tangible evidence to point to, even if they had wanted some.

Regulators also could not keep up with the explosion of new and increasingly complex mortgage loans. Although interest-only, negative-amortization, and subprime loans had been around in some form for years, they had never been offered so widely to all kinds of borrowers in parts of the country where they had never before been available. Regulators didn't have time to evaluate all the new arrangements, let alone determine whether they were appropriate or what to do if they were not.

State regulators were particularly ill equipped to confront lenders, especially in states where housing was at its frothiest. Many state agencies were completely outmanned. At the peak of California's housing boom, for example, no more than 30 state examiners watched over nearly 5,000 consumer finance companies, including some of the nation's most aggressive mortgage lenders.[14] The massive workload effectively reduced examiners to bookkeepers who could only check to make sure that companies had adequate reserves and were not overcharging borrowers. Mortgage companies could expect an examination from state regulators about once every four years. When the bust came, some of the biggest casualties involved subprime lenders that had been examined just a few months before filing for bankruptcy.

Many state regulators also felt pressure from local politicians to keep mortgage credit flowing freely to their constituents. Examiners were asked to strike a difficult balance between regulating and encouraging home buying and lending. When house prices were high and mortgage delinquencies low, it was difficult enough to warn lenders that they might be overdoing it, let alone force them to rein in their lending.

Searching for a Voice

As mortgage loan quality weakened and foreclosures began to mount in 2006, regulators finally got their bearings. Federal agencies jointly issued the October 2006 guidance cracking down on nontraditional mortgage lending and followed in June 2007 with a statement on subprime loans. The Federal Reserve, now under the leadership of Chairman Ben Bernanke, began a series of hearings about protecting mortgage borrowers. HOEPA had given the Fed the authority for this in the mid-1990s, but not until the housing bust was the central bank willing to take on the job in a comprehensive way.

Finally, in December 2007, the Fed proposed some common-sense lending rules. Firms that made "higher-priced" (mostly sub-prime) loans would have to consider the borrower's ability to repay and would have to verify the borrower's income and assets. Prepayment penalties were barred if a homeowner refinanced within 60 days after an adjustable loan reset, and borrowers would have to establish an escrow account for taxes and insurance.[15] Lenders could not compensate mortgage brokers for steering borrowers to higher-rate loans, nor coerce appraisers to overstate home values. Mortgage services would have to credit borrowers as of the date they received payments. None of these rules were radical; indeed, it is hard to imagine that lending standards had eroded so badly that they were even necessary.

The Fed also began working to reestablish its leadership in mortgage and financial regulation. The central bank issued guidance in early 2007 along with other regulators, encouraging lenders to work with borrowers who were struggling to make their payments, particularly those facing steep adjustable-rate interest resets. Later in the same year, Chairman Bernanke threw his support behind expanding Fannie and Freddie's mortgage-lending authority, then still a politically controversial idea. The Bush Administration and Congress eventually followed.

In early 2008, Bernanke also supported helping homeowners whose homes' value had fallen below the amount of their mortgages, a situation called "negative equity." Bernanke argued that such mortgages might have to be written down, reducing the principal until the homeowner no longer owed more than the home was worth. This was a particularly unpopular view in many parts of the mortgage industry and in Washington, DC. Some mortgage holders had agreed to help troubled borrowers by freezing interest rates or extending the term of their loans, but few were willing to shrink the amount of a borrower's debt. Much of the Bush Administration, and some in Congress, also argued that such write-downs would amount to a bailout of bad borrowers and lenders. Bernanke countered that negative equity makes borrowers much more likely to default and that write-downs might be necessary to keep foreclosures from spreading uncontrollably like dominoes, dragging down housing and the wider economy.

Some regulators were particularly forthright in their responses to the subprime shock. FDIC Chairwoman Sheila Bair was one of the first to advocate freezing interest rates for subprime adjustable-rate mortgage (ARM) borrowers facing payment resets; she also proposed writing down borrowers' mortgage debts. John Reich, Director of the federal Office of Thrift Supervision, put forward a plan addressing some of the same concerns. Not only did such efforts illustrate the severity of the subprime shock and its implications for the nation's financial system, but they also testified to the leadership void left over many years by dormant regulators at the Federal Reserve.

Regulators didn't create the subprime financial shock, but they did nothing to prevent it. This was a result of, first, policymakers' distrust of regulation in general and their enduring belief that markets and financial institutions could effectively police themselves; and, second, of the nation's antiquated regulatory framework. The institutions guiding the nation's financial system were fashioned during the Great Depression, and as finance evolved rapidly, they remained largely unchanged. An overhaul is indisputably overdue.

10

Boom, Bubble, Bust, and Crash

June 2, 1995: This is as good a date as any to begin the string of events that led to the subprime financial shock. On this day, the nation's housing market was enjoying a blessedly fortunate set of conditions—the best in at least 30 years, with fixed mortgage rates below 8%, adjustable rates below 6%, and a healthy job market. Combined with the relatively low house prices that prevailed into the mid-1990s, these rates made housing as good a bargain as it had ever been in the United States. Sure enough, home sales, construction, ownership, and prices all climbed steadily through the remainder of the decade—and kept climbing, right through the 2001 recession and into the jobless recovery that followed.

Housing Boom

The period from the mid-1990s through the early 2000s is best described as a housing boom. Consistently strong activity was driven by well-supported demand and disciplined new housing supply. Buyers of second homes or vacation homes had every intention of holding on to them; they weren't "flippers" looking for quick profit. House prices posted solid, steady gains—but those who wanted real action turned to the stock market. Anyone seeking a fast buck was focused on the price of Cisco stock or perhaps eBay—not a Miami Beach condo or San Diego ranch home. Speculation had taken over the stock market, but not yet the housing market.

A single-family home was a bargain in the late 1990s, and the job market was arguably stronger than at any previous time in the nation's history. In 1995, a median-priced U.S. home could be purchased with a monthly mortgage payment of $675.[1] Because mortgage rates had fallen steadily, that monthly payment was no greater than it had been in 1980. Meanwhile, household incomes had more than doubled. Unemployment was falling, too. In 1995, it was near 5.5%, down from 7.5% early in the decade and half the level of the early 1980s. By the end of the 1990s, unemployment had reached a post–World War II low below 4%.

Minority groups were gaining meaningful access to mortgage credit for the first time. African-American and Hispanic households with incomes and savings who may have been unable to obtain mortgage loans in the past now finally could do so. This was a priority for the Clinton Administration; it empowered and then pushed regulators to aggressively enforce requirements on mortgage lenders to extend more loans to previously excluded groups.

Foreign immigration also soared during the 1990s, pushing up the number of households and, thus, the demand for housing. Immigrants were attracted by the surging U.S. economy and all the available jobs, particularly in contrast to their own troubled economies in Latin America, Southeast Asia, and Eastern Europe. The terror attacks of 9/11 were still in the future, and security was a relatively modest concern. Legal and illegal immigrants were adding half a million households a year to the U.S. population; each household required a place to live. Almost one-fourth of the new homes constructed during the housing boom were for immigrants.

Despite the strong demand for new homes, builders were restrained from overbuilding. The large California and Northeast housing markets still felt the effects of the early 1990s savings and loan (S&L) crisis, when many builders failed along with their banks. The S&L bust had hobbled the infrastructure for building homes, from obtaining construction permits to selling completed units.

Even as housing demand improved, it was difficult to put together all the moving parts needed to erect a home. California housing starts in 1995 were a third of their level from a decade earlier. Not until the decade's end did the home-building industry begin humming again.

Housing Bubble

July 4, 2003: What had been a housing boom became a housing bubble (see Figure 10.1). There was no obvious warning: The war in Iraq still looked like an easy win, the domestic job market was finally regaining traction, fixed mortgage rates were closer to 5%, and adjustable rates had fallen firmly below 4%. Despite the solid rise of house prices in the preceding eight boom years, housing was still affordable. But this was also when home buyers, lenders, and mortgage investors began looking skyward, assuming that because house prices had been rising strongly in the recent past, they would continue to do so far into the future. Speculation began to grip the market.

Figure 10.1 Housing boom, bubble, bust, and crash: housing price growth.

The housing bubble was born out of the boom. The boom had been based on solid demand and supply fundamentals, such as affordable homes, strong incomes, and ample household savings. The bubble developed when Americans started buying not simply because they needed someplace to live, but because they thought housing was a great investment. Prices had risen; therefore, they would continue to rise. This is speculation. A bubble develops when an asset's price becomes disconnected from its fundamental value. Stocks derive their fundamental value from future corporate earnings. Housing derives its fundamental value from its future value as shelter or from the rent it generates.

Some regions are more susceptible to bubbles than others. Parts of the country where geography or zoning makes development land scarce—think California, Florida, and the Northeast corridor—are particularly fertile soil for speculation. When strong demand meets a restrictive building environment, houses can be bid up quickly, divorcing price appreciation from the factors that caused the gains in the first place. Some of these areas had seen house-price bubbles in the mid-1970s, and again in the early 1990s. By contrast, in areas where new construction is relatively easy—Texas or Iowa—speculation is less likely. As soon as prices show any strength, builders rush in to add more houses and compete away the gains. Without dramatic price gains to point to, buyers' imaginations never drift toward the skies.

Conventional wisdom stated that although isolated regional housing bubbles might form, a nationwide bubble was all but impossible. The reasoning was based on transaction costs—the incidental expenses involved in buying and selling homes, from realtor fees to taxes. Speculative bubbles, it was believed, require frenzied buying and selling to fuel the price gains. Real estate transaction costs, however, were high enough to short-circuit such activity. Stocks, by contrast, were prone to speculation because the transaction costs involved in trading shares were much lower.

Yet the collapse of the Internet stock bubble at the turn of the century created the fodder for the subsequent national house price bubble. With stocks reeling and the Federal Reserve slashing interest rates, many households wondered what to do with their savings. Because housing was still rising in price, the answer seemed straightforward: Buy a house, or maybe several houses. The idea grew even more appealing following 9/11, as travel began to seem less alluring than a barbecue in the safety of your own backyard.

Besides, almost anyone could get a mortgage loan. For those with unblemished credit histories, the rates resembled those our parents and grandparents talked about, much as they recounted hearing Elvis Presley or Jimmy Dorsey for the first time. Even better, those high transaction costs were falling fast. Competition among mortgage lenders and newfangled Internet technology had made shuffling all those documents much less expensive. There was no place like a brand new home, and sales soared to astonishing levels. At the apex in 2005, fully 10% of all the homes in the country were bought and sold.

How Overvalued?

Economists often debate what constitutes a bubble and how to determine whether one is forming. After all, the price for any asset, from a share of stock to a home, is based on forecasts of future returns by many buyers—and who can say that all those buyers are getting their forecasts wrong? There are some telltale signs, however, and the housing market circa 2005 exhibited all of them: a huge volume of home sales; available easy money for house purchases; and a lot of new theorists arguing that, yes, prices might have gotten too high in the past, but things were different now. To these theorists, the housing market made perfect sense. All you had to do was discard all those antiquated measurements and notions of what constituted an appropriate house price.

One such measure of housing valuation compares house prices with rents.[2] The logic is simple: Households can choose to own or rent their home, and are likely to choose whichever option is more cost-effective. The cost of ownership, of course, is closely tied to the sale price of the home. If house prices rise faster than rents over a long enough period, renting becomes the cheaper option for many people, making house prices look overvalued. (The same relationship works in reverse: If house prices fall relative to rents over time, houses will likely be undervalued.) The relationship between house prices and rents depends on many factors, including interest rates and the availability of mortgage credit. Over sufficiently long periods of time, however, this relationship is quite stable.

Here's another way to think about it: The relationship between house prices and rents is much like a price–earnings ratio for stocks. PE ratios fluctuate as markets change, but since World War II, the PE on the S&P 500 stock index has averaged about 15—that is, stock prices have averaged about 15 times corporate earnings. At times a PE of more than 15 can be justified—such as when interest rates are low—but using the long-term average is a good rule of thumb for identifying whether the stock market is over- or undervalued. Just before the Internet stock bust in 2000, for example, the PE on the S&P 500 peaked around 45. As subsequent events proved, it was clearly overvalued.

Nationally, the housing "price-to-rent" ratio hit an all-time peak of 25 at the end of 2005 (see Figure 10.2). On July 4, 2003, the day I've identified as the start of the housing bubble, the price-to-rent ratio was 18.5. This compares with an average over the past quarter-century of 16.5 and a low of 12.5 during the mid-1980s. Although the overvalued national housing market in 2005 wasn't in the same league as the stock market in 2000, it was close in some metropolitan markets. The highest flyers included Miami, Florida; Washington, DC; Phoenix, Arizona; Orlando, Florida; most of southern California and Sacramento; Las Vegas, Nevada; and Long Island, New York. Before the bubble ended, however, almost every major market in the country was deemed to be overvalued to some extent.[3]

Housing Bust

April 10, 2006: On this chilly and wet day (at least, in my neighborhood in suburban Philadelphia), housing was palpably overvalued from coast to coast. Housing affordability was sinking, dragged down

Housing's price-to-rent ratio

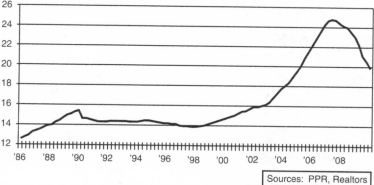

Sources: PPR, Realtors

Figure 10.2 An overvalued housing market.

both by soaring prices and by the Federal Reserve's recent series of interest rate hikes. The economy was looking robust, thanks largely to the soaring housing market, and low interest rates were no longer part of the central bank's prescription for balancing growth and inflation. Rising rates didn't prick the housing bubble immediately; mortgage lenders kept them at bay by offering even easier lending terms to borrowers. Eventually, lenders ran out of tricks for keeping monthly payments down. By the spring selling season of 2006, the housing bubble was starting to leak.

Nationally, house prices didn't fall much in 2006, but even the modest decline that occurred was unnerving. Not since the Great Depression had there been such an overall, coast-to-coast average price decline, and it got people's attention. Small and medium-size real estate speculators stopped buying and began selling—and when no one else showed up to buy, they began mailing their house keys back to their lenders. Mortgage loans made just a few months earlier began to show signs of trouble. Before long, a wave of mortgage defaults began the foreclosure process.[4] The pace of defaults rose from an annualized 775,000 at the end of 2005 to nearly 1 million by year-end 2006 (see Figure 10.3).[5] Many defaults involved recent buyers, who had made only one or two payments—or none—on their loans. Most were "flippers" who had taken out a mortgage expecting to pay it off quickly, after selling the house at a profit. When they couldn't sell or even rent their investment home, they defaulted.

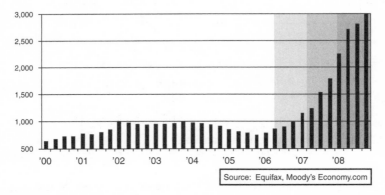

Figure 10.3   Three waves of foreclosures: first mortgage loan defaults, ths, SAAR.

A second wave of defaults and foreclosures began in spring 2007. Subprime mortgage borrowers who had obtained loans two years earlier choked as their mortgage payments jumped higher. Most had so-called 2/28 loans: For two years, the rate was low and fixed; after that, it adjusted generally every six months to levels reflecting prevailing short-term rates. Homeowners who hit their first rate reset in 2007 found themselves facing an average increase of $350 per month: Their average monthly payment shot from $1,200 to $1,550, often an unmanageable amount. The pace of defaults rose from 1 million per year at the end of 2006 to more than 1.5 million by summer 2007.

Nobody in the mortgage business had expected this. Many had understood it *could* happen—under the terms borrowers had agreed to, they could technically face a payment reset that would overwhelm their household finances—but almost no one thought it *would* happen. Surely such borrowers would be able to refinance; doing so was in everyone's interest. Mortgage lenders would collect more fees— often charging both to originate a new loan and to collect a penalty for paying off the old one early. Mortgage investors would be happy to get their money back; they had planned it that way and didn't want to worry about whether these shaky borrowers would default in the future. Borrowers would have a clean start.

Yet as credit conditions weakened, mortgage lenders and investors grew less willing to refinance hard-pressed borrowers facing resets. Suddenly, no one wanted to take on the risk, and subprime borrowers began defaulting en masse.

It was all too much for mortgage investors. They had been judiciously unloading their mortgage security holdings for more than a year, but by summer 2007, panic had set in and the rout was on. The subprime financial shock was in full swing.

Housing Crash

July 30, 2007: As the opening bell sounded on Wall Street, news spread that investment bank Bear Stearns was shuttering two of its hedge funds, both of which had loaded up with subprime mortgage investments. The story pushed the housing market over the edge. Mortgage securities trading shut down; the pipeline from global capital markets to the housing market had been severed. Now mortgage lenders couldn't make a loan even if they wanted to. There were still FHA loans and loans backed by Fannie Mae and Freddie Mac, but they could not fill the void left as private mortgage lending ceased. This was particularly true in places such as California and Florida, where government lending was virtually nonexistent.

Without mortgage credit, home sales plunged. At the start of 2007, new and existing home sales were running close to a 7.5 million unit pace a year, but by the end of the year, the pace had fallen below 5.5 million. Psychology in the housing market had been turned upside down. Until this point, home builders and other sellers had believed that if they were flexible on pricing and were patient, they would make a sale. It might take a few extra weeks or months, and perhaps an incentive such as a built-out basement or retiled roof, but eventually homes would sell for close to their initial asking price. Now, with mortgages and home sales evaporating, sellers realized they had no choice but to slash prices. Of course, those buyers who were still in the market sensed sellers' terror and turned coy; they didn't want to catch the proverbial falling knife.

House prices crashed. The national average price, which had fallen about 5% between the spring 2006 selling season and summer 2007, dropped another 20% by the end of 2008. National house prices had plunged some 25% from their peaks. The declines were much worse around Washington, DC, and on Long Island, where they had declined by more than 30%; in Arizona and Nevada, where they were off by 35%; and in southwest Florida and the Central Valley of California, where the declines were approaching a stunning 50%.

Prices have even farther to fall. Using the price-to-rent analysis as a guide, if the ratio of prices to rents returned to its 25-year average, nationwide house prices are likely to fall at least an additional 10%. This would mean a total drop in house prices of more than 35%, a tumble comparable to the one experienced in the Great Depression. Moreover, some large metro areas (including Miami, Florida; Washington, DC; Long Island, New York; the Bay Area of California; Orlando, Florida; and Phoenix, Arizona) will likely experience price declines measurably larger than this (see Figure 10.4).[6]

Where's the Bottom?

The free-fall in house prices after the subprime financial shock brought on a third wave of mortgage loan defaults and foreclosures. This time, the catalyst for foreclosure was negative equity, the dilemma faced by a homeowner who owes more on a home loan than the home itself is worth.[7] With house prices falling back to 2003 levels, homeowners in most parts of the country who had purchased between 2004 and mid-2007 and put less than 10% down were lucky if they were still above water. By early 2009, close to 14 million

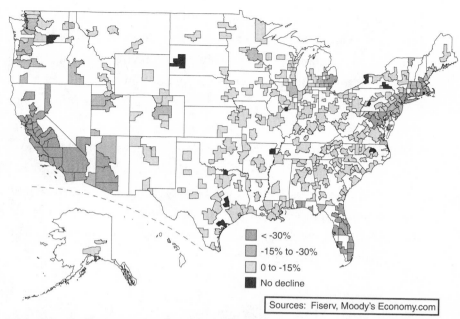

Figure 10.4   Where house prices will decline most: projected peak-to-trough house price decline, U.S. = −36%.

homeowners—more than one in four of all those with a first mort-gage—were indeed underwater. This was up from no more than 7 million a year earlier and just over 3 million the year before that.

Some homeowners chose to just walk away. With their homes' value falling far below the amount of their mortgage, they lost hope of ever getting back their equity and simply handed both mortgage and house back to the bank. This was unusual, however. Most homeown-ers were willing to work hard to stay current and in their homes, even while in negative equity. Many didn't really know their homes' value; others figured it was worth the wait until prices rose once again. It was a tenuous position to be in: One financial mishap, such as a tem-porary loss of income or an unexpected increase in expenses, could mean the loss of a home. The danger was compounded by lenders who couldn't or wouldn't renegotiate or modify the terms of a loan.

Many negative-equity households were also caught up in a rapidly weakening job market. Some were facing layoffs; others were

losing overtime hours or settling for part-time work because full-time
jobs weren't available. Predictably, regions with the worst housing
troubles also saw the most severe job losses. The situation was precarious for those with negative equity: A fender bender, a busted water
heater, or a child's broken arm could push families into delinquency
and default.

From summer 2007 to the end of 2008, first-mortgage loan
defaults soared from more than 1.5 million to 3 million. Nearly 3% of
the nation's households were in default on their mortgages. Default
rates were measurably higher in California, Arizona, Nevada, Florida,
the industrial Midwest, and heavily populated regions of the Northeast corridor (see Figure 10.5).

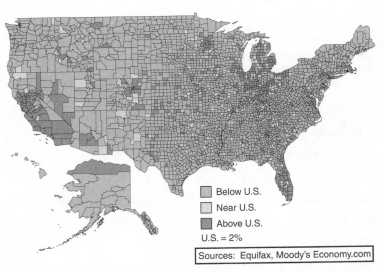

**Figure 10.5   Defaults soar across the country: % of households
defaulting on their first mortgage, '08q4.**

Not all loan defaults forced families from their homes. In good
times, fewer than half of defaults do. Homeowners and lenders are
often able to work out a deal; lenders put homeowners on a repayment plan or modify the loan by lowering the borrower's interest rate
or extending the term to make the loan more affordable. Many homeowners are able to recover and make good on their loans. But during

times of economic weakness, things are different: More than half of defaults cause households to lose their homes. The end could be a short sale, in which the home is sold for less than the mortgage amount; lenders sometimes agree to accept this just to get rid of the problem. It could also be a "deed in lieu," in which the homeowner simply hands the deed back to the lender and is freed from further obligation. More often than not, however, the lender eventually takes possession of the home, putting it into an "other real estate owned" (REO) account from which it is sold.

With so many homes going through this process, the number of vacant homes for sale surged. According the Census Bureau, by the end of 2008, more than 2.25 million homes were vacant and for sale. During the housing boom, there were only 1.25 million such homes. In other words, the bust had turned more than one million homes into "excess inventory."

Such properties were often sold far below prevailing market prices. Lenders were absorbing big losses in maintenance, legal, and carrying costs, and wanted to sell their foreclosed REO properties quickly, even if that meant writing off substantial sums. In early 2009, lenders were commonly selling foreclosed property for 50% below prevailing market prices.

These distressed sales were devastating for the broader housing market. A typical home sold in foreclosure reduces the value of surrounding properties by more than a full percentage point. Rising foreclosures were driving up inventories, which, in turn, were driving down prices and homeowners' equity and, thus, creating more foreclosures. The housing market was trapped in a self-reinforcing negative cycle. This had occurred briefly in California and New England in the early 1990s, but never in so many parts of the country. There was no obvious way out of the cycle—and no guarantee that house prices would stop falling soon.

11

Credit Crunch

Watching a financial crisis feels much like watching a natural disaster—as long as you're watching from a safe distance. The raw, uncontrollable power of each is riveting. Although one is made by man and the other isn't, there is something deeply mysterious about each; it isn't quite clear how, or why, or why now. Of course, each can create enormous damage and can be heartbreaking for those directly involved. The repercussions last well beyond the immediate shock; nearly everyone is affected at least indirectly, and each leaves scars that never entirely disappear.

The subprime shock was as serious a financial earthquake as any the nation had seen since the 1929 stock market crash.[1] There have been some big financial calamities through the years: the collapse of Penn Square Bank in 1982, the savings and loan crisis of the late 1980s, the collapse of hedge fund Long Term Capital Management in 1998, and the Internet stock bust at the turn of the millennium, to name a few. On the financial Richter scale, these other crises might rate a 5 or 6. The subprime shock was off the scale.

This was evident in the size of the losses suffered by global investors. Although the ultimate cost wouldn't be known for years, most reasonable estimates put the tab close to $2.4 trillion.[2] This includes both losses on thousands of defaulting mortgages and the decline in value of the securities backed by other shaky loans. By comparison, the S&L crisis cost the country a mere $250 billion.[3] Even Japan's banking crisis of the 1990s, from which the economy has never fully recovered, doesn't measure up; its losses come in near $750 billion.

Nearly every sector of the financial system has taken a bath because of the subprime shock. Global banks have lost an estimated $1.2 trillion, insurance companies and pension funds another $650 billion, and hedge funds and all other institutions $550 billion (see Figure 11.1). All kinds of institutions saw their residential mortgage and mortgage security holdings hammered by more than $1.1 trillion—no surprise there—but the extent of their other losses was startling. There were write-downs on commercial mortgage holdings and on business loans and credit of all types; even consumer loans such as credit cards, auto loans, and student loans suffered big losses.

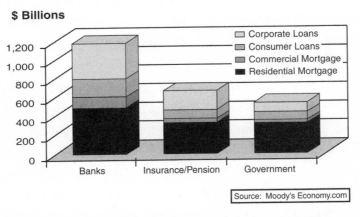

Figure 11.1   Financial sector losses mount: projected losses.

Every corner of the financial system was shaken. Trading in private residential mortgage securities came to a standstill, along with the markets for collateralized debt obligations backed by asset-backed securities and for commercial mortgage securities. Low-rated "junk" corporate bonds and bonds backed by credit card loans were still issued, but investors now held out for a much higher interest rate before parting with their cash. Even the market for municipal bonds, where state and local governments raise money to build schools or sewers, was thrown into turmoil. It wasn't that municipal or state governments were suddenly likely to renege on their obligations, but in panicked times, every deal seemed suspect.

The subprime shock was also noteworthy for its length. There were tremors beginning in early 2007, when the Chinese stock market swooned, but the shock struck hard in July 2007 and was still reverberating nearly two years later. There were moments when the crisis seemed to ebb, but financial markets remained unsettled throughout. Historically, financial market crises begin and quickly abate in just a few days or weeks. Almost none last more than a few months.

The persistent angst that pervaded financial markets during the subprime shock was clearest in the London Interbank Offered Rate (LIBOR) market, where the globe's biggest banks lend each other money for short lengths of time. LIBOR is particularly important because so many other types of loans are pegged to it. For example, most subprime adjustable-rate mortgages carry interest rates tied to the six-month LIBOR rate. Generally, LIBOR rates are not much higher than rates on U.S. Treasury securities of similar maturity. Treasuries are universally viewed as risk-free, and in normal times, big banks don't see much risk in lending to each other, either. When LIBOR rates rise significantly above comparable Treasury rates, it's a signal that bankers are nervous about doing business with each other and want higher rates to compensate for the extra risk. When Long-Term Capital Management collapsed in the late 1990s, for example, the three-month LIBOR jumped to more than a percentage point above the rate on three-month Treasury bills (see Figure 11.2). There it remained for nearly a month. There was a similar increase in the LIBOR–Treasury rate spread in the early 1990s S&L crisis that lasted about three months. In the subprime financial shock, the rate spread sky-rocketed by more than 4 percentage points at its apex in late 2008 and has remained wider than a percentage point for nearly two years.

But the most alarming feature of the subprime financial shock remains the fact that it was triggered by U.S. homeowners. Fifty-one

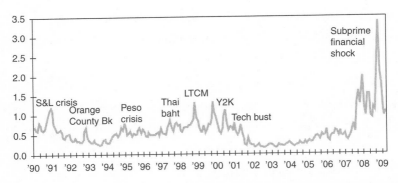

Figure 11.2 In a league of its own: difference between 3-month LIBOR and Treasury bill yields.

million American homeowners have first mortgages, and in a normal year, only about three-quarters of a million of them stop making their mortgage payments and default. In 2006, defaults reached an annual rate of almost 1 million. They rose to nearly 1.5 million in 2007 and more than 3 million by year-end 2008. This was a calamity for those losing their homes and also for the banks and mortgage security investors who owned their mortgages. Conservatively estimated, all those defaults would cost mortgage owners more than $1.1 trillion.[4]

Even at that size, it is still difficult to see how mortgages could have been the catalyst for such a wrenching financial crisis. In fact, $1 trillion in mortgage losses equals not quite 10% of the $11 trillion in total U.S. mortgage loans outstanding, and that's not even a meaningful percentage of the $140 trillion in loans and debt securities held by banks, insurance companies, pension funds, hedge and mutual funds, sovereign wealth funds, and other institutions around the world.[5] How could the entire global financial system be undermined by subprime mortgage loans?

Reevaluating Risk

It wasn't the mortgage losses, per se, that ignited the shock, but what they meant more broadly: Global investors had taken on too much risk, not simply in their subprime mortgage security holdings, but arguably in all their investments. The mortgage losses crystallized what had long been troubling to many in the financial markets: Namely, that assets of all kinds were overvalued, from Chinese stocks to Las Vegas condominiums, to the British government bonds known as "gilts" (short for gilt-edged securities). The subprime meltdown was simply a catalyst for a top-to-bottom reevaluation of risk: Were investors being adequately compensated for the risks they were taking? Many quickly concluded that the answer was no.

Global investors suddenly saw the entire U.S. housing and mortgage market in a new light. Although the number of homeowners struggling with mortgage payments was relatively small—only a few million—investors began to question the ability or willingness of all 52 million U.S. mortgage borrowers—subprime, alt-A, and even prime—to meet their obligations. The $11 trillion in U.S. residential mortgage debt outstanding had become a significant global financial influence, accounting for more than 8% of all the bank loans and securities in the world. In short, the world had made a huge bet on U.S. homeowners. In the mid-1990s, few overseas investors had ventured into the U.S. mortgage securities market. Those who did owned mostly debt backed by Fannie Mae and Freddie Mac, which was not much different than owning a U.S. Treasury bond. A decade later, foreign investors held some $3 trillion in mortgage securities, almost one-third of all their U.S. financial holdings, including stocks. Some of this was backed by the U.S. government, but most was supported simply by the financial rectitude of the U.S. homeowner. This was seen as safe: Investing in an American household with a home and a mortgage wasn't supposed to cost investors any sleep—much less their shirts.

Investors also began looking critically at their other holdings, such as corporate bonds. It wasn't that businesses were defaulting on their obligations; the economy was still strong at the time. The problem was that investors were receiving returns that suggested no firm would ever default again. The rates were razor-thin compared to the potential risks. The difference between rates on risk-free Treasury bonds and rates on low-rated or junk corporate bonds narrowed to an all-time low in spring 2007 (see Figure 11.3). This interest rate difference—the spread—measures how much compensation investors receive for the risks they take with their money. Not only was there not much of a spread in the prices of corporate bonds, but many bonds came with terms considered remarkably loose by historic standards. Traditionally, firms that issue bonds have to meet strict conditions, maintaining a certain level of cash flow or other financial benchmarks, to assure investors that they can meet their interest payments. If the benchmarks aren't met, creditors have the right to demand their principal back. But in the 2000s, investors were so eager to throw their money around that many bought so-called "covenant-lite" bonds, which had fewer conditions and benchmarks for issuers. Terms became so easy that some businesses were allowed to make interest payments on their bonds by issuing additional bonds instead of paying in cash.[6]

Sources: Federal Reserve Board, Moody's Economy.com

Figure 11.3 Junk spreads hit lows prior to shock: interest rate difference spread between junk corporate bonds and treasuries.

With corporate bond rates so low and terms so lax, it was incredibly cheap for private equity firms to finance their purchases of public companies. Firms such as the Carlyle Group, Blackstone, Cerberus, and Apollo Management were borrowing this cheap debt to buy out stockholders and take companies private. The plan was typically to reorganize a business, hopefully making it more profitable in the process, and later take it public again at a much higher price. Buyouts often worked purely because it cost so little to borrow in the bond market. To be more precise, private equity firms financed their purchases with bank loans that were then paid off after the bought-out business issued their junk bonds.[7] The bank loans were intended to be short-term bridge loans. These deals were all the rage in the lead-up to the subprime financial shock, and they helped drive global stock markets to record highs as private equity firms bid up stock prices.

The subprime meltdown brought it all to a swift end. Investors no longer wanted to buy corporate bonds with interest rates that effectively assumed there would never be another default. They had good reason: Such an assumption couldn't be right. Publicly traded automakers, retailers, and media companies were being taken private using a lot of debt. These were cyclical businesses—sales rise and fall, as do profits and the cash flow needed for interest payments. Some of these companies wouldn't make it and would default. Investors lost interest in some deals entirely; for others, they wanted more compensation in the form of higher interest rates. The private-equity buyout mania fizzled, junk bond issuance fell off, and the spread between junk bonds and Treasury rates soared. By late 2008, the yield spread was more than 20 percentage points. Investors were now expecting corporate bond default rates to approach those last seen in the Great Depression.

Investors were also nervous about their holdings of commercial mortgage-backed securities (CMBS). As with a residential mortgage security, a CMBS is backed by interest and principal payments on mortgages—but these are mortgages on office, retail, and industrial buildings, as well as hotels and apartments. Similar to the residential mortgage securities market, the CMBS market had expanded rapidly prior to the subprime shock as investors willingly purchased securities at increasingly narrow rate spreads. The CMBS market became a huge source of cheap cash for commercial property owners, who aggressively bought up office towers and strip malls. Property prices surged, encouraging even more borrowing in the CMBS market—backed, of course, by the higher-priced properties.

It sounded all too familiar to investors. If the residential securities market was unraveling, CMBS couldn't be too far behind. CMBS issuance came to a standstill, and the yield spread between CMBS and Treasury bonds widened sharply. Even though commercial property markets weren't choking on empty space and rent growth was still holding up in most areas, investors weren't willing to make fine distinctions between the commercial real estate market and the housing market. Commercial property prices were too high, vacancy rates were just beginning to rise, rent growth was sure to weaken significantly, and investors wanted compensation for the risk.

The new attitude toward risk rolled through other global financial markets, affecting everything from emerging debt–bonds issued by developing nations such as Argentina and Turkey; to asset-backed securities, based on credit cards, auto loans, and student loans; to municipal bonds. Although the impact on these markets wasn't quite as harsh as in the junk bond or CMBS markets, fewer new bonds of any type were issued, and interest rate spreads widened across the entire credit market.

When Insurers Need Insurance

Not all investors had been reckless. Some had limited their purchases of mortgage securities to the top-rated Aaa tranches, and to be even more conservative, they had also purchased insurance. The insurance came from financial guarantors, also known as monoline insurers. These firms had traditionally insured municipal bonds against default; now they were also insuring the highly rated tranches of mortgage securities. The guarantors themselves were rated by the credit-rating agencies—guarantors had promised to make investors whole if anything went wrong with their bonds, so it was important that they be rock-solid Aaa firms. Yet after the subprime shock, the guarantors began to appear markedly less solid than their ratings had indicated. Monolines weren't failing to make payments on defaulting bonds, but with the pace of defaults soaring, it looked increasingly likely that some might not be able to meet their commitments in the future. As the mortgage securities they had insured were down-graded, odds increased that the guarantors would eventually have to make big payouts—bigger than their executives, investors, or clients had ever imagined would be necessary.

The rating agencies warned the guarantors to raise more capital or risk losing their Aaa rating. It was a potent threat: Without that super-safe rating, the guarantors would be out of business and their insurance meaningless. No investor would trust them to be able to make payouts if needed. Most guarantors took the warning to heart and raised more capital. This wasn't easy or cheap because potential investors knew there was a reasonable chance the insurance firms might not survive. Nevertheless, the two biggest monolines, MBIA and Ambac, held on tenuously to their Aaa ratings.

The guarantors' problems exacerbated the nervousness in financial markets. A chain of events that had once seemed unimaginable suddenly began to loom as a possibility. It would work like this: Many large institutional investors, such as pension funds and insurance companies, are barred by law or their own rules from buying any securities rated less than Aaa. Without bond insurance, many securities would lose their Aaa ratings; thus, pension funds and insurance companies would be forced to sell them. If a guarantor went out of business—or even lost its own Aaa rating—the securities it had insured could suddenly face such a downgrade. As the monolines' problems grew, so did the odds they would lose their Aaa ratings. The prospect of institutional investors suddenly flooding the markets with massive amounts of bonds began to haunt financial players.

Such worries reinforced the free-fall in mortgage securities and also pushed the formerly staid municipal bond market into turmoil. Perfectly solvent state and local governments and authorities found

themselves having to pay interest rates reserved for high-risk borrowers. This was most clearly demonstrated by the disruption of the auction-rate securities market. In this out-of-the-way market, certain
long-term municipal bonds were treated as if they were short-term
investments, with interest rates set once a week in an auction run by
large Wall Street investment banks. The rates were typically lower
than for comparable fixed-rate bonds, making them attractive to
municipalities issuing debt. The weekly auctions effectively turned
long-term municipal bonds into more liquid short-term bonds, which
appealed to investors such as money market funds. Both features,
however, depended on the success of the weekly auctions. So important were these auctions that, to ensure their smooth functioning, the
investment banks would step in and buy the debt themselves if they
failed to attract enough outside bidders.

In early 2008, spooked by the potential failure of the monolines
and other worries, investors stopped participating in the auctions,
causing scores of them to fail. Even the investment bank sponsors,
worried about their own financial exposure, refused to play their
usual backstop role. As a result, the interest rates on auction-rate
securities surged. Municipalities were suddenly forced to pay rates
far higher than even junk corporate borrowers. Trust had broken
down so thoroughly that municipalities couldn't even count on their
own investment bankers. The subprime financial shock had engulfed
even state and local governments.

Leverage and Liquidity

If the subprime shock involved no more than a massive reevaluation of risk, it still would have been a garden-variety financial event
and not a global crisis. Investors took a hit, but this was seen early on
as a healthy antidote to the housing bubble. Risk-taking had gotten
out of control; financial decisions made less and less economic sense.
For instance, the private-equity firm Cerberus's leveraged buyout of
the Chrysler Corporation, which involved piling a lot of debt onto the

balance sheet of a very cyclical vehicle manufacturer struggling to sell big cars in the face of steadily rising gasoline prices, might be a case in point. Officials at the Federal Reserve and other central bankers weren't unhappy to see such excesses being wrung out of the financial system.

Views quickly changed as the shock's nasty side came into clearer relief. As the shock wore on and losses mounted, investors who borrowed money to pump up their returns in the good times came under increasing pressure to reduce their leverage. As this process of deleveraging gained momentum, the subprime financial shock turned from a therapeutic to a destructive process. To see the corrosive, self-reinforcing nature of financial leverage, consider the hypothetical example of an investment fund that bought mortgage securities by borrowing 85% of the purchase price, using its own equity for only 15% (see Table 11.1). The fund's leverage can be expressed as 85/15, meaning that the power of its own investment has been magnified 5.7 times by leverage. Now suppose that the securities the fund owns fall in value by 5%. This isn't a very large decline, but it reduces the fund's equity to 10%, and its leverage jumps to 85/10 or 10.5 times. Because the fund agreed when it borrowed money from a broker-dealer to maintain at least 15% equity, it receives a notice known as a margin call, requiring it to either put up more cash or sell as much of the portfolio as necessary to get back to the agreed margin. Most funds are reluctant to put up more cash, particularly in a declining market, so they take the second option and sell. Brokers, meanwhile, can demand higher margins; if they believe the value of the underlying collateral is eroding, they might decide that the original 15% is too low. If in this example the broker increases the margin to 25%, the funds have even more selling to do. Things get measurably worse if the fund's own investors start pulling out their money. These redemptions force more portfolio sales. In our example, the fund's value is ultimately slashed by more than 60%

and its leverage plunges to three times. When leverage is involved, even a modest decline in asset values can provoke a rout.

TABLE 11.1 **Corrosive Power of Leverage**

	Asset Value	Equity	Borrowing	Leverage	Margin
Initial	100.0	15.0	85.0	5.7	15.0
5% loss of value	95.0	10.0	85.0	8.5	10.5
After margin call with a 15% margin	66.7	10.0	56.7	5.7	15.0
Increase in margin to 25%	40.0	10.0	30.0	3.0	25.0
10% redemption rate	36.0	9.0	27.0	3.0	25.0

Source: IMF

Now consider what happens when there are many such funds, and all receive margin calls and redemptions at the same time. The wave of forced selling drives prices for assets such as mortgage securities sharply lower, further exacerbating investors' collective problems. This is exactly what happened as 2007 ended. Some funds, backed by larger financial institutions that were worried about their reputations, put up their own cash to meet margin calls. Others stopped accepting redemptions, to try to stem the bleeding. None of it worked. They were overwhelmed by the tidal wave of deleveraging.

No financial institution avoided the fallout from the imploding securities markets. The list of casualties ranged from small boutique investment funds to the giant Swiss banks UBS and Credit Suisse, to Wall Street titans Citigroup and Merrill Lynch. Each day seemed to bring another high-profile blow-up. Financial disaster seemed to lurk in practically every deal. Even making an overnight loan could be a mistake; a borrower could run aground between today and tomorrow.

An often-cited strength of the global financial markets had been their capability to diffuse risk widely; now this strength had become part of the problem. Risk was so widely scattered across the financial system that it was hard to tell who was bearing how much and what the danger of failure really was. Without clarity about which institutions had the bad investments and how much more financial damage was likely, there would be much less borrowing, lending, buying, and selling. As more institutions stumbled, the risk fog grew thicker until liquidity began to evaporate.

Liquidity—the ability to move money in and out of investments or among markets quickly and smoothly—is vital to all financial institutions. Some need it simply to survive. Banks, with their relatively stable deposit bases, weather liquidity storms best. Depositors tend not to move their money quickly (U.K. mortgage lender Northern Rock being a notable exception),[8] and even in times of crisis, they tend to stick with banks, particularly those covered by government deposit insurance. This gives such banks a reliable source of liquidity: money the bank can use to make loans or use for other purposes whenever needed.

Other financial institutions also need ready sources of liquidity. Asset-backed conduits and special investment vehicles (SIVs)—institutions that warehoused and invested in mortgage and other securities—obtained theirs by issuing short-term commercial paper. When money market funds and other investors became too worried to buy these IOUs, the conduits and SIVs lost their liquidity and were quickly forced out of business. Broker-dealers such as Bear Stearns and Lehman Brothers also relied on being able to raise money quickly. Because they were big, rich, seemingly healthy Wall Street firms, they typically had no trouble getting investors to buy their IOUs. It seemed unimaginable that this confidence would ever be shaken, yet in early 2008, Bear Stearns lost the faith of its creditors. By the middle of March, its funding sources had gone completely dry and the Federal Reserve stepped in to arrange an emergency sale of Bear Stearns to JPMorgan Chase.

Bad Marks

The entire banking system was now under pressure to reduce leverage. When conditions are good and borrowers are making their loan payments faithfully, banks are eager to increase leverage by building up their assets of both loans and securities relative to their capital. Higher leverage leads to big profits, at least in good times. When conditions grow difficult and borrowers fall behind on their debts, banks seek to cut back on leverage to limit losses and protect their capital. This ebb and flow in banking lending defines the credit cycle and gives rise to the old saw that a banker will give you an umbrella when there is plenty of sunshine, but wants it back as soon as it begins to rain.

Amplifying the credit cycle during the subprime financial shock was the use of an accounting standard called "mark-to-market."[9] It's based on a simple principle: When the market value of an asset changes, the bank or business that owns it must reflect that change on its books. Thus, if a bank makes a loan or buys a security, and after a time that loan or security is worth only 50¢ on the dollar, the bank has to declare that on its balance sheet. Financial regulators adopted mark-to-market rules in response to the S&L crisis and expanded and solidified them after the corporate accounting scandals of the early 2000s when it came to light that Enron and other firms had been manipulating their books to disguise huge losses.

On the face of it, mark-to-market seems like a way to keep the financial system healthy as well as honest. If asset prices decline, those asset owners should have to acknowledge the losses and move on. Had more businesses done that in the 1980s, America might have avoided the S&L debacle and Japan might not have lost a decade of growth during the 1990s, when its banks were paralyzed by all the bad loans they refused to recognize and the economy starved for credit.

But as appealing as the theory behind mark-to-market is, it can present serious problems in practice. Sometimes, such as during the subprime financial shock, marking to market is almost impossible because there are no market prices that make much objective sense. In the midst of the shock, prices for mortgage and other securities bounced around wildly or simply flat-lined as trading in these assets froze. Even the Aaa-rated tranches of mortgage-backed securities, which remained highly unlikely to suffer losses in the long run, were being traded at steep discounts or were not traded at all. Yet under mark-to-market accounting rules, the banks that held these securities had to write down their securities drastically. The distressed prices could have reflected investor fear or a temporary gap in trading and would thus eventually right themselves, but the banks nonetheless had to record the lower prices.

Some institutions tried a different tack: Instead of using mark-to-market, they used "mark-to-model." In the absence of a functioning market for some highly complex securities, they turned to their own in-house mathematical models to calculate what the securities' values *should* be under normal conditions. Of course, these models typically concluded that prices should be higher; nonetheless, this tactic didn't play well with regulators, and the modelers eventually had to slash the value of their holdings as well. The losses were huge, at least on paper. By early 2009, the globe's biggest banks had collectively written down their assets by more than $1 trillion (see Table 11.2). The losses were a direct hit to the banks' capital.

TABLE 11.2   Total Write-Downs and Credit Losses on U.S. Financial Assets (Write-Downs Since January 2007)

Banks		$ Billions
1	Wachovia	95.5
2	Citigroup	67.2
3	Merrill Lynch	55.9
4	UBS	48.6
5	Washington Mutual	45.6
6	HSBC	33.1
7	Bank of America	27.4

TABLE 11.2   Total Write-Downs and Credit Losses on U.S. Financial Assets (Write-Downs Since January 2007)

Banks		$ Billions
8	National City	26.2
9	JPMorgan Chase	20.5
10	Lehman Brothers	16.2
11	Royal Bank of Scotland	15.8
12	Morgan Stanley	15.7
13	Bayerische Landesbank	14.8
14	Wells Fargo	14.6
15	IKB	14.4
16	Credit Suisse	14.2
Total	**Worldwide**	**741.2**
Insurers		
1	AIG	60.9
2	Ambac	10.6
3	Hartford Financial	7.9
4	Metlife	7.2
5	Allianz	4.5
6	Prudential Financial	4.4
7	Allstate Corp	4.4
8	MBIA	4.3
9	Swiss Re	4.2
10	Aegon	3.8
Total	**Worldwide**	**146**
Government Sponsored Enterprises		
1	Freddie Mac	58.4
2	Fannie Mae	56
Total		**114.4**
	Grand Total	**1,001.6**

Sources: FT, Bloomberg

The banks' problems were aggravated further by the fact that even as losses eroded their capital, their assets were growing rapidly. This wasn't a conscious choice by the banks, and it made them appear even weaker and more risk prone by increasing their leverage just when they needed to reduce it. Many had agreed earlier to prop up the asset-backed conduits, structured investment vehicles, and broker-dealers in case they needed funds. Now these troubled institutions needed funds desperately, and some drew down long-standing credit lines with the banks. In other cases, bridge loans the banks had made to finance private equity deals just prior to the subprime shock were effectively converted into long-term loans; the troubled junk bond market had made it impossible to refinance or sell off the loans as originally planned. Banks were dragged into becoming the lenders-of-last-resort for much of the financial system. They didn't view it as an honor.

By mid-2008, the net result was that banks were hemorrhaging capital and were awash in assets they didn't want. Their leverage was rising at a time when they desperately wanted to reduce it. They had two choices: either raise more capital or shed any assets they could. They did both. With each quarterly round of earnings announcements, bank after bank reported billions in losses and followed this by announcing they had found an investor willing to take an equity stake in the bank. Many of these white-knight investors were sovereign wealth funds, large investment pools set up by foreign governments such as Abu Dhabi, Singapore, China, Korea, and Qatar, filled with the dollars these governments had earned from soaring energy prices and trade with the United States. They were the only investors with the ready cash needed to fill at least some of banks' capital hole.

Even the sovereign wealth funds didn't have enough capital to rescue the banks. By year-end 2008, some of the global financial system's most venerable institutions, such as Lehman Brothers, Merrill Lynch, Wachovia, and Washington Mutual, had not survived. And those that remained going concerns were effectively nationalized such as Fannie Mae, Freddie Mac, and AIG, or were getting capital infusions from U.S. taxpayers. Even this wasn't enough to lift the intense financial pressure to reduce their leverage and pull back on their lending. They aggressively ratcheted up their standards for all new potential borrowers. New, rigid lending criteria applied not just to subprime or alt-A mortgage loans—those were simply unavailable under any circumstances—but also to prime mortgage borrowers, credit card and student loan borrowers, and businesses of all sizes and stripes. Borrowers who in more normal times would have no problem getting a loan now couldn't get any bank's attention. According to a quarterly Federal Reserve survey of senior loan officers at the nation's major banks, lending standards were tighter than at any time since Jimmy Carter temporarily imposed credit controls on lending in 1980 (see Figure 11.4).[10] Marking to market, a much-praised feature of the modern banking system, had instead become part of the problem, reinforcing a vicious and self-reinforcing credit crunch.

Net %

Figure 11.4   Credit crunch: net % of banks tightening consumer loan standards.

12

Timid Policymakers Turn Bold

Policymakers' early response to the subprime financial shock was sometimes halting and, other times, confused. They misjudged the extent of the shock's economic and financial damage and were hamstrung by its complexity. They also feared bailing out undeserving homeowners, mortgage lenders, and investors; this would be unfair to people working hard to stay current on their mortgages and would embolden more reckless risk-taking in the future. But instead of dousing the turmoil, the tentative policy response fanned it. Investors didn't expect to be bailed out, but they were distressed by the government's reluctance to provide help.

As financial and economic fallout spread, policymakers were forced to take stronger and more dramatic steps to combat the crisis. The Federal Reserve and U.S. Treasury gracefully resolved the Bear Stearns collapse in spring 2008, but their takeover of Fannie Mae and Freddie Mac and the decision to let Lehman Brothers declare bankruptcy in September 2008 set off a chain of events that brought the system to the edge. The economic downturn intensified, becoming the key issue in the 2008 presidential campaign. The new president and Congress had to do much more, and soon did.

By early 2009, the Federal Reserve had slashed interest rates effectively to zero. The Fed had also devised a range of novel mechanisms to help not only the commercial banks it regulated, but also the investment banks and insurance companies it technically did not oversee. Finally, the central bank began effectively printing money.

With trillions of newly created dollars, the Fed began to buy every-thing from corporate commercial paper to Fannie Mae and Freddie Mac mortgages, to Treasury bonds. Adopting a strategy most econo-mists had known only from theoretical papers and economic history books, the central bank essentially "monetized" the nation's debt.

At the same time, the newly installed Obama Administration was pushing a massive fiscal stimulus through Congress. The legis-lation included hundreds of billions in aid to hard-pressed state and local governments, more help for those losing their jobs, tax cuts for households and businesses, and increased spending on infrastruc-ture—roads and bridges, the electric grid, even the Internet back-bone. The new stimulus was nearly five times as large as the one the Bush Administration and Congress had cobbled together a year earlier.

To stem surging foreclosures and their pernicious effect on house prices, the Obama Administration also launched the most aggressive effort to stem foreclosures since the financial shock first hit. The new plan proposed to subsidize mortgage payments for strapped home-owners, aiming to make house payments affordable and thus keep thousands of households from defaulting on their loans.

But the biggest and most difficult problem facing the Obama Administration remained cleaning up the banking system. The nation's biggest banks were choking on trillions in toxic assets, leaving them dangerously short of capital. The only way to restore normal lending, and thus begin to heal the economy, was to provide banks the capital they needed and rid them of their problem loans and secu-rities. The administration planned to use a combination of taxpayer funds and private investor dollars to get the job done.

Financial markets gave these actions an initial thumbs-up, yet by spring 2009, markets remained anything but normal. Policymakers would need to do still more—another round of fiscal stimulus, a fore-closure plan that reduced the principal amounts homeowners owed, direct purchases of banks' bad assets—but a comprehensive policy response to the subprime financial shock was finally in place. It would take a few months more to determine how well it was working.

Taking so many major policy steps in such a short period incurred substantial costs. The federal budget deficit was ballooning and soon would dwarf anything experienced since World War II. Although deflation was a real near-term concern, creating trillions of new dollars raised the specter of inflation down the road. It also would not be easy for the government to unwind its sizable ownership stake in the financial system. And unintended consequences would surely flow from some of the policies enacted or even merely considered, such as letting bankruptcy judges reduce mortgages, taxing financial institution bonuses, or bailing out the auto industry. But although these concerns couldn't be ignored, they also could not lessen the overwhelming necessity for government to tame the crisis. Unless government stepped into the breach left by panicked investors, businesses, and consumers, the economic suffering would be much more severe and, ultimately, much costlier to taxpayers.

Fiddling While Markets Burned

The 2007 subprime financial shock seemed to surprise policymakers. The crisis had begun in earnest in mid-July, but the Federal Reserve didn't respond until more than a month later. Policymakers cut the federal funds rate target in September and then again in October and December, but the total reduction by year-end amounted to only 1 percentage point. More important for investors, the Fed hinted that each rate cut might be the last, saying inflation was too high to risk accelerating it by lowering rates aggressively. Even with the mid-December 2007 rate cut and financial markets clearly on edge, Fed officials were still hand-wringing about the inflation threat:[1]

> Readings on core inflation have improved modestly this year, but elevated energy and commodity prices, among other factors, may put upward pressure on inflation. In this context, the

Committee judges that some inflation risks remain, and it will continue to monitor inflation developments carefully.

The crisis also surprised the Bush Administration. The President maintained consistently that the economy was "fundamentally sound" for months after the shock hit. Treasury Secretary Paulson confidently forecast that the housing market had hit bottom just weeks before markets began to unravel. "I don't see [subprime mortgage market troubles] imposing a serious problem," Paulson argued. "I think it's going to be largely contained."[2]

The administration didn't respond concretely to the crisis until the end of August. Recognizing that foreclosures were mounting, the President proposed legislation to make it easier for troubled homeowners to sell out before they faced foreclosure. This was usually a preferable option, saving both homeowners and their lenders a costly trip through the legal system—but the tax code discouraged it by treating any mortgage debt forgiven by a lender as taxable income. A lender might be willing to let a distressed homeowner sell at a loss, writing off the difference instead of foreclosing, but the homeowner would need to pay taxes on that difference. Distressed homeowners with no cash to pay their tax bill had the Hobson's choice of going through foreclosure or stiffing the IRS. The Bush bill proposed to fix this by eliminating the tax liability on mortgage debt forgiven in a so-called short sale.

The President also unveiled a new program called Federal Housing Administration (FHA) Secure, designed to help homeowners who were delinquent on their mortgage loans as a result of a payment reset.[3] To qualify for the program, homeowners had to have been current on their payments prior to the reset, made at least a 3% down payment, and have sufficient income and a stable job. In announcing the plan, the president declared that "it's not the government's job to bail out speculators or those who made the decision to buy a home they knew they could never afford." Despite being well-intentioned, it quickly became clear that FHA Secure would be of little real help;

the hardest-pressed homeowners didn't have the down payment or the necessary income to qualify. Even under the best of circumstances, the administration expected the program to help only a quarter-million households avoid foreclosure—a trivial number as foreclosure forecasts surged into the millions.

The administration followed up in October with a second program, called Hope Now. This was a consortium of mortgage lenders, services, and investors brought together to find an efficient way to modify mortgage loans. Millions of subprime borrowers were facing large mortgage payment increases at the time; the average reset was expected to be $350 per month, an overwhelming amount for most ordinary working families. The Hope Now agreement established rules to let lenders keep mortgage rates frozen temporarily, enabling these homeowners to keep paying under their original loan terms. The Treasury Department played a vital role, bringing together the diverse range of players who set loan terms, each with its own financial interests and understanding of the process. No one had ever contemplated the need to revise (or "modify") many millions of mortgage loans at once, and the system didn't seem up to the task on its own.

Hope Now helped open communications between stretched homeowners and mortgage servicers, but not as much as expected. Instead of substantially modifying many loans, mortgage services put most delinquent homeowners on repayment plans. This provided no relief; the plans simply let delinquent homeowners resume paying their mortgages with no change in terms; they also had to make up any missed payments and pay the associated penalties. Monthly payments actually rose in most of these repayment plans. Hope Now also failed as the nature of the problem changed. As the Fed aggressively lowered interest rates, the pending mortgage resets (which were tied to prevailing short-term interest rates) began to look less dire. Instead, homeowners now were struggling with plunging housing prices and negative mortgage equity. Hope Now's program did not involve lowering the principal on distressed mortgages; it only tinkered with their interest-rate terms. Now, with millions of home-owners underwater (their home's market value was less than the loan amounts), defaults rising, and policymakers searching for new ideas to keep people in their homes, financial markets began to writhe.

Policy Paralysis

Policymakers had significantly misjudged both the severity of the shock and its broader economic implications. At most, they assumed this would be a normal, even therapeutic, correction of financial markets that had simply become overvalued. They reasoned that although the housing market had been struggling for more than a year, housing prices had only begun to decline, and stock and bond prices had been rising almost continually since just after the tech-stock bust.

Markets were overextended, but policymakers had no idea how much. Prices had risen sharply in nearly all markets—not just housing, and not just in the United States. Prices for everything from Chinese stocks to European corporate bonds, to U.S. commercial real estate were juiced up. Leverage had helped drive asset prices sky high; investors were borrowing aggressively to finance their trades. And this wasn't a matter of investors asking their friendly local banker for a loan; instead, investors were issuing short-term IOUs to faceless financial institutions across the globe. The web of financial relationships had grown so complex that it was hard to tell who was taking how much risk and what would happen if bets went bad. When they did go bad, a simple, healthy market correction rapidly turned into a rout, and policymakers were caught unaware.

Policymakers' confusion was exacerbated by their inability to gather timely and accurate information. Unlike past financial crises, when most of the players involved were regulated and had to report regularly on their risks and financial health, rapidly evolving institutions that had little or no regulatory supervision were driving this crisis. Policymakers knew little to nothing about them. Global regulators had discussed whether and how these new institutions should report on their activities, but they had gotten nowhere. U.S. Treasury officials were particularly uninterested in restricting the financial system; they believed the marketplace could discipline itself. The Bush Administration's philosophy was to keep government out; financial markets should work out problems on their own. Yet without a regulatory structure in place, policymakers at the U.S. Treasury, the Federal Reserve, and elsewhere had no way to judge the severity of the shock, and they lacked the expertise to respond to it.

Adding to the policy paralysis were the Federal Reserve's worries about inflation. The Fed's legal mandate is to keep both inflation and unemployment low, but policymakers appropriately believe that focusing mainly on inflation is the most efficient way to ensure both objectives in the long run. Stable prices let the economy function efficiently, ultimately creating more jobs and holding down unemployment. Yet the broader forces shaping inflation had turned less positive as the benefits of the Internet boom began to fade and productivity growth slowed. Soaring oil and other commodity prices were adding to the inflationary pressures. As the subprime shock loomed in 2007, interest rates were still low by historical standards, and with oil prices hovering over $100 per barrel, Fed officials reasoned that aggressively lowering rates in response to a financial crisis would only fan inflation more broadly. That was the last thing they wanted to do.

Policymakers also worried about something called moral hazard. This is a principle with roots in the insurance industry: It says that people are more likely to take risks if they are insured against the consequences. If your car is 100% covered against theft, you're less likely to lock your doors. Similar principles govern financial markets: If investors believe the Federal Reserve will cover or lessen their losses, for example, they will take greater investment risks. It is reasonable to argue that when the Fed cut rates aggressively in response to the 1987 stock market crash, the collapse of hedge fund Long-Term Capital Management in 1998, or even the tech stock bust in 2001, it planted the seeds of moral hazard, which led to the latest financial crisis. Therefore, Fed officials feared that lowering rates quickly in response to the subprime shock would only set the stage for bigger financial problems in the future, with complacent investors taking even bigger risks.

Other federal policymakers were less concerned about the moral hazard issue. The Democratic leadership in Congress wanted to do more to respond to the subprime shock, but acting quickly was all but impossible. Congress could pressure banking regulators to toughen their oversight of unscrupulous mortgage lenders, but passing legislation was a different matter. Some in Congress worried that they would overreach, citing Sarbanes–Oxley, the act that changed accounting and corporate governance rules in the wake of the Enron and Arthur Andersen scandals. Mortgage and financial service industry lobbyists also worked hard to slow any legislative action.

Policymakers were also receiving conflicting messages from their constituents. Homeowners who were facing foreclosure pleaded for government help, but others who were struggling but managing to stay current on their mortgages questioned the justice of such government assistance. Why provide relief to people who had gotten in over their heads with a big house purchase, while prudent families in smaller homes got nothing?

But while the government dithered, the financial turmoil worsened. The longer policymakers delayed acting, the more investor panic spread. The subprime shock had begun in the residential mortgage securities market, but now it was infecting the corporate bond market, the market for commercial mortgage securities, and even the normally low-risk municipal bond market. The stock market, which had held up well in the weeks following the shock—the Dow Jones Industrial Average hit a peak in early October 2007— now stumbled badly. By early 2008, stock prices had fallen almost 20% (see Figure 12.1).

Figure 12.1   Stock investors lose faith: Dow Jones Industrial Average.

Even major global banks became reluctant to lend money to each other, demanding hefty interest rates for loans of any length. It was astonishing, but the world's largest financial institutions had suddenly become nervous that they wouldn't get their money back. Banks also worried that they might need the cash if their own investments went bad and their own long-standing lenders cut them off. The cash squeeze became particularly acute as the end of the year approached, normally a season when the demand for cash is greatest. LIBOR, the interest rates banks charge each other for short-term funds, spiked.[4]

Outside the Monetary Box

At the Federal Reserve, theoretical concerns over inflation and moral hazard were quickly being overwhelmed by practical concerns that a credit crunch was developing. Not only were people with clear credit problems no longer able to get loans, but even borrowers with solid credit histories faced usurious rates and onerous terms. This raised a new set of alarms among policymakers: Tighter credit for weak borrowers would slow the economy, but a crunch that affected creditworthy borrowers as well would likely bring on a recession.

The Fed began trying to ease pressures in money markets by encouraging banks to use its discount window. This part of the Federal

Reserve provides a way for some, but not all, financial institutions to borrow cheap money in times of need.[5] Although the subprime shock was clearly a time of need, institutions were reluctant to use the discount window. Historically, borrowing from the Fed that way had been a signal that a bank was in precarious financial health, and bankers feared it would scare away customers and other financial institutions, worsening their problems. The Fed tried lowering the rate on discount-window borrowing, permitted borrowing for a longer term, and even cajoled a few too-big-to-fail money center banks to use the discount window, just to show others it was okay. Nothing worked. Banks were hungry for cash, but they didn't approach the discount window, for fear of being seen as losers whom the market would let starve.

With the banking system increasingly cash-strapped and discount-window borrowing at a standstill, the Fed became creative. In mid-December, the central bank unveiled an alternative to the discount window, which it called the Term Auction Facility (TAF). It enabled institutions to bid for short-term funds by putting up a wide range of securities, including mortgage-related instruments, as collateral (see Table 12.1).[6] In a TAF auction, the bids begin at a rate above the federal funds rate but well below the discount rate, thus providing institutions with at least the cover of a reason to borrow funds from the Fed other than potential financial stress. It worked: Because no apparent stigma was attached to borrowing from the TAF, response was strong, beginning with the first auction. Although money markets were still not functioning normally by mid-2008, worries that the banking system might grind to a halt for lack of cash had faded.

In late January 2008, Fed officials took even more convincing action. In an unscheduled emergency meeting, the Federal Open Market Committee (FOMC) slashed the Fed funds rate target by three-quarters of a percentage point, the biggest such reduction in decades (see Figure 12.2). At their regularly scheduled January meeting a few days later, the committee cut rates again, by an additional

TABLE 12.1   What's in the Federal Reserve's Monetary Toolbox?

	Who Can Borrow?	Accepted Collateral	Term of Loan	Interest Rate	Type of Loan from Fed	Reserve Impact
Primary Dealer Credit Facility (PDCF)	Depository institutions	Treasuries, investment-grade municipal bonds, MBS and ABS for which a market price exists	Overnight	Discount rate	Money	Yes
Term Securities Lending Facility (TSLF)	Primary dealers	Treasuries, agencies, and AAA RMBS, CMBS, and CMOs	28-day funds auctioned weekly, up to $200 billion	Minimum fee bid set by the Fed	Treasuries	No
Term Auction Facility (TAF)	Primary dealers	Wide, ranging from Treasuries to CDOs	28-day funds auctioned bimonthly; size determined by the Fed	Minimum bid rate set according to expected fed funds rate over the term of the loan	Money	Yes
Discount Window	Depository institutions	Wide, ranging from Treasuries to CDOs	Maximum maturity is 90 days	Discount rate	Money	Yes
Open Market Operations	Primary dealers	Treasuries, agencies, and agency MBS	Repos or reverse repos for a term up to 65 days	Fed funds rate	Money	Yes

TABLE 12.1   What's in the Federal Reserve's Monetary Toolbox?

	Who Can Borrow?	Accepted Collateral	Term of Loan	Interest Rate	Type of Loan from Fed	Reserve Impact
System Open Market Account	Primary dealers	Treasury bills, notes, bonds, and TIPS	Overnight and auctioned daily	Minimum fee bid of 50 basis points	Treasuries	No
Term Asset-Backed Securities Loan Facility (TALF)	U.S. businesses	ABS that have the highest long-term or short-term investment-grade rating category from two or more NRSROs, U.S. dollar-denominated cash	3-year maturity	Fixed rate: 100 basis points above 3-years LIBOR swap rate; floating rate: 100 basis points above 1-month LIBOR	Money	Yes
Asset-Backed Commercial Paper (ABCP) Money Market Mutual Fund (MMMF) Liquidity Facility	Depository institutions, bank holding companies, or U.S. branches and agencies of foreign banks	Rated not lower than A1, F1, or P1 by two or more NRSROs	120 days for banks, 270 days from non-bank borrowers	Primary credit rate in effect at the Boston Fed offered to depository institutions	Money	Yes

TABLE 12.1 What's in the Federal Reserve's Monetary Toolbox?

	Who Can Borrow?	Accepted Collateral	Term of Loan	Interest Rate	Type of Loan from Fed	Reserve Impact
Commercial Paper Funding Facility (CPFF)	Through the primary dealers, U.S. issuers of commercial paper	U.S. dollar-denominated commercial paper (including ABCP), rated at least A1/P1/F1 by an NRSRO	Maximum 3 months	Unsecured commercial paper: 3-month OIS +100 basis points; asset-backed commercial paper: 3-month OIS +300 basis points	Money	Yes
Money Market Investor Funding Facility (MMIFF)	Money market mutual funds managed or owned by a U.S. bank, insurance company, pension fund, trust, SEC-registered investment advisor or U.S. state or local government	U.S. dollar-denominated CDs, bank notes, and commercial paper	Between 7 and 90 days	Primary credit rate	Money	Yes

Sources: Federal Reserve Board, Moody's Economy.com

half percentage point. For the FOMC, changing interest rates in between its normally scheduled meetings was a clear signal that the financial system was in crisis. And added together, the two rate cuts in January were unprecedented.[7]

The Bernanke-led Fed was sharply departing from the Fed's pattern under former Chairman Greenspan, in which rate changes were

Figure 12.2   The Fed goes on high alert: federal funds rate target.

typically incremental moves of one-quarter of a percentage point. Greenspan had cut rates by as much as half a point in times of stress, but never more. He had worried that if a larger cut didn't prove effective, his policy would be questioned, undermining confidence in the Fed. Chairman Bernanke jettisoned this concern; he signaled that he was willing to adjust monetary policy whenever the Fed's forecasts for inflation and growth changed.

Those forecasts were changing fast in early 2008. In just a few weeks, policymakers went from expecting the economy to slow modestly, to believing it would come close to stalling, to thinking a recession was likely.[8] Historically, when the economy has been in recession, the real federal funds rate goes negative—the benchmark interest rate falls below the rate of underlying inflation.[9] The real funds rate went negative in spring 2008 as the Fed lowered the nominal rate to 2%, about the same rate as inflation (see Figure 12.3).

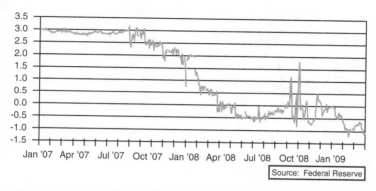

Figure 12.3   The Federal Reserve girds for recession: real federal funds rate target.

The Federal Reserve was now fully engaged in staunching the bleeding from the subprime shock, but its actions couldn't keep the crisis from spreading to other parts of the financial system over which the central bank had less influence. Most worrisome were the rumors swirling about potential liquidity problems among Wall Street's so-called broker dealers. These companies are investment firms that buy and sell securities, both for customers and for themselves (see Table 12.2). They often are highly leveraged, borrowing to make big bets on securities ranging from U.S. Treasury bonds to exotic and risky securities backed by mortgages. When they bet right, their profits can be huge—but when they bet wrong, they can end up as Bear Stearns did in mid-March 2008.

TABLE 12.2   Who Are the Broker-Dealers?

BNP Paribas Securities Corp.

Banc of America Securities LLC

Barclays Capital Inc.

Cantor Fitzgerald & Co.

Citigroup Global Markets Inc.

Countrywide Securities Corporation

Credit Suisse Securities (USA) LLC

Daiwa Securities America Inc.

Deutsche Bank Securities Inc.

TABLE 12.2   Who Are the Broker-Dealers?

Dresdner Kleinwort Wasserstein Securities LLC

Goldman, Sachs & Co.

Greenwich Capital Markets, Inc.

HSBC Securities (USA) Inc.

JPMorgan Securities Inc.

Lehman Brothers Inc.

Merrill Lynch Government Securities Inc.

Mizuho Securities USA Inc.

Morgan Stanley & Co. Incorporated

UBS Securities LLC

Bear Stearns bet big on the residential mortgage market. It not only issued mortgage securities, but it also had acquired mortgage-lending firms that originated the loans that went into those securities. Bear "made a market" in mortgage securities, meaning it would either buy or sell—whichever a customer wanted. It prospered during the housing bubble, but as the housing and mortgage markets collapsed, each of Bear's various business segments soured in turn, and confidence in the firm's viability weakened. Unlike commercial banks that collect funds from depositors, a broker-dealer relies on other financial institutions to lend it the money it invests. If those other institutions lose faith and begin withdrawing their money, the broker-dealer's only options are filing bankruptcy or, as in Bear Stearns' case, selling out.

During a tumultuous weekend in March 2008, the Federal Reserve engineered the sale of Bear Stearns to JPMorgan Chase. The Fed acted out of fear of what a bankruptcy could have meant for the financial system, given Bear's extensive relationships with banks, hedge funds, and other institutions around the world. Policymakers were legitimately worried that the system would freeze up. When it was finished, the Fed had agreed to absorb any losses on $29 billion in risky Bear Stearns securities that JPMorgan acquired in its takeover of the failed firm.

To quell fears that other broker dealers might follow Bear Stearns, policymakers established two new sources of credit for them: the Term Securities Lending Facility (TSLF) and the Primary Dealers Credit Facility (PDCF). The TSLF enabled broker-dealers to borrow Treasury securities from the Fed in exchange for various other securities, including Aaa residential mortgage-backed securities, for up to a month. The PDCF provided overnight loans to broker-dealers at the discount rate and accepted an even wider range of securities as collateral. The TSLF and PDCF provided much-needed liquidity to the broker-dealers and stabilized financial markets, at least temporarily.

Economic Stimulus I

As the struggling economy soared to the top of voters' lists of concerns in early 2008, it quickly dominated the policy debate in Washington, DC. The sense of political urgency was highlighted in early February, when in just a few days, the Bush Administration and Congress came to terms on a sizable and reasonably well-designed fiscal stimulus package.[10] It was an astonishing show of bipartisanship; not only was there broad agreement that this was necessary, but very little debate occurred about what should be in the plan. Policymakers felt it critical to get something done quickly.

The package was worth $168 billion, equal to a little more than 1% of the gross domestic product (GDP). It included tax rebates for lower- and middle-income households, with checks to be mailed between May and July 2008, and tax incentives to spur business investment and put people to work. Economists debated just how large a boost the stimulus would provide—the administration said it would add about half a million jobs—but few believed the medicine would provide more than temporary relief if the housing market and financial system didn't begin to recover as well.[11]

The stimulus package did include some modest housing help; it significantly raised the caps on mortgage lending by the FHA, Fannie Mae, and Freddie Mac.[12] The previous caps made it all but impossible for these agencies to provide mortgage credit in areas of the country where high housing prices required large home loans.[13] These included places such as California, southern Florida, New York City, and Washington, DC (see Figure 12.4). Because private lenders weren't making loans, perhaps these federal lenders could fill at least part of the void. This was a striking policy reversal for the Bush Administration; only a few weeks earlier, the White House had emphatically said no to such a move. Until the crisis, administration officials had been intent on reining in these agencies, demanding that Congress pass reforms before expanding their lending powers. That the administration could forget its long-running feud with Fannie and Freddie—both institutions traditionally had much stronger Democratic support—and let them take on such a prominent role in solving the subprime financial shock was proof of how events had unnerved politicians of nearly all stripes.

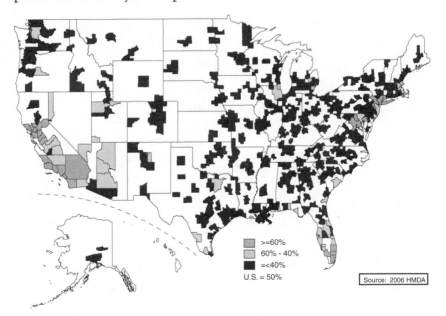

Figure 12.4   Government lending helps most here: nonconforming share of '06 mortgage originations.

The administration even went along with relaxing Fannie and Freddie's capital requirements. This had been a contentious political issue earlier in the decade. A serious accounting scandal occurred at the two lending agencies; their books were so tangled that for years no one knew how much they were earning or losing. OFHEO, the agency that oversaw Fannie and Freddie, had issued penalties in the form of higher capital requirements—in effect, giving them less money to play with.[14] But now both institutions were suffering their own credit problems, and losses were making it harder for them to grow. The administration realized that unless it reversed OFHEO's rule and relaxed the capital requirements, Fannie and Freddie wouldn't be able to ramp up their lending and help ease the mortgage crisis.

The administration didn't stop there; it also granted Fannie and Freddie permission to increase their purchases of mortgage loans and securities. OFHEO had put limits on the growth in their holdings—also punishment for their past bad behavior—but with no one else buying, the mortgage securities market was choking. The Federal Home Loan Banks were also permitted by their regulator, the Federal Housing Finance Board, to substantially increase their security holdings.[15]

The Bush Administration quickly retreated from its long-held positions in an effort to stem the financial crisis and developing recession. Markets weren't figuring it out by themselves—they needed government help. And the parts of government most valuable in addressing the crisis were the very ones the administration had previously wanted to restrict or dismantle. The administration viewed the FHA, Fannie Mae, Freddie Mac, and the Federal Home Loan Banks as, at best, anachronistic and, at worst, risks to the financial system. These institutions were now the centerpiece of the policy response to the subprime finance shock.

Government Misintervention

This strategy turned shaky almost immediately during summer 2008, as the financial health of Fannie Mae and Freddie Mac grew more tenuous. The mammoth mortgage lenders had ventured off their traditional low-risk turf, where they specialized in lending to borrowers with good credit scores and ample down payments; now they began investing in riskier alt-A securities. The loss rates on Fannie's and Freddie's loans were still low by industry standards, but they were rising and starting to threaten the institutions' very thin capital cushions. The average commercial bank held $10 worth of assets for every $1 of capital; Fannie and Freddie's ratio was as high as 70 to 1. The two firms had never been thought to need as much capital as ordinary banks, since they were lending to such good borrowers; now that they were lending to less creditworthy borrowers, their capital appeared inadequate.

The investors who owned Fannie and Freddie stock and debt began to openly worry they might fail. The two firms' share prices plunged and their borrowing costs rose. All this made it difficult to extend mortgage credit, which policymakers were counting on to help stabilize the sinking housing market; rates on their mortgage loans also began to rise, just the opposite of what policymakers were hoping. Treasury Secretary Paulson aimed to shore up investor confidence when, in July 2008, he reaffirmed and expanded Fannie's and Freddie's lines of credit with the Treasury. Investors were only briefly appeased and grew even more convinced that Fannie and Freddie were headed toward insolvency. In early September 2008, the Treasury placed Fannie and Freddie in conservatorship, effectively nationalizing them. Debt-holders were safe, but shareholders were wiped out.[16]

The financial crisis that had begun a year earlier unraveled into a panic. The seizure of Fannie and Freddie signaled to investors that their stakes in even the largest financial institutions were at risk.

The weakest link in the financial system, broker-dealer Lehman Brothers, came under immediate pressure as shareholders sold their stock, and short-sellers took advantage of the downdraft. Lehman had access to cash, thanks to the TSLF and PDCF, but one by one, Lehman's business partners dropped away, seeing the firm as too risky to do business with. The company was spiraling toward bankruptcy.

The Treasury and the Fed worked feverishly to find a buyer for Lehman but came up short. Treasury officials decided not to intervene, arguing that they couldn't bail out every financial institution and that Lehman's counterparties had plenty of time to prepare after the Bear Stearns collapse months earlier. The Fed went along, arguing that it could not, by law, loan Lehman any more without collateral.

The Treasury and the Fed made a grievous mistake; they misjudged the fallout from the Lehman bankruptcy. One of the nation's oldest money market funds, the Reserve Primary Fund, was choking on its investments in Lehman paper. The Reserve Fund "broke the buck" (the value of its assets fell below what it owed its investors), which, in turn, broke the psyche of small investors, who thought of a money fund as one step removed from a mattress. Redemptions from money funds surged. Money funds are the largest buyers of commercial paper, the short-term IOUs issued by the largest companies, and when the funds stopped buying and started selling commercial paper to pay off scared depositors, the market seized up. Stock investors were terrified; if companies couldn't issue commercial paper, many couldn't meet payrolls, finance inventories, or pay vendors. A huge amount of commerce would simply cease.

Other major financial institutions were teetering. Fearing Lehman's fate, venerable broker-dealer Merrill Lynch hastily sold itself to Bank of America. Shakier banks suffered silent runs as scared depositors with more than the FDIC insured limit of $100,000 moved their funds. Wachovia, a top-five commercial bank, was forced to sell itself to rival Wells Fargo, and WAMU, the nation's largest Savings & Loan, was folded into JPMorgan Chase. In the midst of this turmoil, insurance colossus AIG told policymakers it, too, was in serious financial trouble. The company had been aggressively writing insurance on mortgage-backed securities via the credit default swap market. As the value of those securities declined and the cost of the insurance it was providing rose, the credit-rating agencies downgraded AIG debt. Other financial institutions that had bought the credit insurance demanded more collateral, which AIG didn't have. Fearing another Lehman-like event, the Fed extended AIG a multibillion-dollar loan in exchange for a majority ownership stake. The financial system seemed about to shut down.

In late September, a visibly shaken Treasury Secretary Paulson and Fed Chairman Bernanke appeared before Congress with a plan to calm the mounting turmoil. They called it the Troubled Asset Relief Program (TARP). Paulson and Bernanke wanted Congress to devote $700 billion to rescuing the financial system. For such a huge sum, the plan was shockingly short on details. Why $700 billion? This was roughly equal to the system's likely losses. What would the money be used for? No restrictions would govern how the money could be deployed, but Paulson's plan was to buy "toxic" assets from distressed banks. Who would oversee how the money was spent? That would be worked out at some point in the future. Would any restrictions be placed on institutions that benefited from the TARP money? That, too, would be determined at a later date, but policymakers argued that restricting executive compensation at firms receiving help would be a mistake because it could dissuade them from participating.

TARP brought about a groundswell of protest among taxpayers, who simply couldn't understand why they should pay for Wall Street's mistakes. Banks had made the bad loans; they should fix them. Asking taxpayers for $700 billion to clean up the mess was beyond the pale. Congress was flooded with calls opposing the plan.

Despite the uproar, the Democratic leadership in the House thought it had just enough votes to squeak TARP through and called a vote. Although many in Congress didn't fully understand the gravity of Secretary Paulson and Chairman Bernanke's warnings, the election six weeks away made taxpayers sound loud and clear. Congress voted down the TARP. The consequences were evident immediately: The stock market cratered. The House reversed its vote a week later, but in the furor, Paulson's plan for using the TARP money changed. Instead of buying toxic assets, the Treasury decided to buy equity directly in the nation's largest banks. To sell this idea, however, policymakers had to convince the public that these banks were too large to fail. Meanwhile, to further shore up confidence, the FDIC insurance limit was increased to $250,000, insurance was provided to money funds, and the government guaranteed bank-issued debt.

A tenuous calm prevailed in financial markets through the presidential election. Money fund redemptions slowed, bank runs ended, and no other major failures occurred. Even the stock market held its own after its September downdraft. That lasted until mid-November, when Secretary Paulson said he no longer planned to use TARP money to buy toxic assets. Market prices for residential and commercial mortgage securities tanked on the news. Banks that owned these assets—notably including once-mighty Citigroup—came under immediate intense pressure. The Treasury and Fed once again were forced to step in to stop a bank failure, this time by guaranteeing hundreds of billions of dollars' worth of Citigroup holdings.

The Bush Administration had taken office early in the decade holding the belief that financial markets would effectively police themselves; if they got into trouble, it was on them to get themselves out. Government intervention would only create moral hazard, encourage imprudent risk-taking, and lead to worse problems in the future. By the time Bush left office, however, his administration had jettisoned its scruples about moral hazard and was intervening aggressively. Washington had mis-stepped badly, letting a severe yet manageable financial crisis become an uncontrollable panic. The financial system was a shambles and the economy was in its worst downturn since the Great Depression.

Printing Money

The Fed was already thinking well outside its monetary policy box, working overtime to invent new tools for combating the crisis. Policymakers had dropped their main benchmark interest rate, the so-called federal funds rate, effectively to zero and said publicly it would stay there indefinitely. Even more dramatic, the Fed was ramping up a policy called "quantitative easing," essentially creating money by fiat to buy financial assets. The central bank had already been buying commercial paper and securities issued or guaranteed by Fannie Mae and Freddie Mac. Policymakers also signaled that they could soon be buying long-term Treasury bonds and thus monetizing the nation's debt.

In addition to stepping up security purchases, the Fed expanded its lending via a parade of new lending facilities, essentially offers to provide cash under specific terms to different groups of financial institutions. The first, called the Term Auction Facility (TAF), began in late 2007 to get short-term cash to banks. The newest, as of spring 2009, was called the Term Asset-Backed Securities Loan Facility (TALF) short. This aimed to give private investors the wherewithal to buy newly issued Aaa securities backed by residential and commercial mortgages; credit card debt; and student, auto and small business loans. The Fed was also willing to guarantee troubled assets to backstop struggling financial institutions, a tactic used successfully with Bear Stearns, AIG, and Citigroup.

The Fed took unprecedented steps to deal with an unprecedented financial and economic crisis. Yet despite more than a year of aggressive government policy, credit markets remained frozen and the banking system was still in disarray. Except for Treasury yields, which had never been lower, interest rates that consumers and businesses face remained disconcertingly high. Given the collapse in bond issuance and the tightened lending standards, many borrowers couldn't obtain credit at any price.

The recession was intensifying, due to the credit crunch, crumbling confidence, and the loss of wealth. The Real GDP was falling sharply, with no sign of stabilization in housing, consumer spending, or business investment. Deflation was a mounting threat as businesses were forced to cut prices to make sales. Core consumer price inflation came to a standstill in early 2009 and looked set to go negative. Businesses had little choice but to cut jobs and investment, which only exacerbated the decline in sales and threatened to push the economy into a pernicious, self-reinforcing deflationary cycle.

Quantitative easing would ultimately succeed in short-circuiting the deflationary cycle and reviving the economy. This was already evident in the commercial paper market. After the Fed began buying commercial paper directly from issuers, rates fell and issuance picked up. The Fed's program was so successful that it grew measurably smaller over the first quarter of 2009.

The decline in long-term Treasury yields and fixed mortgage rates also showed how much power the Fed still had. After the Fed said it would buy long-term government bonds, 10-year Treasury yields plunged to near 3%. Fixed mortgage rates fell to just above 5%, pulled down by both lower Treasury yields and narrowing mortgage spreads after the Fed bought debt and mortgage securities from Fannie and Freddie. If spreads kept falling toward their long-run averages, fixed-rate mortgages seemed likely to approach 4.5%. That seemed enough to ignite a new refinancing boom—most existing mortgage loans carried rates around 5.5%—and to support stronger home sales when the downdraft in the job market abated.

Just how far the Fed would need to take quantitative easing and its lending facilities would depend on how quickly the financial system responded. It was not hard to imagine the Fed ultimately extending its reach to all asset markets, from mortgage-backed securities to municipal bonds and corporate debt.

All this added to concerns that the Fed wouldn't be able to gracefully unwind its massive intrusion into the financial system. Many worried that the Fed's strategy would ignite runaway inflation after the crisis abated. After all, inflation is a monetary phenomenon, and the Fed was printing dollars by the trillions.

Although inflation could well grow uncomfortably high at some point, it was not likely to validate such fears and was certainly not a reason for the Fed to hold back in its response to the crisis. Money ignites inflation only if it first leads to more and less costly credit, fueling tight labor markets and sending utilization rates up against capacity constraints. Policymakers would have time to respond before this transpired; in the wake of the crisis, it might be years before credit flowed freely again and the economy found its way back to full employment.

Also important was that most of the Fed's liquidity was in the form of very short-term loans—less than 90 days. When the financial system and economy found their footing, policymakers could without much difficulty allow these programs to simply fade away.

The Fed was expected to begin normalizing interest rates by summer 2010. By that time, the financial crisis will have subsided, and house prices and the broader economy will be stabilizing. Policymakers will be reluctant to keep rates too long too low, a mistake that the Fed seemingly made coming out the tech-stock bust early in the decade. This contributed to the housing bubble at the root of the epic financial crisis.

Economic Stimulus II

The new Obama Administration also swung immediately into crisis management. Just a few weeks after Obama took office, the administration and Congress came to terms on a massive fiscal stimulus plan. It included tax cuts and increased government spending totaling nearly $800 billion, to be mostly distributed through the end of the decade. This equaled 3% of the GDP in 2009 and 2010, the largest stimulus since the New Deal of the 1930s.

Of the $800 billion, some $300 billion was in tax cuts to individuals and businesses, $250 billion in aid to fiscally strapped state and local governments, $150 billion in various kinds of infrastructure spending, and $100 billion in additional income support to workers who were losing their jobs.

Income support and aid to state and local governments was intended to provide quick help to the economy. Without this relief, workers who were losing their jobs had little choice but to immediately slash spending, costing the economy even more jobs. In most cases, state and local governments struggling with falling tax revenues must balance their budgets by cutting payrolls and programs and also raising taxes, adding to the economy's burdens. Federal help for the unemployed and for state and local governments was thus intended to prevent even worse job losses.

Tax cuts stimulate job creation as individuals spend and businesses invest some of their new cash. But the near-term economic benefits of individual tax cuts are diluted because some is saved and some is used to repay debt. These aren't bad things in themselves, but they don't help the economy as much as spending the money quickly. The stimulus plan also helped the troubled housing and auto industries with tax breaks, including a nonrefundable tax credit worth up to $8,000 for first-time home buyers who made a quick home purchase, and a write-off of state sales taxes and interest on loans to buy new vehicles.

The economic benefits of infrastructure spending are generally not quick—it takes time to get these projects underway—but they are significant, particularly for the depressed construction and manufacturing industries. The economy was expected to struggle well into the next decade, so this spending was expected to be particularly welcome in 2010 as the impact of the other stimulus efforts faded. The stimulus plan drew criticism for its mixed bag of infrastructure targets, from roads and bridges to the electric grid and the Internet backbone. But given the uncertain returns on such projects, diversification is probably a plus. Moreover, the Japanese experience during their "lost decade" of the 1990s showed there are diminishing returns to infrastructure spending. Investing only in bridges, for example, ultimately produces bridges to nowhere.

Concerns arose that the stimulus plan's price tag was too large. It would be paid for with borrowed money, adding significantly to the government's already swelling debt load. But without a stimulus, the economy would sink further as consumers and businesses retrenched, undermining tax revenues and fueling more government spending, producing even larger deficits and debt burdens. Fortunately, the United States is still the global economy's triple-A credit; even though the subprime financial shock began in the United States, global investors still preferred the safety of U.S. Treasury bonds. The United States was thus still able to borrow at record-low interest rates.

Indeed, a more significant criticism of the stimulus plan was that it was too small. The struggling economy was set to produce nearly $1 trillion less than it was capable of during 2009 and will almost surely fall short again by as much in 2010. The $800 billion in spending and tax cuts to be distributed during this period will not fill this expected hole in the economy. Nonetheless, the hope was that, when combined with the other aggressive policy steps being taken, the stimulus plan would go a long way toward curtailing the downdraft in the economy.

Foreclosure Mitigation

With the economic stimulus plan in place, the Obama Administration turned its focus on foreclosure mitigation. Foreclosures undermine house prices because foreclosed property is dumped on the housing market at deep discounts. They also choke the banking system, as losses on defaulted mortgages mount. There had been a string of policy efforts to stem foreclosures by facilitating mortgage refinancings and loan modification, dating back to late 2007 with FHA Secure and Hope Now, but these efforts had been overwhelmed. So within just a few weeks of taking office, the administration put forth a comprehensive plan to shore up the housing market and stem the foreclosure crisis.

Broadly, the administration's housing policy aimed to support single-family housing demand by lowering the cost and increasing the availability of mortgage credit. At the same time, the initiative worked to control housing supply by offering refinancing and mortgage loan modifications as alternatives to foreclosure.

More specifically, the plan made mortgage credit cheaper and more widely available by empowering Fannie and Freddie. Because these institutions were now part of the federal government, they had no shareholders to appease and making profits was no longer a priority—making more and cheaper mortgage credit was. One way Fannie and Freddie were asked to do this was to refinance loans that they owned or insured but had been precluded from refinancing because the homeowner didn't have the requisite 20% down payment because of falling house prices.

A major mortgage refinancing boom looked imminent in spring 2009. With the Federal Reserve aggressively buying Fannie and Freddie debt and mortgage securities, conforming mortgage rates were drifting below 5%. About $3 trillion in Fannie and Freddie loans (more than one-fourth of all mortgage loans outstanding) carry mortgage rates higher than 5% and would be good candidates for refinancing if rates fell much lower. This would do less to prevent foreclosures—subprime, alt-A, and jumbo borrowers are having the most trouble making payments—but it would reduce mortgage payments and save borrowers tens of billions of dollars, adding more stimulus to the economy.

The administration's housing policy also included a large mortgage-modification plan targeted primarily at owner-occupied homes with troubled subprime and alt-A loans. The plan involved using tens of billions in taxpayer dollars to provide lucrative incentives to homeowners, mortgage servicers, and mortgage owners to engage in substantial loan modifications. There were lower mortgage payments and subsidies for homeowners who stay current on modified loans, payments to servicers who successfully modify loans, and, in some circumstances, payments to mortgage owners who agree to the modifications.

Ultimately, the number of loans modified will be up to mortgage owners. Owners of subprime and alt-A mortgage loans are mainly global financial institutions that invested in mortgage securities backed by the loans. These owners benefit only if a modification significantly reduces the chance of default. Thus, their calculation is sensitive to the borrowers' probability of default before and after the modification. The probability of default, in turn, depends on the equity position of the homeowner. A deeply underwater homeowner will still be liable to default, even with a lower monthly payment. Add one financial setback—say, a leaky roof—and default may be a rational choice. Indeed, loan modifications to lower monthly payments have not worked out particularly well thus far. The OCC said more than half the loans modified in this way in early 2008 had defaulted again six months later. The bottom line is that, given the complexity of the calculation for mortgage owners, ultimately there may be fewer modifications than the administration hopes for, and it could take longer for modifications to get going in earnest. Still, the plan will substantially increase loan modifications and reduce foreclosures.

The administration's housing initiative also included legislation to change bankruptcy law, allowing homeowners in a Chapter 13 filing to have the principal on their first mortgage reduced—crammed down—to the home's current market value. Under current law, bankruptcy judges may reduce most consumer debts, but not a first mortgage. The logic is that by not allowing first-mortgage cram-downs in bankruptcy, mortgage rates remain lower and credit stays more available.

Policymakers likely hoped the proposed change would not increase bankruptcy filings, but rather encourage mortgage owners to modify more loans. Bankruptcy judges have significant latitude to rearrange households' finances and could impose greater losses on mortgage owners than they would face by participating in the modification plan. The bankruptcy law would be the stick persuading mortgage owners to take the financial carrots in the modification plan.

Even so, a change in the law could lead to substantially more Chapter 13 filings. Some homeowners would find this alternative more attractive than a loan modification, particularly those significantly underwater or with high total debt loads. Indeed, bankruptcy could put some homeowners on firmer financial ground and thus lower the chance of future default more than modification would.

Some concerns about such bankruptcy legislation are misplaced. The change would not significantly raise the cost of mortgage credit because the change would apply only to loans already originated. The likelihood that abuses by distressed homeowners would increase is also low, given that a workout in Chapter 13 is financially painful. Indeed, the number of bankruptcy filings has remained surprisingly low since the late-2005 bankruptcy reform, reflecting the much higher costs to households filing for Chapter 13.

Yet it is reasonable to worry that rising bankruptcies would hit other consumer lenders hard. Unsecured credit card lenders, in particular, could lose substantially as judges significantly reduce or eliminate credit card debts. If a million more households filed for bankruptcy because of cram-down legislation and the average household had $50,000 in credit card debt, the potential loss to credit card lenders would be $50 billion. Complicating matters further, most credit card debt has been securitized; these securitizations could fall apart if the losses are great enough.

Changing bankruptcy law to allow for first-mortgage cram-downs would forestall more foreclosures and thus help alleviate the housing crisis. But there will be costs, some known and some still unknown.

The administration's housing policy came under fire from various critics, with the most vitriolic arguing that it rewarded bad behavior by homeowners and mortgage owners, that bankruptcy reform abrogates contracts, and that the plan will hurt the financial system. Others argued that the plan's cost to taxpayers, estimated at $275 billion, was too high.

These criticisms have some merit, but without such a plan, everyone's cost will be higher—in soaring foreclosures, lower house prices and household wealth, a measurably weaker financial system and economy, and even greater costs to taxpayers. In certain respects, the administration's housing policy was not aggressive enough, and an even larger policy response might ultimately be needed.

Financial Stability

Solving the nation's banking crisis was the Obama Administration's most intractable problem. There hadn't been a major financial failure since late 2008, but many banks didn't have enough capital and were reluctant to make loans to consumers and businesses. Until the banks' capital hole was filled, the credit crunch would strangle the economy.

New Treasury Secretary Geithner had presented the rough outlines of what he called a financial stability plan in February, but this did more harm than good because the outline was so rough that it suggested to financial markets that there was no real plan. The stock market hit a new low in early March, some 50% below its peak in late 2007. Household nest eggs had literally been cut in half.

The stakes were thus extraordinarily high when the Treasury unveiled substantially more details on the plan in mid-March. It would combine as much as $100 billion from the Troubled Asset Relief Program with private investment and debt financing guaranteed by the FDIC, and have the capacity to buy up to approximately $1 trillion in toxic assets. The plan also involved expanding the Fed's Troubled Asset-Backed Securities Lending Facility program to purchase legacy (previously issued) securities on banks' balance sheets. TALF had originally been designed only for newly issued securities.

Toxic assets are loans, or securities backed by loans, on which the borrowers are behind or in default. The assets are thus worth a lot less than when the loans were originally made. The resulting loss cuts into the banks' capital, the financial cushions they need to remain in business. Making the problem worse is that banks don't know how toxic these assets will ultimately prove to be: Will a delinquent borrower eventually default? Given that uncertainty, banks are unsure how much capital they will need (particularly because raising new capital from investors is nearly impossible at this time) and, therefore, are nervous about making new loans. The key idea in the Treasury's plan was to have the federal government finance the purchase of these toxic assets and create certainty for the banks so they could resume lending normally.

One attractive feature of the plan was that it relied on only a handful of private investors; their job would be to bid for toxic assets that willing banks put up for auction, to determine a fair price. The government would then finance purchases of these assets on a large scale at these prices. Private investors should be attracted to the auctions, given the potentially high return on their money, the limited downside (because the federal government is also participating), and efforts to ensure that they would not face compensation and other management restrictions, unlike institutions receiving TARP money. The logic was that there was a difference between receiving taxpayer dollars directly, via the TARP, and partnering with taxpayers, as was being proposed.

This was important, given the furor over retention bonuses paid to AIG traders, the very same people who had driven the insurer into the ground and cost taxpayers a couple hundred billion dollars. Contracts between AIG and some of its traders had been signed before the government had stepped in. And although the government now owned nearly 80% of the company because it had not gone into bankruptcy, those contracts were still enforceable. It was absurd, but the Treasury felt that it had no legal recourse but to allow the bonuses to be paid. Congress was infuriated and considered legislation to tax the bonuses away. The Treasury's financial stability plan would work only if private investors participated, and they wouldn't participate if they thought Congress might at some point impose retroactive taxes or other penalties. Policymakers had to assuage those concerns.

Another attractive feature of the Treasury's plan was that the FDIC played a key role, conducting the auctions and guaranteeing the debt financing for the purchases of toxic assets. The FDIC sells assets all the time as part of its resolution of failed banks. Using the FDIC for debt financing also did not require the Treasury to go back to Congress for approval, which could have been problematic in the current political environment. Private investors will manage the assets after buying them in the auctions.

Purchasing $1 trillion in toxic assets wouldn't be enough to solve the banking system's problems; the program probably needed to be at least twice as large. The volume of toxic assets on U.S. bank balance sheets that had not already been written down was between $2 trillion and $2.5 trillion. To cover losses on these assets, the government would ultimately need an additional $300 billion to $400 billion (on top of the $700 billion already spent on TARP). The up to $100 billion they planned to commit on this plan was a good start, but officials would eventually have to ask Congress for more. If things worked well enough, however, Congress would likely provide more money to solve the banking problem once and for all.

There were reasons to worry that the plan would not work as well as hoped. Banks could be reluctant to offer assets for sale in the auctions, believing they still wouldn't obtain a good price. Private investors could stay away, rather than risk incurring the wrath of Congress if they made too much money down the road. Weak banks could be pushed under if they were forced to mark the value of their own assets to the prices determined in the auctions, thus putting pressure on taxpayers to come up with more assistance. Given these uncertainties, it would be quicker and more efficient for the federal government to buy the toxic assets directly. But given the various political constraints on this approach—most significantly, the worry that the government would overpay for the toxic assets if it bought them directly—the Treasury's financial stability plan was a good second-best option.

Indeed, Wall Street liked the plan. Finally some optimism seemed to emerge regarding the prospects for the financial system and the economy. As banks unload their toxic assets and taxpayers provide more capital, the system should slowly begin to pump more credit through the economy. Combined with Washington's fiscal stimulus (which would take effect in spring 2009), a potentially massive refinancing boom during the summer (as mortgage rates fall firmly below 5%), and fewer foreclosures (as the administration's mortgage-modification plan kicks in during late 2009), chances were rising that the economy would stabilize by early 2010.

Adding Up the Costs

The government's unprecedented intervention throughout the financial system and economy was necessary to quell the financial panic and stabilize the economy, but the costs to taxpayers were enormous. By March 2009, the commitments policymakers had made to combat the crisis totaled an astounding $12 trillion, of which nearly $4 trillion had already been used (see Table 12.3).

TABLE 12.3   Government Response to Financial Crisis: $ Billions, through March 2009

Federal Reserve	Committed	Provided
Term auction credit	900	469
Other loans	Unlimited	135
Primary credit	Unlimited	64
Secondary credit	Unlimited	0
Seasonal credit	Unlimited	0
Primary Dealer Credit Facility	Unlimited	20
Asset-Backed Commercial Paper Money Market Mutual Fund	Unlimited	8
AIG	43	43
AIG (for SPVs)	9	0
AIG (for ALICO, AIA)	26	0
Rescue of Bear Stearns (Maiden Lane)**	27	26
AIG-RMBS purchase program (Maiden Lane II)**	23	18
AIG-CDO purchase program (Maiden Lane III)**	30	28
Term Securities Lending Facility	200	18
Commercial Paper Funding Facility**	1,800	241
TALF	1,000	0
Money Market Investor Funding Facility	540	0
Currency swap lines	Unlimited	329
Purchase of GSE debt and MBS	1,250	285
Guarantee of Citigroup assets	286	0
Guarantee of Bank of America assets	108	0
Purchase of long-term Treasuries	300	0
Treasury		
TARP	700	547
Fed supplementary financing account	479	479
Back stop of Fannie Mae and Freddie Mac	400	0

Federal Deposit Insurance Corporation

Guarantee of U.S. banks' debt°	1,400	201
Guarantee of Citigroup assets		10
Guarantee of Bank of America assets		2.5
Transaction deposit accounts	500	0

Federal Housing Administration

Refinancing of mortgages	100	0

Congress

Economic Stimulus Act of 2008	170	170
American Recovery and Reinvestment Act of 2009	787	787

Joint Fed, FDIC, and Treasury

Public-Private Investment Fund	1,000	0
Total	**12,077**	**3,746**

Sources: Fed, Treasury, FDIC, FHA, Moody's Economy.com
*Includes foreign-denominated debt
**Net portfolio holdings

This isn't the final bill for taxpayers—it will be less. Taxpayers will ultimately recoup some of the trillions they lay out as the government sells the assets it accumulates and presumably privatizes its large ownership stake in the financial system. The final price tag isn't small, however: It could easily approach $3 trillion, equal to more than 20% of the current GDP. For context, the United States savings and loan crisis during the early 1990s cost taxpayers some 7% of GDP, and the Japanese banking crisis that weighed on that economy throughout the 1990s cost Japanese taxpayers at least 10% of the GDP.

Two-thirds of the $3 trillion in expected taxpayer costs is the direct cost of the government response to the financial crisis. This includes nearly $1 trillion in total economic stimulus and another $1 trillion in net costs of what the government has committed to support various financial institutions and markets via such things as $700 billion for TARP, $400 billion for recapitalizing Fannie and Freddie, and more than $2 trillion in Federal Reserve loans and loan guarantees. The remaining one-third of the costs reflects the economic downturn and resulting loss of tax revenues and increased government spending.

The federal government's fiscal situation, which was already weakening before the crisis, will be extraordinarily worrisome in the wake of it. The nation's federal-debt-to-GDP ratio, a good measure of the nation's fiscal health, will increase from close to 45% of GDP (about the average over the period since World War II) to more than 65%. And unless big changes in tax and spending policy come soon, this ratio will move steadily higher even after the financial crisis abates. In just a few years, the outsized baby boom generation will retire en masse and require more healthcare. The costs of Social Security, Medicaid, and Medicare will balloon. This will be untenable. Policymakers must credibly address these long-term budget concerns soon or risk losing the confidence of global investors—the same investors who are buying the trillions in Treasury bonds currently being issued to finance the government's response to the crisis.

Many other costs from the government's interventions are difficult to determine. A taste of this is evident from the difficulties created by the government's big ownership stakes in the nation's largest financial institutions. Determining appropriate compensation packages for senior management might look easy in comparison to some of the decisions policymakers might yet have to make regarding the operations of these firms. Selling off these stakes somewhere down the road won't be easy, either. Consider that privatizing Fannie and Freddie could mean somewhat higher mortgage rates and less ample mortgage credit; will future policymakers have the political will necessary to take this step? The list of potential repercussions goes on and on.

The government response to the subprime financial shock had gone from timid to bold. In summer 2007, the Federal Reserve had been uncomfortable lowering interest rates and the Bush Administration had thought giving the FHA the authority to refinance a few hundred thousand troubled mortgage loans would be enough to quell the crisis. By spring 2009, policymakers were engaged in the largest government intervention in the financial system and the economy since the New Deal. The failure to act decisively early in the crisis and a series of policy errors in the middle of it ultimately led to the need for unprecedented government action. The costs of all this are daunting, but the costs of governmental inaction would be measurably greater.

13

Economic Fallout

The subprime financial shock hit in summer 2007, and by early 2008, the U.S. economy had come unhinged. Economists and policymakers debated whether the nation was in recession, but for most Americans, there was no debate. They were worth measurably less and their incomes didn't stretch nearly as far.[1] For them, this was a recession.

By summer 2008, little was going right: Job losses were intensifying, and part-time work was replacing full-time. The stock market was down and, for the first time since the collapse of the tech-stock bubble early in the decade, was having trouble getting back up. Gasoline prices were rocketing past $4 per gallon. The cost of bread, milk, and other staples was rising quickly as well. Millions were losing their homes to foreclosure, and house prices were in free-fall. American consumers, whose collective spending had powered the global economy since World War II, had no choice but to tighten their belts.

Americans' anxiety steadily mounted. As 2008 came to a close, it was as if everyone were running to take shelter in the proverbial bunker. Home Depot reported that its biggest-selling item in November was home safes, presumably to store the cash people were pulling out of the stock market. Surveys of consumer sentiment concurred that the collective psyche had never been so frayed, at least not since such surveys began in the 1960s. Households were even more upbeat in the early 1980s, when inflation and unemployment were both in double digits.[2] Though both inflation and employment were still relatively low at this point, it was telling that people felt things were worse than they had been in that earlier dark period.

For the economy to be pushed into recession by scared consumers was unprecedented. Historically, recessions had been caused by businesses that had overextended in the good times and had to pull back when things didn't go as planned. An event such as 9/11 or the Gulf War could trigger a recession, as they had in 2001 and 1990. Disruptions in oil supplies did the trick in 1973 and 1980. Those downturns began when firms had been forced to lay off workers and cut investment. But that wasn't the cause in 2007 and 2008. First, homeowners stopped paying their mortgage bills and other debts; then they stopped spending altogether. Economists had long counted on the American consumer to power the economy's growth—as they put it, to never underestimate the hedonism of the American consumer. That old adage no longer appeared to hold true.

Yet the subprime financial shock's significance goes beyond the severe economic downturn it started. The shock was, in fact, an inflection point in the nation's economic history. Before it hit, most households saved little, and many borrowed aggressively and spent beyond their incomes. Between 1980 and 2005, the personal saving rate—the percent of after-tax income that is not spent—fell steadily from 10% to essentially nothing (see Figure 13.1). The decline was due partly to wealthier households saving less. Affluent Americans had built up their nest eggs during years of strong stock and real-estate gains. The 1987 stock market crash, the tech-stock bust, and the housing crash had been only temporary setbacks.[3] Millions of families didn't have to worry about paying for the children's college education or their retirement, so they were set. Why save?

Saving also declined as the borrowing power of poorer households increased. Steadily falling interest rates since the early 1980s and financial innovation had made credit available to households that had not previously had access to credit cards, car loans, or mortgages. By going from a three-year to a five-year car loan or taking on a 2/28

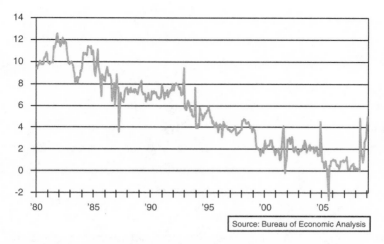

Source: Bureau of Economic Analysis

Figure 13.1   Personal saving fades away: personal saving rate.

subprime mortgage, these households could add debt without seeing their monthly payments rise, at least for awhile. Borrowing allowed them to maintain a level of spending despite having tenuous jobs and volatile incomes.

The subprime shock signaled an end to all this. No longer would wealthier families be able to count on outsized gains in the stock or real-estate markets to do their saving for them. No longer could poorer households easily get another loan when the cash from the previous one ran out. The subprime shock marked the denouement of a half-century of global economic history driven by the American consumer.

Housing's Tentacles

The bursting of the housing bubble and the waves of mortgage defaults that followed brought on the subprime shock. Conversely, the shock and subsequent credit crunch accelerated the housing crash. With mortgage lending at a standstill, home sales collapsed and foreclosures soared, forcing builders to cease construction and home sellers to slash prices. Because housing is such an essential part of the economy—no other industry is arguably as important to the business cycle—the housing crash choked the economic expansion. Recession followed.

The severity of the housing crash was without parallel, except perhaps for the Great Depression. By early 2009, housing starts had fallen nearly 80% from their peak three years earlier; home sales were off 35% (and closer to 60% if foreclosure and other distress sales were excluded), and house prices had dropped by 25% on average nationwide. For historical context, during the housing downturn of the early 1980s, the industry's previous low-water mark, although housing starts fell 60% peak to trough and home sales fell by about 50%, the sales price of American home prices never declined.[4]

The most obvious link between housing and the economy is construction. During the housing boom, residential investment, which includes the value of home building, renovation, and remodeling, steadily rose. When home building peaked in early 2006, its value as a percentage of GDP was at an all-time high; residential construction had never been more important to the economy.[5] Three years later, building as a share of GDP was plumbing a record low.

The wild swing in home building had a dramatic impact on the nation's overall growth. Residential construction had added nearly half a percentage point to real GDP steadily during the boom; it *subtracted* a full percentage point from yearly growth during the crash. In 2007, real GDP growth came in at 2.2%, but it would have been 3.2% if home building had simply remained unchanged that year. But this is just a partial measure; it doesn't count all the ripple effects that occur when home building falls off: Demand, and thus production, falls for steel, cement, gypsum, lumber, tools, plumbing fixtures, and electrical apparatus; for surveyors, truckers, and retailers have less work; fewer roads, bridges, and schools are built; and on and on.

A less obvious link between housing and the economy runs through state and local government finances. Property taxes account for more than two-thirds of local governments' tax receipts, while states depend on various transfer fees and capital gains taxes on home sales for their revenue. Government coffers overflowed during the housing boom as rapidly rising house prices fueled gains in revenue.

Those coffers didn't dry up right away, thanks to the time lag between house prices, property assessments, and tax payments. But it was clear the housing crash would be a drag on government finances for a long time.

Budgets for the fiscal year 2009 already showed the first effects. More than half the nation's states reported sizable shortfalls for fiscal year 2009, and nearly all will have budget problems in fiscal year 2010. States had been relatively prudent during the boom and had fattened up their rainy-day funds. But states have largely spent those monies now, and with most states having constitutional balanced budget requirements, they are being forced to cut back spending and even raise taxes to balance their books. All government services, from schools and universities to hospitals and roads, are being pinched. In addition to the institutional pain this causes, the economy as a whole feels the ill effects. Government isn't generally a huge contributor to the economy's growth, but it is a consistent one, and when other sources of growth fall off, it can be important.

Perhaps the least understood link between housing and the economy is house prices and their impact on homeowners' wealth. As we saw in Chapter 4, "Chairman Greenspan Counts on Housing," the wealth effect of rising house prices lifted consumer spending during the housing boom. During the crash, this wealth effect went into reverse. Because a home is most households' most important asset, a drop in real estate prices affects consumers' sense of their own net worth and strongly influences decisions on spending. When house prices were high, for example, the equity in a home might have been enough to pay for a year or two of a child's college—but with prices down, there was enough for room and board, at best. With the echo-boom generation reaching late teens and the credit crunch suddenly making student loans more difficult to get, there was no other option but to spend less and save more—and quickly.

Amplifying the financial angst was the extra debt many home-owners had taken on during the boom via home equity lines and cash-out refinancing deals. When prices were soaring, this had seemed essentially like free money. Even if some thought their rising real-estate wealth was a bit too good to be true, they were confident that, at worst, house prices would only plateau rather than fall. It was inconceivable that home values would drop and keep dropping, past 10%, 20%, or even 30%. The average homeowner's equity was roughly $75,000 when house prices peaked in spring 2006.[6] By early 2009, this figure had fallen to almost $45,000. And house prices were still declining. If nationwide average home prices bottomed out 35% below their peak—the widespread consensus among economists at the time—then an average homeowner would have only $40,000 left in equity.[7] But these numbers mask a wide distribution in homeowners' economic fortunes. Millions of wealthier and generally older homeowners had built up hundreds of thousands of dollars in equity through the years. Millions more owned no equity at all—they owed more than their homes were worth. As of early 2009, an estimated 8 million households had more than $200,000 in homeowners' equity. Another 14 million were completely underwater on their homes.

To fully appreciate the implications of the negative wealth effect on consumer spending and the economy, consider the behavior of three types of households: renters; lower- and middle-income households who dipped into their home equity for cash during the boom; and wealthier homeowners who did not. The saving rate for those who rent has long been close to zero (see Figure 13.2).[8] Rising and falling house prices mean little to them directly, so ups and downs in the housing market do not directly affect their spending and saving. Renters account for about one-third of the population, but only 10% of consumer spending.

This is not the case for lower- and middle-income homeowners who cashed out. For them, movements of house prices are crucial; nothing affects their financial decisions more. As prices took off in the early 2000s, they borrowed so aggressively that their saving rate reached an astounding −10%—in other words they were collectively

Figure 13.2   Cashing out homeowners dis-save: personal saving rate.

spending 10% more than their income. Rising home equity was fueling this binge. As the fuel ran out in the housing crash, they were forced to become more prudent spenders, at the very least, matching their spending with their income. This was a tough adjustment for an economy whose growth had become dependent on these consumers' earlier profligate habits.[9] These homeowners account for one-third of the population and a roughly equal share of consumer spending.

Wealthier homeowners who did not cash out their homeowners' equity are much less influenced by shifting housing values than on the stock market. This group had a zero saving rate during the housing boom, but this had more to do with the period's record stock prices. They also had a zero saving rate when the tech-stock bubble was its most inflated at the turn of the millennium. As the stock market began to crumble under the weight of the financial shock in late 2007, panic began to set in. Their nest eggs weren't big enough for retirement after all—not even close. They significantly cut back on their spending, and their saving rate soared to a positive 10% in early 2009. Although this group accounts for the remaining one-third of the population, it accounts for a disproportionately large nearly 60% of consumer spending. How much they decide to spend or save has a big impact on everyone.

Economists have long wanted U.S. consumers to save more, but not to begin saving more all at once. The dramatic increase in saving in such a short-period of time was too much for the broader economy to adjust to. A big hole formed in the economy. Retailers, manufacturers, wholesalers, shippers, and a range of other firms had built their businesses on certain amount of consumer spending. With consumers not buying, they had no choice but to slash their payrolls and investment, further weighing on consumer spending. A vicious cycle developed, with households pulling back on their spending, which forced businesses to cut jobs, which scared consumers to rein in their spending even more. What seemed to be a garden-variety recession unraveled into the worst economic downturn since the Great Depression.

Falling $, Record Oil

It is important to note that the economy might have been able to avoid such a severe downturn if not for the dramatic fall in value of the U.S. dollar early in the financial crisis. The subprime shock and the weakening dollar were related: The housing bust had occurred in the United States at a time when financial and economic conditions elsewhere around the world were measurably better. Global investors who had been eager to put their cash into U.S. markets before the shock were now just as eager to get out. As a result, the dollar tumbled in value against other major world currencies. The euro moved up from $1.35 to almost $1.60; the Canadian loonie rose from 85¢ to $1-for-$1 parity (the first time since the early 1970s); and instead of needing 125 Japanese yen to make $1, traders needed only 100. Together, the dollar's value (measured against the currencies of America's major trading partners) fell more than 10% in just a few months in late 2007 and early 2008. This was on top of a 15% decline during the Iraq invasion and deflation scare earlier in the decade. The dollar was worth about one-fourth less than at its peak.

This wasn't an entirely bad thing. The weaker dollar had clear economic benefits. When combined with still-strong growth overseas, the U.S. trade deficit narrowed. The imbalance between U.S. imports and exports had, in fact, peaked with the housing market in late 2005; by early 2008, it had been cut by a fourth.[10] The nation's agriculture, aerospace, machine tools, and technology industries gained new market power overseas and shipped record amounts of goods to Asia, South America, and Europe. After years of weighing down the economy, trade had become a vital source of growth.

The dollar's sharp drop at the start of the financial turmoil did more damage than good, however. It helped ignite another surge in oil, food, and other commodity prices. Since most commodities trade globally in dollars, a fall in the dollar's exchange value means the dollar price of these commodities must rise to maintain a balance between global demand and supply. Given the increasing values of the euro, yuan, and rubble vis-à-vis the dollar, without a higher dollar price for oil, wheat, and copper, the Europeans, Chinese, and Russians will consume more, throwing demand and supply off-kilter. As a result, a barrel of oil that sold for $65 in the weeks leading up to subprime shock had doubled in price by spring 2008.[11] The dollar price of other commodities, ranging from gold and wheat to copper and coca beans, didn't rise quite as much, but most were still hitting record highs.

Commodities weren't being powered by a weaker dollar alone. The financial bedlam created by the subprime shock also contributed. Global investors were truly confused about where to put their money. Real estate was certainly out, bonds seemed like landmines, and stocks appeared shaky, at best. Each new explosion in the financial markets drove investors to seek safer investments—mainly U.S. Treasury securities and commodities. Some investors reasoned that commodity prices tended to move in the opposite direction of other asset prices and would thus help diversify their portfolios. Other short-term investors, so-called momentum players, simply bet that because commodities had been consistently rising in price, they would rise even further. The commodity markets were like any other asset market in an age of easy trading and excess liquidity; here too, prices could be subject to speculation and bubbles.

For the economy, surging oil and other commodity prices were too much to bear. The price of a gallon of regular unleaded gasoline, which had averaged $2.75 nationwide on Labor Day 2007, reached $4 by Memorial Day 2008 and kept rising. Each penny increase pushed up Americans' driving costs by more than $1 billion. Washington's $100 billion tax rebate—part of the fiscal stimulus passed a few months earlier to try to stave off recession—began arriving in Americans' mailboxes just as gasoline crossed $4, and was effectively gobbled up by the higher cost of fuel. Observers noted a bitter irony: The U.S. Treasury had sold bonds to raise the cash to pay the tax rebates, which were spent to buy oil from the same nations that had purchased the bonds. It's not much of an exaggeration to say that countries such as Saudi Arabia had essentially financed the purchase of their own oil.

Energy wasn't the only thing that was rising quickly in price. Food prices were also up sharply. This was driven partly by the higher cost of moving farm products to store shelves as diesel prices soared, but it also reflected the weak dollar and strong global demand for all U.S. agricultural products. Imported goods of all kinds cost more. Even prices for goods coming from China, which had fallen for years, were now on the rise. It was the reverse of the late 1990s, when the Asian financial crisis had sent investors scurrying to the safety of the United States. This lifted the dollar and slashed the price of imports to U.S. consumers. The subprime financial shock induced global investors to flee American markets, undermining the dollar and raising prices for anything not made in the United States. Consumers were rightly panicked, realizing that there was no way out and that recession was unavoidable.

Cracked Nest Egg

A temporary period of slack in U.S. growth was hardly the net impact of the subprime shock, however. Henceforth, American consumers would have to find ways to live within their means. Their unlimited freedom to spend, as well as their dominant role in the global economy, had reached an end.

The era of U.S. consumer dominance can be tracked through the rise of household spending as a share of the total economy. In 1980, consumer spending stood at 62% of GDP, about where it had been since the end of World War II (see Figure 13.3). By 1990, that share had risen to 66%; by the turn of the millennium, it was 70%.[12] This is the flip side of the falling personal saving rate. Consumer spending rose as a share of GDP throughout this period because households were willing and able to spend above their incomes.

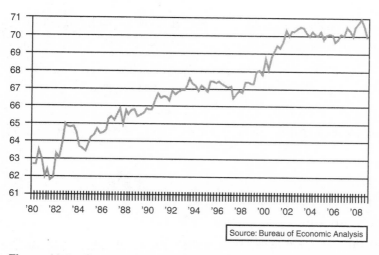

Source: Bureau of Economic Analysis

Figure 13.3   Consumers power the economy: consumer spending share of GDP.

Underpinning this quarter-century of aggressive consumer spending was the steady deceleration in inflation and the resulting decline in interest rates. The early 1980s was a period of stagflation, characterized by double-digit inflation, unemployment, and interest rates. The oil-price shocks of that time—the Iranian revolution had occurred in 1979—had ignited a spiral in which rising prices begat increased wages, which begat yet higher prices. Consumer price growth and the ten-year Treasury bond yield both peaked about this time at close to 15%. Almost 25 years later, inflation had been wrung out of the economy by years of stringent monetary policy, stable and low oil prices, and China's rapid ascent. Inflation and interest rates fell into the low single-digits.

These conditions helped ignite an increase in asset prices: Stocks, bonds, and real estate all increased smartly in value. Interest rates play a crucial role in determining any asset's value because they affect the present value (what it's worth today) of the asset's future income. For a share of stock, for instance, that income is the future profits of the company that issued it. For real estate, it's rents for landlords and the benefits of living in the home for homeowners. When interest rates fall, the present value of this future income rises and, thus, so does its price. Lower rates mean asset prices will rise relative to the future income they are expected to generate—the price-to-earnings ratio (PE) increases. As the ten-year Treasury yield fell from 15% in 1980 to less than 5% in 2005, asset prices rose strongly, and the economy's collective PE ratio—measured by the ratio of the value of all household assets to GDP—went from 3.5 to more than 5 (see Figure 13.4).[13]

The increase in asset prices and PE ratios is evident in the stock market. The S&P 500 PE rose from less than 10 in 1980 to closer to 20 by 2008. Stock prices rose about 10% annually during this period, despite some major setbacks such as the 1987 crash and the bursting of the Internet stock bubble. House prices also enjoyed a solid run, rising more than 5% annually. As with stocks, the housing PE rose from a low of 10 to near 20, even after including the post-2005 housing market crash.

The financial benefits of these outsized asset price gains have gone almost entirely to higher-income households. The data is a bit

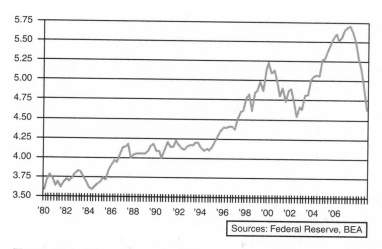

Sources: Federal Reserve, BEA

Figure 13.4   The economy's PE has peaked: ratio of value of household assets to GDP.

sketchy, but households that are among the highest 20% of income earners saw their share of overall wealth rise from 65% to 70% in the nearly 20 years between 1989 and 2007.[14] The median net worth of these households was above $750,000 in 2007, up from less than $425,000 20 years earlier. The share of wealth going to the lowest 80% of income earners fell commensurately, from 35% to only 30% (see Table 13.1). Their median net worth of $50,000 in 2007 had not changed very much during the 1990s and so far this decade.

TABLE 13.1   The Wealthy Get Wealthier, the Poor More Indebted

	Share of Wealth		**Share of Debt**	
	1989	**2007**	**1989**	**2007**
Percentile of Income				
0–20	2.6	3.8	1.1	2.71
20–40	7.2	4.8	5.2	5.62
40–60	10.8	7.6	12.0	14.39
60–80	14.4	13.4	26.9	26.59
80–100	64.9	70.4	54.8	50.69

Source: Federal Reserve Board

About the time the housing market peaked in 2005, many wealthy Americans thought they were financially set. If their nest eggs were not quite large enough to sustain a comfortable retirement and meet other obligations, they would be assuming that asset prices continued their recent pace. This seemed a reasonable assumption: Assets had risen on average in the high single-digits for as long as this generation could remember.

The subprime financial shock put an end to this kind of thinking. The super-wealthy had no concerns. They were indeed set, but the simply well-to-do realized now that their nest eggs were insufficient. The subprime shock dashed beliefs and hopes that asset prices would consistently appreciate faster than the income those assets were likely to generate. This was clear in the post-shock collapse in house prices. The tech-stock bust had similarly made it clear in the stock market. With interest rates unlikely to go lower for long, the most reasonable assumption was that asset prices would grow about as fast as the income those same assets generated. That is, PEs would not continue to rise. Across all asset classes—stocks, bonds, and real estate—the best forecast was that asset prices would increase at a mid-single-digit pace, about the same as the expected growth in GDP. Even higher-income households had some saving to do.

Debt Millstone

Lower-income households faced a far more difficult adjustment. For a quarter-century, these households benefited from steadily increasing access to credit. By borrowing more, they could supplement their constrained incomes to maintain their spending at a relatively high level. The subprime financial shock signified the end of such free-flowing credit. Lower-income households had little choice but to match their spending with their incomes; their living standards would inevitably suffer.

It was tough to get a loan in the early 1980s. For most households, that period's double-digit interest rates made borrowing prohibitively expensive. Credit cards were still new (they were not mass-marketed until the late 1960s) and still only a minority of households used them. Vehicle loans lasted, at most, three years and were exclusively intended for car buyers with pristine credit. Mortgages were almost entirely plain-vanilla 30-year, fixed-rate loans.

Over the subsequent 25 years, the availability of credit ballooned, powered by steadily declining interest rates, rapid financial innovation, and government policy. The lower rates were vital to increased borrowing because households could take on more debt and not have to make larger payments. Lenders also extended the length of loans to keep payments down; minimum payments on credit cards fell, most car loans evolved into 5-year loans, and 40-year mortgages became increasingly common. Credit scoring, direct marketing, and securitization came into their own, and lenders grew emboldened to provide credit to new groups of consumers. Risk-management techniques improved dramatically, enticing lenders to provide more credit to less creditworthy borrowers. Mounting regulatory pressure also emerged to provide more credit to minority and disadvantaged borrowers. Ongoing changes to the bankruptcy laws, making them steadily more lender-friendly, might have also empowered lenders to extend more credit.[15]

Although all income groups took on more debt, lower-income groups were particularly burdened. In the 20 years between 1989 and 2007, households in the bottom 20% of income earners increased their indebtedness by a whopping 8-fold.[16] Those in the next-lowest 20% bracket boosted their debt levels 6 times. Households in the top 20% of income earners also borrowed more, but their debt increased by less than 2 times.

Some of this reflects a judicious use of credit by households getting their first taste of it. Higher-income households have long had the luxury of financing purchases of big-ticket items—a car, a dishwasher, or even a big-screen TV—that they will consume over a long period. They use debt to more efficiently pay as they consume, laying out cash (via debt repayment) as they go. Of course, this plan includes interest charges, but for many, it is well worth it. Lower-income household should enjoy the same privileges, and that's how many have used their access to credit.

Over time, lower-income households have increasingly used debt to supplement their constrained and volatile incomes. It's not hard to understand why: After inflation, incomes for those on the bottom rungs of the income and wealth ladders barely grew after the early 1980s and didn't grow at all through the late 1990s to the mid-2000s. Although globalization—including immigration and trade—had been a boon to the overall economy, it was hard on those with lesser skills and education. In the competition with cheaper labor from all corners of the world, lower-skilled U.S. workers were losing. Borrowing more took the financial sting out, and although debt burdens were getting weightier, these households could manage it as long as lenders continued to extend them credit.

By the time the subprime financial shock hit, debt loads were at record highs. The average American household was paying almost one-fifth of its after-tax income on financial obligations—everything from the mortgage payment to the auto lease—to avoid going delinquent on those obligations. For subprime homeowners, who were forking over more than 35% of their after-tax income to meet their obligations, this was an overwhelming burden (see Figure 13.5). It all came undone in the housing crash and the subprime financial shock. Many poorer households were now completely cut off from credit. Although lending to this group would eventually be reborn, these households would no longer be able use credit as a ticket to a better lifestyle.

Figure 13.5   Weighty household debt loads: financial obligation ratio, % of disposable income.

14 ————————————

Back to the Future

As this is being written, the financial and economic crisis rages on. While progress has been made in quelling the panic in the financial system, it remains far from normal and the global economic downturn remains intense. The global economy will likely continue to shrink in 2009; the last time that occurred was during World War II. The subprime financial shock thus continues to reverberate.

Continued sharp declines in house prices are particularly unnerving. With no clear bottom in sight for the residential real-estate market, financial institutions remain unsure of their losses on mortgage loans and securities. Many have already written down their portfolios by large amounts, subtracting from their balance sheets both the estimated losses from defaults and declines in the market value of their remaining loans and securities. Some institutions believe that the market has grown overly pessimistic and that those securities will eventually rise again in value; thus, the write-downs might simply reflect a temporary hysteria from the subprime shock. Whether this ultimately proves correct depends on how far house prices eventually fall. Another wave of financial turmoil looms if house prices don't soon find a bottom.

Also disconcerting is the fact that many banks don't have the capital they need to withstand the credit losses that are still coming— even after the hundreds of billions of taxpayer dollars that have been put into them. The nation's biggest banks will get what they need from taxpayers to survive, but hundreds of community and regional banks won't and will be taken over by the FDIC as credit problems spread from residential mortgages to other types of lending. Never have there been so many auto repossessions, and credit card and student loan delinquencies are rising quickly. Banks also have loans out to troubled home builders and have sizable commercial loan portfolios that will soon face serious problems from weakening rents and falling commercial property prices.

Even with government help, the big banks will remain hobbled and unable or willing to extend the credit that businesses and households need to hire, invest, and spend. Until these institutions are able to work off the mountain of very troubled loans and securities on their balance sheet, they won't have the wherewithal or inclination to provide the credit the economy needs to function well. The hope is that the banks can make significant progress in ridding themselves of these toxic assets in coming months, but it's not difficult to imagine this taking years.

Parts of the global financial system that have held up reasonably well also could ultimately give way under future waves of the subprime shock. One likely candidate is the mammoth market for credit default swaps. Although CDS on mortgage-related securities are relatively well understood, a much larger portion of the market involves default swaps on corporate bonds. These have been unaffected thus far because corporate bonds have experienced relatively few credit problems. However, as corporate bond defaults rise, which they will, the default-swaps market will surely be tested. Work is being done to get CDS trading on exchanges so they can be monitored (CDS trading has been historically done over-the-counter and, thus, not on well-organized and regulated exchanges), forestalling a problem, but these efforts might not be enough.

Nervousness about the soundness of the banking system elsewhere in the world, particularly in Europe, is also well-founded. Many Western European banks, which are among the largest in the world, made big loans to Eastern European businesses, households, and banks. Many of these loans were in euros, which seemed like a deal when things were going well and euro interest rates were much lower than rates on credit denominated in Polish zlotys or Hungarian forints. As the financial crisis has gone global and there has been a flight-to-quality, Eastern European currencies have fallen sharply in value. Polish homeowners who have euro-denominated mortgages have seen their monthly payments in zlotys soar. A U.S.-style foreclosure problem could soon roil Eastern Europe. German, Austrian, and French banks that are struggling to digest their bad U.S. investments could choke on their Eastern European loans. The vortex engulfing the global financial system will grow wider and deeper.

Other potential new shocks could emerge as well, but it remains unclear which pose the greatest threats and to which institutions. Financial markets remain disturbingly opaque, making it hard for financial players to identify or prepare for additional threats. If financial institutions are worried and uncertain, they will remain cautious and will restrict credit and raise its cost for nearly everyone, good borrowers as well as bad. Until credit flows more freely and cheaply, the economy will not get its groove back.

Policymaking in the Crisis

The bad news is that the global financial and economic crisis is sure to be the most severe since the Great Depression. The good news is that what we are experiencing will be nothing like those times. That dark period lasted more than a decade, and U.S. unemployment topped out at 25%. Unemployment in this downturn could well reach into the double digits and the economy might not return to full employment—generally thought to be 5%—in President Obama's first term, but this is far from the endless breadlines and mass exodus of homeless families we suffered during the 1930s.

Much was learned during that trying time, and many financial and economic safeguards were put in place to prevent such an occurrence from ever happening again. The Federal Reserve now knows that it must take extraordinary steps to forestall a deflationary cycle—in which falling prices and wages force businesses and households to pull back, causing prices and wages to fall even more—even printing trillions in dollars to buy those things no one else can or is willing to. Policymakers also know that putting up trade barriers and engaging in financial protectionism such as restricting cross-border investments result in the global tit-for-tat that undermines economies even more.

Many of the safeguards put in place during the Great Depression are working admirably now. The FDIC was born out of the ashes of the thousands of Depression-era bank failures, and the FDIC has forestalled bank runs and major failures during this crisis. Unemployed workers are getting unemployment insurance benefits, food stamps, and soon even help with COBRA payments to pay for their health insurance so that they don't panic (along with everyone they know) because of their lost job. The unemployment insurance system was erected in response to the Great Depression.

The most fundamental lesson of the Great Depression for today's crisis is that government must be extraordinarily aggressive. In normal times, government must be strong but little seen; in times of crisis, it must be overwhelming and everywhere. Policymakers working fast and taking big steps will make mistakes, even mistakes that can make matters worse. But with consumers, businesses, bankers, and investors panicked and pulling back, only government has the resources and the will to fill the resulting void.

Policymakers in the current crisis were slow to heed this lesson but have grown increasingly bold. Their actions now have become increasingly unconventional and even unprecedented. Yet their best efforts have not been able to end the turmoil—far from it. A prudent approach thus dictates that policymakers plan as if their current efforts will be insufficient to the task ahead and prepare for what to do next.

For the Federal Reserve, this could well mean that it will have to effectively become the nation's financial system—the principal and, in some cases, only source of credit—at least for awhile. This requires printing trillions of dollars and using those dollars to purchase a wide array of assets, make loans to other financial institutions, and guarantee assets owned by other financial institutions. The Fed has aggressively stepped up its buying to include commercial paper issued by blue-chip companies and Fannie and Freddie's debt and the mortgage securities they insure. They are even buying longer-term Treasury bonds—monetizing the nation's debt, as they say. Buying corporate bonds and equity would be a stretch but could be necessary if businesses have difficulty funding themselves. The Bank of Japan has gone down this path. Although the Fed is prohibited from directly buying municipal securities, it would likely find a creative way to do so if municipalities were at risk of defaulting on their debts.

The Fed is also lending cheap money to hedge funds and other investors for purchases of financial securities backed by auto loans, credit cards, student loans, small business loans, and even residential and commercial mortgage loans. This Term Asset-Backed Securities Lending Facility (TALF) has the potential to restart frozen securities markets so that credit can resume flowing to consumers and businesses. To make it more effective, TALF might have to be expanded to include many other existing and lower-rated securities. Investors might also need assurances that if they participate in TALF and thus receive taxpayer-subsidized funds, they will not receive the kind of withering scrutiny and restrictions that other financial institutions receiving taxpayer help have received.

Teetering financial institutions could need the Fed to guarantee that the losses on their toxic assets don't increase to the choking point. The Fed did this for Citigroup, Bank of America, and AIG, helping to forestall their collapse. This would be particularly important if other efforts to get the bad assets off institutions' balance sheets, such as TALF, fall flat.

The Obama administration and Congress also need a Plan B and perhaps Plan C. The financial system will certainly require more taxpayer dollars to put it on a sound footing. The first dose of help via

TARP cost taxpayers $700 billion. The second dose will cost at least that. The additional funds will be needed to fund the Treasury's private-public bank, which, like the TALF, will provide cheap loans to hedge funds and other investor groups to buy, in this case, troubled loans that financial institutions own. However, even more than TALF, the private-public bank seems at risk of failing. Investor groups might have an appetite to buy securities that institutions have marked down to depressed market values due to mark-to-market accounting rules, but that appetite might not be there for loans whose values are determined by models and, thus, haven't been marked down nearly as much. Unless the private-public bank is up and running by summer 2009, the Treasury could have no choice but to directly buy the bad loans. The political will has been lacking for this, given the worry that the Treasury will overpay for the loans, but it will cost taxpayers much more if the bad loans continue to fester and impair the ability of financial institutions to resume lending.

Another round of fiscal stimulus seems like a real possibility. The $100 billion in tax rebates mailed in summer 2008 proved less potent than hoped because much of the money was used to pay for record-high gasoline prices. The $800 billion stimulus that began working its way into the economy in spring 2009 might also not provide the economic pop needed. Although it's big, it's not big enough: The money will be spread out over more than two years, and the economy's problems have only gotten worse since its passage. Stimulus 3, if needed, should be mostly temporary tax cuts. A payroll tax holiday for both employees and employers—say, during the first half of 2010—would be especially effective. This would be costly, about $450 billion, but it would be a significant cash infusion for strapped households and small businesses that will be out of cash by then. Temporary tax cuts don't provide the same boost to jobs as, say, infrastructure spending, but the money can get into the economy much more quickly.

Given the failure of each successive policy attempt to promote work-outs between mortgage lenders and troubled homeowners from

Hope Now and Project Lifeline to Hope for Homeowners, the current attempt in President Obama's housing and foreclosure mitigation policies could also fall short. These efforts are being overwhelmed by the magnitude of the problem and the shifting forces behind it. When Hope Now was established in late 2007, the main driver of foreclosures seemed to be the prospect of huge interest-rate resets on subprime ARM loans. Yet this possibility faded as the Fed's aggressive rate cuts drove down current interest rates: By the time their reset clocks ran out in early 2008, many subprime homeowners ended up facing no big jump in payments at all. Foreclosures have continued to increase, but now the biggest problems are negative homeowners' equity and rising unemployment. Hope Now was not designed to tackle these issues, and Hope for Homeowners, which was designed for this, has turned out to be too complicated and too costly to get much participation by mortgage lenders. The administration has high hopes that its housing policy will forestall millions of foreclosures by modifying loans so that homeowners have much lower monthly payments. However, the policy does not reduce the negative equity homeowners are laboring under.

The next policy effort to forestall foreclosures should include loan modifications that reduce the mortgage principal underwater homeowners owe. Only when homeowners feel like they have a stake in their home will they work hard to make their mortgage payments. The criteria for being able to participate in such a modification should be strict, applying only to owner-occupying homeowners who were put into inherently unaffordable loans when they were originated. The monthly payments on these loans were too high from the start. These were loans that shouldn't have been made, and regulators should have stopped them. Because they didn't, taxpayers now arguably bear some responsibility to help. Even if taxpayers feel no such responsibility, it doesn't make much economic sense for them to let these loans go through foreclosure. The foreclosures drive down house prices, making all homeowners less wealthy. Foreclosures also add to the financial system's burden for exacerbating the credit crunch, resulting in more lost jobs and tax revenues. If troubled homeowners do not receive financial help, the costs to taxpayers will almost certainly be greater than the cost of bailing them out.

Preventing the Next Crisis

Policymakers understandably have had little room to consider how to ensure that something like this never happens again. The crisis hit its apex when the Bush presidency was winding down and the Obama presidency was getting off the ground. Both were very short-staffed at a time when an army of policymakers would have had an impossible time keeping up with events. But after the panic subsides and the crisis is quelled—and it will—policymakers must quickly refocus their attention to preventing the next crisis.

What follows is a "top ten" list of what I believe needs to be done, starting with the most pressing items and ending with the most complex. The list has changed a bit since the first edition of the book was released in fall 2008 because policymakers have already implemented a few of the suggestions. Most notable is the Federal Reserve's adoption of clear guidelines for appropriate mortgage lending: Under the Fed's new rules, lenders must consider the borrower's ability to repay and also verify the borrower's income and assets. Prepayment penalties are barred if a homeowner refinances within 60 days after an adjustable loan reset, and borrowers must establish escrow accounts for taxes and insurance. These common-sense lending rules apply to all mortgage lenders, given the Fed's broad authority.[1]

Policy Step #1: Modify Mark-to-Market Accounting

Past financial crises have often resulted from lax accounting rules. Ironically, the subprime financial shock is partly the result of too-rigid rules. Mark-to-market accounting standards, implemented widely in recent years, need to be adjusted. The rules put pressure on financial institutions to quickly adjust the book value of their assets to reflect market prices. The practice stems from the reasonable argument that it is better to deal with problems quickly and move on, even if the adjustment is painful. But what happens when institutions own assets whose prices can't be found, or for which the market price reflects temporary panic? In the midst of the subprime shock, trading in the mortgage securities market literally froze. With no buyers, even Aaa-rated prices for these securities went into free-fall.

Of course, such a plunge could—and did—reflect weakening housing and mortgage markets, but depressed prices could also simply reflect fear and distressed selling. If so, these prices would eventually rebound, but not until after institutions marked down their assets. In the subprime shock, markdowns were so large and cut so deeply into some institutions' capital that it threatened their survival.

To keep this from happening in the future, mark-to-market accounting rules could be tweaked most importantly for securities that financial institutions don't ever plan on selling. These are known as held-to-maturity securities, and financial institutions—including all of the Federal Home Loan Banks and many depository institutions—hold hundreds of billions of them. If these institutions will hold on to these securities until they mature and their auditors think they will never be forced to sell them, why should they mark these securities to current market values? It is reasonable for institutions to value these securities based on expectations of any losses they might eventually suffer, but it isn't reasonable to value these securities using prices they would get if they sold them today. Without some quick relief on this mark-to-market accounting rule, the FHLB system could soon be insolvent, putting an added unnecessary burden on taxpayers.

Policy Step #2: Reinstate the Uptick Rule

The downdraft in stock prices, particularly for financial institutions, has been dizzying. Much lower stock prices for these companies are surely justified, given the near-collapse of the financial system and the subsequent infusion of taxpayer capital, but there is a justifiable (albeit difficult-to-prove) concern that stock prices have been manipulated lower by short-sellers. Short-sellers borrow stock and sell it with the intent of buying back the stock in the future at a lower price. With financial stocks so vulnerable in this crisis, short-sellers often at least implicitly teamed up, borrowing and selling the stock and driving prices ever lower. Rumors—some perhaps true, but many that weren't—often swirled as financial stocks were barraged by short-selling.

The uptick rule is an attempt to throw a bit of sand into a short-selling frenzy. With this rule, a short seller would be able to sell the stock only at a price above the price at which the immediately preceding sale was effected, or at the last sale price, if it is higher than the last different price. This rule had been in place since the Great Depression, when Joseph Kennedy, the first SEC commissioner instituted it; it was dropped in summer 2007, just about the time financial stock prices began heading south. The research done on the rules' effect is inconclusive, but the logic for it seems compelling. The only downside to reinstating the uptick rule is a worry that it could reduce the number of transactions and, thus, liquidity, making it more difficult to come up with an accurate price for the stock. This concern seems stretched.

Policy Step #3: Expand Data Collection

A lack of timely and accurate information hobbled policymakers' ability to respond to the subprime financial shock. Data on mortgage delinquencies and defaults comes from a variety of mostly private sources, making it nearly impossible for regulators or others to see the crisis as it grew. No government agency tracks the number of mortgage foreclosures, for example, and the various private sources of such information are limited in various ways.

A ready mechanism for expanding the government's data collection already exists under the data-collection efforts required by the

Home Mortgage Disclosure Act (HMDA). HMDA requires most mortgage originators to report some information on all loan applications and approvals. This includes data on the lender, location, income, and ethnicity of the borrower; whether the loan is a first or second lien; whether it is a purchase loan or refinancing; and the loan's amount and interest rate.

Reporting requirements should be expanded to include mortgage servicers, who, in most cases, are also the lenders already reporting under HMDA. Servicers can provide information on delinquencies and defaults, as well as information on whether various types of loans and borrowers are having credit problems. Reporting under HMDA should be more frequent—it currently occurs annually—and data releases should be accelerated. The HMDA data for 2006 wasn't fully released until fall 2007. More frequent updates and more rapid reporting would help policymakers and lenders spot credit quality problems earlier and allow them to respond better to developing problems.

Policy Step #4: Reform the Fractured Foreclosure Process

The current mortgage foreclosure system is a complex mélange of laws and rules that varies substantially from state to state. The foreclosure process generally entails three steps: first a loan default, no more than six months after the first missed loan payment; then a foreclosure auction; and finally a sale of the property by the bank. The average time between the first and last steps ranges from about 7 months in Virginia to 20 months in New York City.

The federal government streamlined the bankruptcy code in 2005 to make it more uniform across states, and it should do the same for foreclosures. A federal foreclosure system would substantially reduce the cost of the foreclosure process, be more equitable to borrowers and lenders, and allow for the more accurate collection of data and information.

A federal foreclosure process should standardize the time between a mortgage loan default and an auction. One year would be reasonable because that is approximately the median current length of time among states. A year would be sufficient to give borrowers who have hit hard times—perhaps because of unemployment or illness—a meaningful opportunity to work with their lenders and turn things around. It also allows lenders to foreclose within a reasonable time if borrowers are unable or unwilling to meet their obligations.

A federal process should also favor the nonjudicial form of foreclosure. This is a change in my thinking, given the current mess in states with judicial foreclosures. The Florida courts, for example, have been woefully inadequate in handling the state's tsunami of foreclosures. At first the courts let a massive backlog of cases develop, and then they worked through the backlog so quickly that distraught homeowners failed to get any hearing at all. Deficiency judgments, which hold borrowers liable for the difference between the price a home fetches in a foreclosure sale and the amount of outstanding debt,[2] should be severely restricted, as should the right of redemption, which gives the original homeowner a chance to repurchase a foreclosed home for up to a year after it is auctioned. This right can add delay and uncertainty to the process and reduce the value of the foreclosed home. A one-year period between default and foreclosure offers homeowners sufficient time to negotiate with lenders or to find the cash to keep their homes, if they are able.

Policy Step #5: Invest in Financial Literacy

Americans aren't as smart about money as we should be. Financial illiteracy was a fundamental cause of the subprime financial shock. Yes, many people knowingly stretched to buy an expensive home with a subprime ARM loan, figuring they could either sell quickly at a profit or refinance before the payment reset hit. But many more barely understood what they were getting into. According to Federal Reserve surveys done before the subprime shock, almost half of lower-income home buyers (mostly subprime) couldn't describe basic features of their mortgage, such as how their interest rate was determined or whether it was capped. Many trusted their brokers to get them a mortgage they could afford, believing it was the broker's responsibility to look after their financial interests.

The nation's general financial illiteracy contributes to a wide range of poor decisions on borrowing, saving, and investing. This might have been less dangerous 10 or 25 years ago, when there were fewer financial products to choose from and it was harder to make a financially catastrophic mistake. But ignorance of the basics is certainly perilous today. Some of the mortgage options presented to home buyers during the housing boom were mind-numbingly complex and confusing; even an economist adept at manipulating spreadsheets would have had trouble calculating future payments on an interest-only or "option" ARM loan.

It is both bizarre and tragic that American high schools today are more likely to offer students cooking classes than personal finance courses. Such courses should be required—period. A meaningful investment in the financial acumen of young people would pay enormous dividends by reducing the likelihood that future households will take out bad mortgages or not save adequately for retirement.

Policy Step #6: Raise Financial Transparency and Accountability

Both transparency and accountability are vital to a well-functioning financial system. Both were thought to be present until the subprime financial shock occurred.

Transparency means timely, meaningful, reliable, and complete information is available regarding financial products, institutions, and markets. In transparent markets, financial players borrow, lend, and buy and sell aggressively. In opaque markets, players are uncertain and tend to panic in times of trouble, just as they did during the subprime shock.

Financial products were anything but transparent. Complex mortgage loans were offered to home buyers, and nearly incomprehensible mortgage securities were sold to investors. Too many financial institutions hid in the shadows and outside the regulatory light. Large global banks took on risks that they kept off their books until forced to take responsibility. No one really knows what most hedge funds are up to. At times it was all but impossible to reasonably price most mortgage securities. Even the integrity of the LIBOR interest rate, a daily financial benchmark used to calculate financial costs all over the world, has been called into question.

Accountability means someone is ultimately responsible if mistakes are made. No one bore responsibility for the performance of mortgage loans made during the housing boom; as a result, many bad loans were made. The mortgage securities market remains in disrepair partially because it is unclear how to apportion responsibility for the performance of the underlying loans. Someone must have enough financial skin in the game to want to be sure that good loans are originated and securitized.

Ensuring transparency and accountability requires confident regulatory oversight, which, in turn, must be empowered by Congress and the executive branch. Now that the Federal Reserve has explicitly backstopped the broker-dealer industry via its new credit facilities and its resolution of the Bear Stearns collapse, the *quid pro quo* should be a more watchful and questioning eye on that industry's capital and activities. This will also provide a better window into the hedge fund industry. In addition, the SEC must become more aggressive about policing financial statements, audit opinions, credit ratings, and analyst reports.

A balance must be struck between the benefits of transparency and accountability and the costs of greater disclosure by financial players. The subprime shock showed how unbalanced things have become. Regulators must set it right.

Policy Step #7: Fix Securitization, Don't Scrap It

The process of securitization clearly broke down during the housing boom and bubble. The originate-to-distribute model, in which lenders made a loan they quickly sold to investment bankers, who packaged it into a rated security and offloaded it to global investors, has collapsed. No one involved in the process had enough at stake if the loan went bad, so many bad loans were made. This applied more or less to all types of securitization, from residential and commercial mortgages to auto and student loans.

This doesn't mean that securitization should be abandoned. The fundamental logic underlying the process is sound; it parses up the risks in lending and matches these risks with the risk tolerance of investors. More investors can thus participate, allowing more credit to flow to consumers and businesses throughout the global economy. Securitization should be fixed, and it can be.

The Fed's TALF program is a crack at resurrecting the process of securitization. Investors get cheap loans from the Fed to buy various kinds of securities, and their downside—the amount they can lose if the securitization goes bad—is capped. The lenders participating in the program—the auto lenders and credit card companies, for example—hold on to the riskier parts of the securitization. If they make too many bad loans, they will suffer. That's a good reason to make good loans. Whether securitization lives on after the TALF ends is debatable unless other more fundamental changes in the process occur.

One idea with some traction is the covered bond. It is a securitization, but the loans backing the security remain on the lender's balance sheet. If loans go bad, the lender is responsible for replacing them with well-performing loans. If a lot of loans backing the security went delinquent and investors in the security stopped getting all their money, they would have the ability to go after the lender's other assets. Lenders would have a very strong incentive to make sure that the loans are properly underwritten. For the covered bond idea to really get going, it might need both regulatory and taxpayer help.

It would be a mistake to scrap securitization altogether and go back to the simple originate-to-hold model that banks followed in times past. Credit would be much less ample and more costly, even for very creditworthy borrowers. Moreover, no guarantee ensures that this will forestall future financial missteps. Remember that the savings and loan crisis of the early 1990s was caused by the most plain-vanilla of lending institutions.

Policy Step #8: Overhaul Financial Regulation

The regulatory framework overseeing the nation's financial system needs a top-to-bottom overhaul. The current byzantine regulatory structure contributed to the subprime financial shock, allowing the most aggressive lenders to avoid regulatory scrutiny. Regulators were also hamstrung in efforts to impose greater discipline on the industry, given the difficulties coordinating among themselves.

Regulatory oversight tends to be pro-cyclical. That is, when credit quality is good and lenders are aggressive, regulators have difficulty imposing discipline; when quality is poor and lenders are tightening, the disciplinary screws are tightened. This tends to exacerbate shifts in lending standards and credit availability. Partly it stems from regulators' inability to respond quickly, but it also reflects the influence of politics on regulation. Lenders find it much easier to keep regulators at bay when credit conditions appear robust, although this is generally when increased regulatory oversight would be most beneficial.

The current fractured regulatory structure overseeing the financial system should be reworked into three principal agencies. The basic concept of regulation would shift: Instead of agencies monitoring specific types of financial institutions, regulators would specialize in various types of risks and activities. The Federal Reserve would look out for the stability of the entire financial system; its mandate would include any risk that threatened the system, whether it involved banks or hedge funds. The Fed is uniquely suited for this task, given its central position in the global financial system, its significant financial and intellectual resources, and its history of political independence. A second regulatory agency would oversee any financial institution that received an explicit government guarantee. Lenders couldn't choose their regulator, as they do now, and would have consistent standards to work with. The biggest financial institutions, those that are "too big to fail," would receive more stringent scrutiny; if they will get taxpayer help when things don't go well, the *quid pro quo* is more oversight in the good times. The third regulatory agency would aim to protect consumers by monitoring how all financial institutions market their products. Certain government agencies watch over food, drugs, and the safety of consumer products; financial services need a similar type of watchdog.

Financial institutions and their products no longer fit in narrowly defined boxes. The risks they take cut across markets and extend around the globe. The regulatory structure needs to adapt, or it will be as irrelevant in the next financial crisis as it was in the subprime financial shock.

Policy Step #9: Pay Attention to Asset Bubbles

Conventional wisdom has long held that the Federal Reserve should not worry about asset bubbles and should set monetary policy without regard to the price of investments such as stocks or real estate. Those who hold this view doubt that it's possible to identify investment bubbles anyway. Thus, they believe the Fed should stick to worrying about inflation and the real economy; if a bubble does burst, the central bank's role is to clean up afterward and limit the economic damage.

Recently, this prescription has not worked particularly well. In the wake of both the late-1990s tech-stock bubble and this decade's housing bubble, the Fed was forced to slash interest rates, with doubtful consequences for both financial markets and the real economy. The Fed's ultra-low rates after the stock bubble burst helped inflate the subsequent housing bubble, and the low rates in the wake of the housing collapse could contribute to a developing bubble in energy and other commodity markets. Ignoring bubbles could abet their creation.

Cleaning up the economic mess from bursting bubbles has also proved difficult for the Fed. The financial system is the key conduit between monetary policy and the economy, and it is invariably a casualty of plunging markets. Lower rates can't help a struggling economy if they don't quickly translate into more and cheaper credit for businesses and households.

In fact, it might be possible to accurately identify bubbles. Not only are these characterized by rapidly rising prices, but they also involve increased leverage, surging trading volumes, and the arrival of less sophisticated buyers to a market in which they have little experience. Bubbles are always born out of something fundamental—for example, the Internet's debut for stocks, low interest rates for housing, or Chinese demand for oil—making it difficult to conclude in real time that they are actual bubbles. Yet policymakers are often asked to make judgments of equal, if not greater, difficulty. Will record oil prices undermine inflation expectations and result in higher underlying core inflation? Is a zero funds rate target and the purchase of Treasury bonds an appropriate response to the subprime shock? Was putting the Fed's balance sheet on the line to resolve the Bear Stearns collapse and save Citigroup and AIG beyond the Fed's mandate? Asking whether there is a bubble in the housing market is not a more difficult question than these.

Yet policymakers might argue credibly that higher interest rates are too blunt an instrument to wield against bubbles. And so we are back to a regulatory response. Bubbles need lots of leverage, and regulators have many ways to affect the amount of leverage being used. A Federal Reserve that determines the nation's monetary policy and is also its chief financial regulator could reduce the odds of future financial crises through deft use of its regulatory powers. However, this requires the central bank to also demonstrate the courage of its convictions.

Policy Step #10: Adopt a Bold Long-Term Budget for the Federal Government

Addressing the nation's long-term fiscal problems is the most important and most intractable policy step on the top-ten list. Federal government debt is piling up quickly. The deficit will be close to $2 trillion in 2009 and about the same in 2010. This massive borrowing is necessary to quell the financial and economic crisis, but it will leave the government with a crushing debt load. Total federal government debt will increase from about 40% of the gross domestic product (GDP) before the crisis to as much as 70% in its wake. And unless big changes are soon made to the tax code and in government spending, the nation's debt-to-GDP ratio will continue to rise rapidly as the aging baby boomers put increasing demands on Social Security, Medicare, and Medicaid. The math is unambiguous and daunting. Without big policy changes, global investors will demand increasingly higher interest rates to buy our debt and, at some point, will stop buying it altogether. The resulting financial and economic crisis will be worse than the current one.

Reducing our long-term budget deficits will require healthcare reform that successfully reduces the growth in healthcare costs, cuts in Social Security and medical benefits, and higher taxes. Although President Obama's first budget is ambitious in many respects, it doesn't go nearly far enough. The plan does raise taxes on higher-income households, but the additional revenues go to lower-income households and aren't used to reduce future deficits. The plan does hold out the possibility of substantive healthcare reform, but instead of reining in medical benefits, it expands them. The plan is silent on Social Security.

Of course, it is too early to harshly judge the new President's ability to address our long-term budget problems. He could well have the political fortitude and skill necessary to tackle them. However, he doesn't have much time to convince global investors that he has what it takes. They have given us a pass on all the borrowing we will be doing in the next couple years. They understand this is necessary to end the crisis and reestablish economic growth—besides, a Treasury bond remains the world's safest investment, at least for now. But investors fully expect that once the economy finds its footing, the borrowing will quickly become more judicious. The President needs to come up with more than an ambitious budget—he needs a bold one.

Personal Challenge

Policymakers won't enact all the reforms on my top-ten list soon. Nevertheless, some substantive policy changes are coming. The financial and economic damage emanating from the subprime financial shock is a powerful catalyst for change. The mortgage-lending industry will face new rules, and Wall Street will live with new standards and oversight. Work will also begin in earnest on making the regulatory framework more effective in a globalized financial system.

Financial institutions and markets have also begun the task of repairing themselves. Wall Street is reengineering the subprime loan (soon to have a new name) and is refashioning the process of securitization. Banks are feverishly writing off bad loans and repairing their tattered balance sheets. Funds are raising billions from institutions and wealthy individuals to prepare to buy up distressed properties and securities.

Policymakers' efforts, along with investors' renewed enthusiasm, will eventually prevail; financial markets will settle and the worst economic downturn since the Great Depression will end. Although the next financial crisis is not in sight, there is no question that another one will arrive eventually. If the subprime financial shock has one lesson to teach, it is that that, no matter how sophisticated financial institutions, markets, and products become, those animal spirits—aka hubris—cannot be kept down long. Future generations will again come to believe that this time things are different, but they will ultimately overstep.

The most daunting challenge is thus a personal challenge. We must each prepare for the next financial crisis by carefully considering the condition of our own balance sheets. No longer can we count on rapid gains in stock and house prices. Lenders will be less forthcoming with credit, particularly to those who already have taken on their share. Social Security and Medicare benefits will almost certainly be cut for most of us. We will all have to save more and invest more carefully. Instead of piling into the next new thing, we should be diversifying away from whatever is appreciating quickly. These are simple principles that have long been the basis for sound personal finance and high finance—principles that many of us seemed to forget in the frenzy that produced the subprime financial shock.

Endnotes

Chapter 2

1. This is based on data from the Federal Reserve Board's Flow of Funds.

2. The FHA is part of the Department of Housing and Urban Development.

3. FICO is named after the firm that invented it, Fair Isaac, who recently changed its name to FICO given the widespread recognition of the name of its credit score.

4. This is based on data collected from the 2006 Home Mortgage Disclosure Act.

5. This is based on credit scores calculated by credit bureau Equifax and is analogous to the more ubiquitous FICO score.

6. This is based on data from the Mortgage Bankers' Association.

7. Loans held in bank portfolios are likely to be less than prime, given the thin spread between rates on prime loans and their cost of funds. They are also likely to be of higher quality than securitized loans, given the risk of holding them on their balance sheet.

Chapter 3

1. Between the late 1800s and 1940, the homeownership rate remained essentially unchanged, at just less than half of households.

2. Like the FHA, Fannie Mae, and Freddie Mac, the VA does not originate mortgage loans but provides insurance on loans to veterans originated by private mortgage lenders.

3. The Bureau of Labor Statistics' Consumer Expenditure Survey is the basis of this statement.

4. The Federal Reserve Board's Flow of Funds is the source of this data.

5. Although sizable, this is down from $105,000 when house prices were at their peak.

6. The Treasury loses approximately $85 billion a year from the mortgage interest deduction, $20 billion from the deduction for property taxes, and $30 billion from the favorable treatment of capital gains.

7. This is based on a 6.5% fixed mortgage rate.

8. The FHLB was established in 1932, the FHA in 1934, and Fannie Mae in 1938. Freddie Mac was established in 1968, when Fannie Mae was converted into a private corporation to provide competition to Fannie and further facilitate the availability of cheap mortgage credit.

9. This is well documented in "Do Homeowners Know Their House Value and Mortgage Terms?" by Brian Bucks and Karen Pence, Federal Reserve Board of Governors (January 2006). www.federalreserve.gov/pubs/feds/2006/200603/200603pap.pdf.

10. This is based on data from the Bureau of Census. www.census.gov/const/C25Ann/sftotalmedavgsqft.pdf.

11. The sources and uses of cash from mortgage equity withdrawal are presented in this Federal Reserve study, at www.federalreserve.gov/pubs/feds/2007/200720/index.html.

12. This is based on data collected as part of the Home Mortgage Disclosure Act.

Chapter 4

1. This assumes a 20% down payment and property tax payments equal to 1.5% of the home's value.

2. In 1982, the Federal Home Loan Bank gave savings and loans explicit authority to originate adjustable-rate mortgages.

3. As of 1980, the S&L industry held approximately half of all residential mortgage debt.

4. See "Understanding Household Debt Obligations," speech by Alan Greenspan to the Credit Union National Association 2004 Governmental Affairs Conference, 23 February 2004. www.federalreserve.gov/boarddocs/speeches/2004/20040223/default.htm. As it turns out, the basis for Greenspan's argument that ARMs are a bargain for homeowners (at least, the one he provided in the speech) is incorrect. He estimated that fixed-rate loans had an option-adjusted spread that was as much as 1.2 percentage points greater than that of an ARM loan. In other words, he said, even after accounting for the benefit to borrowers from being able to refinance a fixed-rate loan, a fixed-rate loan still costs borrowers substantially more than an ARM. However, there was no meaningful difference between the OAS spread on a fixed-rate loan and an ARM loan. Greenspan's analysis was improperly based on the OAS between 30-year fixed-rate mortgage-backed securities and Treasuries. This was significantly biased, however, by the dramatic decline in Treasury yields during the period when the federal government was running a surplus and the supply of Treasury bonds was dwindling.

5. Cost of Fund Index ARMs (or COFI ARMs) were prevalent in the western United States and are based on an average of the cost of various types of deposits at savings and loan institutions.

6. In this case, the so-called user cost housing is negative. That is, buyers believe that they will make a profit, given that the return on owning the home is greater than their cost of financing it. Moreover, the greater buyers' conviction in future house prices gains, the greater their incentive becomes to take on as large as mortgage as possible.

7. The real funds rate, which equals the difference between the funds rate and expected inflation, and is a better gauge of just how aggressive the Fed is conducting monetary policy, declined from 4% in late 2000 to −1.5% by early 2003. At only a handful of times since World War II has the real funds rate been as high as 4% and as low as −1.5%.

8. Stock investors borrow from their brokers to finance the purchase of more stocks. Investors currently can borrow up to half the value of their stock holdings in margin debt.

9. See "Monetary Policy and the Economic Outlook," testimony before the Joint Economic Committee, U.S. Congress, 17 June 1999. www.federalreserve.gov/boarddocs/testimony/1999/19990617.htm.

10. See "Home Mortgage Market," speech before the annual convention of the Independent Community Bankers of America, 4 March 2003. www.federalreserve.gov/boarddocs/speeches/2003/20030304/default.htm.

11. See "Issues for Monetary Policy," speech before the Economic Club of New York, 19 December 2002. www.federalreserve.gov/boarddocs/speeches/2002/20021219/default.htm.

12. This is effectively as low as the federal funds rate can go without creating substantial problems for various parts of the financial system.

13. It is also worthwhile to point out that the deceleration in inflation experienced during the period was also likely due to the monetary easing itself. See Andrew Bauer, Nicholas Haltom, and William Peterman, "Examining Contributions to Core Consumer Inflation Measures," working paper, Atlanta Federal Reserve Board, April 2004. www.frbatlanta.org/invoke.cfm?objectid=27CDD5D8-E72D-7303-E60DDF476993E68E&method=display.

14. According to the Federal Reserve's Flow of Funds, the value of housing owned by households rose from $10.4 trillion at the start of 2000 to $18.7 trillion by year-end 2005.

15. The most recent paper is "Sources and Uses of Equity Extracted From Homes," by Greenspan and Kennedy, Finance and Economic Discussion Series, Federal Reserve Board of Governors, March 2007. www.federalreserve.gov/pubs/feds/2007/200720/index.html.

16. The transaction costs include everything from points on the mortgage to the cost of title insurance.

17. The home equity line of credit has generally been more popular. It has an adjustable rate that moves with the prime rate and is thus more attractive when short-term rates are lower. The prime interest rate was historically the rate charged a bank's best business customers. In more recent years, it has became a commonly used rate for consumer loans, such as the home equity line of credit; banks set it to 3 percentage points over the federal funds rate.

18. The increase in home equity debt outstanding also reflects the increasingly popular use of piggy-back seconds during the housing boom as a way to avoid paying mortgage insurance.

Chapter 5

1. Chairman Greenspan dubbed it a "conundrum" that long-term rates remained so low throughout this period despite much stronger economic conditions. In early 2005 testimony before Congress, he speculated that this was at least partly because of the global forces considered in this chapter. See www.federalreserve. gov/boarddocs/hh/2005/february/testimony.htm.

2. The Chinese authorities determine the value of the yuan and have intentionally kept it cheap relative to other currencies such as the U.S. dollar to promote exports and foreign investment in their country. Since summer 2005, the Chinese have been allowing the yuan to appreciate slowly in value, but it still remains undervalued by an estimated 20% to 25% against the dollar.

3. Chinese exports of certain products to the United States, such as women's lingerie, doubled within a few months. U.S. textile producers objected loudly, setting off a trade dispute some called the "bra war." It ended quietly, with some import restrictions being reimposed on Chinese textiles.

4. More precisely, Chinese imports accounted for 11% of consumer spending on nonenergy and food durables and nondurables.

5. Treasury bonds are also owned by various government entities that are not publicly traded. The most significant is the Social Security trust fund.

6. It could be argued that Chinese purchases of U.S. Treasury bonds have effectively financed the U.S. war efforts in Afghanistan and Iraq. The cost of those wars now totals about $500 billion, which equals the increase in Chinese Treasury holdings.

7. The U.S. economy accounts for approximately one-fourth of global output, and the remaining fourth is in other developed economies, including Europe, Canada, and Japan.

8. Most emerging economies have also managed their new riches well, paying off their previously existing debt and investing the rest.

9. The average central bank target rate is calculated as a weighted average of target rates across central banks, where the weights are equal to the nation's GDP on a purchasing power parity basis.

10. The Bank of Japan felt it had to strongly commit to its zero interest rate policy and the strong money growth it implied to rid the economy of deflation.

11. Global financial liberalization has been important in breaking down the so-called home bias in investing, in which populations have a bias in investing in their own countries. This bias had been fading until the current subprime financial shock.

12. The stock PE ratio in the United States had risen, but well below the record high set in the technology stock bubble of the late 1990s. This is a key reason U.S. stock prices have not fallen more sharply in the wake of the financial shock.

Chapter 6

1. Depository institutions are financial institutions that take deposits insured by the FDIC. Most depositories are commercial banks, thrift institutions, and credit unions.

2. Most have a license for those who want to be a "broker associate," a "brokerage business," and a "direct lender."

3. Since 2005, a third of the top 30 have either been acquired (Countrywide is now part of Bank of America), filed for bankruptcy, or been liquidated.

4. This is from the Federal Housing Finance Board. It might overstate the decline, because the period was characterized by a refinancing boom, and fees and points on refis were lower than on loans made for the purchase of a home.

5. Interstate banking became a reality with passage of the Riegle–Neal Interstate Banking and Branching Efficiency Act of 1994. More specifically, the legislation allowed adequately capitalized and managed bank holding companies to acquire and merge with banks in any state.

6. The largest refinancing boom in history occurred in 2002–2003. Some 30 million homeowners, with $5 trillion in mortgage debt, refinanced their mortgage during those two years.

7. A REIT is a corporation that invests in real estate that allows its owners to avoid corporate income taxes. For this benefit, REITs are required to distribute 90% of their income to the owners of the firm. REITs were designed to provide a similar structure for investment in real estate that mutual funds provide for investment in stocks.

8. Gresham's law is named after Sir Thomas Gresham, an English financier in Tudor times. Gresham's law says that any circulating currency consisting of both "good" and "bad" money (both forms required to be accepted at equal value under legal tender law) quickly becomes dominated by the "bad" money. This is because people spending money will hand over the "bad" coins instead of the "good" ones, keeping the "good" ones for themselves.

9. Fannie Mae's AU model is known as Desktop Underwriter; Freddie Mac's model is called Loan Prospector.

10. Perhaps as important (at least, from their perspective), if they were misjudging, then their competitors with less capable models were certainly doing worse.

11. The most common credit score is known as the FICO score, named after Fair Isaac, the company that commercialized credit scores. Each credit bureau also constructs scores that it sells, as do most large lenders, which customize the scores for their own specific purposes.

12. Credit bureaus and scoring companies have gotten wise to this practice and are working to shut it down.

Chapter 7

1. "Banks" is used here to refer to all depository institutions, including commercial banks, savings and loans, and credit unions. This is the traditional banking system in which institutions use households' deposits to at least partly finance their lending and other investment activities.

2. The consumer price index and prime interest rate were consistently in the double digits between the early 1970s and early 1980s.

3. The banks were largely recycling "petro-dollars" from the Middle East and other oil-producing nations earned in the period's high and rising oil prices to Latin American nations. This bears some similarity to the recent experience, as flush oil producers were putting their cash to work financing U.S. subprime mortgage loans.

4. The Resolution Trust Corporation was established in 1989 and closed its doors in 1995. It ultimately resolved close to 750 thrifts with assets of nearly $700 billion in today's dollars. The total cost of the S&L crisis for taxpayers was ultimately $250 billion.

5. This occurred in the large 1986 tax reform law.

6. This is a form of credit enhancement, which also includes overcollateralization, in which the face value of the securities is less than the value of the underlying loans.

7. In investment management vernacular, diversification benefits accrue if returns on the bonds are not correlated.

8. Ironically, the first CDO was issued in 1987 by the infamous investment bank of junk bond fame, Drexel Burnham Lambert.

9. Synthetic CDOs were constructed so that the CDS included in the CDO mimicked the cash-flow patterns of the residential mortgage securities being insured.

10. The first Basel Accord on minimum capital standards for banks was reached in 1988 and implemented globally during the 1990s. Basel II provides much more comprehensive guidelines and was implemented during the early 2000s.

11. The Treasury deal involved establishing a "super-SIV" that would be funded and owned collectively by the big global banks and would buy assets from the failing SIVs at some undetermined discounted price.

12. The ABX is an asset-backed securities derivatives index constructed by Markit.

13. The hedge funds were euphemistically called the Bear Stearns High-Grade Structured Credit Fund and the Bear Stearns High-Grade Structured Credit Enhanced Leveraged Fund.

14. These securities are said to be negatively correlated.

Chapter 8

1. This calculation does not include the current housing bust.

2. Pent-up demand represents the demand for a product that develops during recessions as nervous and financially pressed households put off spending they would normally do, given their income, wealth, and demographic circumstances.

3. The passage of the Monetary Control Act of 1980 phased out Regulation Q.

4. Nationwide, land prices accounted for an estimated 60% of housing values as of 2005. This varied from 30% in Pittsburgh, Pennsylvania, to more than 90% in San Francisco, California. This calculation is based on a methodology presented in "The Price of Residential Land in U.S. Cities," by David and Palumbo, Finance and Economic Discussions Series, Federal Reserve Board, May 2006. www.federalreserve.gov/pubs/feds/2006/200625/200625pap.pdf.

5. The Bureau of Census estimates that legal immigration averages approximately 1 million annually and illegal immigration averages about 250,000.

6. The 1.8 million homes in annual fundamental demand consist of 1.25 million in household formations, 200,000 in second homes, and 350,000 in obsolete homes.

7. Home building peaked in early 2006 partly because of rebuilding in the wake of Hurricane Katrina, which had destroyed more than a quarter-million homes in New Orleans, Louisiana, and Gulfport–Biloxi, Mississippi.

8. The homeowner vacancy rate hit a record 2.9% in the first quarter of 2008, according the Census Bureau. The long-run average of the vacancy rate was 1.7%.

Chapter 9

1. The definition of *predatory mortgage lending* is clearly defined in this January 2001 regulatory guidance: www.federalreserve.gov/boarddocs/press/boardacts/2001/20010131/default.htm.

2. Regulators issued their "Interagency Guidance on Nontraditional Mortgage Product Risks" in October 2006. www.federalreserve.gov/newsevents/press/other/20061018a.htm.

3. Regulators issued their "Statement on Subprime Mortgage Lending" in June 2007. www.federalreserve.gov/newsevents/press/bcreg/20070629a.htm.

4. Former Fed Governor Susan Bies did warn early on of pending mortgage credit problems. See "A Supervisor's Perspective on Mortgage Markets and Mortgage Lending Practices," 14 June 2006. www.federalreserve.gov/newsevents/speech/bies20060614a.htm. FDIC Chairwoman Sheila Bair was also outspoken on the topic before most others. See www.fdic.gov/news/news/speeches/archives/2006/chairman/spsep2706.html, 27 September 2006.

5. This is through the doctrine of preemption, which was extended in an early 2007 Supreme Court ruling clarifying that federal regulation applies to operating subsidiaries of national banks, not just the national banks themselves.

6. These entities can be regulated both in the state where they are headquartered and in other states where they operate.

7. See the Boston Federal Reserve study "Mortgage Lending in Boston: Interpreting the HMDA data," working paper, October 1992.

8. HMDA has been amended since the 1970s to increase the mortgage lenders required to report on their lending activity and also to expand the information reported.

9. See the Boston Fed Study. For a critique of this study, see "Is the Boston Fed Study on Mortgage Discrimination Flawed?" Mark Zandi, *American Banker*, March 1993.

10. The largest bank to fail the Fed's discrimination test was Shawmut Bank, based in Hartford, Connecticut. Soon after that, it was denied permission to acquire another smaller bank and was acquired by the Bank of Boston.

11. Gramlich's views on subprime lending are expressed in a December 2000 speech, "Subprime Lending, Predatory Lending." www.federalreserve.gov/boarddocs/speeches/2000/20001206.htm.

12. The Greenspan–Gramlich disagreement came to light in *The Wall Street Journal* interviews with both on June 9, 2007. See http://online.wsj.com/article/SB118134111823129555.html?mod=todays_us_money_and_investing. Gramlich later stated that he generally thought subprime lending was positive because it supported increased home ownership, and he probably even thought the criticism Chairman Greenspan received on the subject was unfair. Still, his view that the Fed should take on a leadership role in addressing predatory lending practices was rebuked.

13. HOEPA was passed in 1994 as an amendment to the Truth in Lending Act in response to congressional testimony about predatory home equity lending practices in poor and other underserved markets.

14. In California, the Department of Real Estate oversees mortgage brokers and the Department of Corporations is responsible for finance companies, in addition to regulating more than 300,000 corporate entities in a wide range of financial businesses.

15. A higher-priced mortgage was defined as a loan with an annual interest rate of 3 percentage points or more above a comparable Treasury note. These rules apply to first mortgage loans secured by the borrower's principal dwelling.

Chapter 10

1. This assumes a 20% down payment and a fixed-rate mortgage at prevailing rates for a prime borrower.

2. Another common approach is to compare house prices with household incomes. Because people generally want as much housing as they can afford, given their incomes and saving, it makes sense for incomes and house prices to increase at about the same rate. More sophisticated econometric approaches also apply, but all of them reach roughly the same conclusions.

3. This is of the nation's 60 largest metropolitan areas, based on population.

4. The mortgage foreclosure process is long and complicated and varies substantially across states. The average length to move through the entire foreclosure process from default to a home sale is about one year.

5. These are first-mortgage loan defaults based on consumer credit file data supplied by credit bureau Equifax. They are measured at an annualized rate—the number of loans that would default over a year, given the default rate at that time.

6. Given the house price declines that have already occurred, this analysis undervalues a few markets, including Detroit, Michigan; Cincinnati, Ohio; Cleveland, Ohio; and Indianapolis, Indiana.

7. See "Mortgage Put Options and Real Estate Markets," Pavlov and Wachter, April 2008, forthcoming in the *Journal of Real Estate and Finance*.

Chapter 11

1. The 1929 stock market crash leading to the Great Depression was measurably more serious because it was part of a global financial and economic meltdown. The subprime financial shock has affected the entire globe, but not nearly to the same degree.

2. The IMF has also come up with a similar loss estimate. See "Global Financial Stability Report," October 2008. www.imf.org/External/Pubs/FT/GFSR/2008/01/index.htm.

3. These loss estimates are in 2007 U.S. dollars. The $2.4 trillion loss estimate includes both cash-flow losses on loans and mark-to-market losses on security. For example, for mortgages, it includes the losses on defaulted mortgages and the losses on the value of mortgage securities.

4. This is based on the assumption that national house prices would fall 35% from their peak. It includes about $350 billion in losses on mortgage loans and $800 billion in losses on mortgage securities.

5. According to the IMF, in 2006, total global bank loans were more than $70 trillion and the value of debt securities was just less than $70 trillion.

6. These are known as payment-in-kind (PIK) bonds.

7. The banks' loans were also securitized into collateralized loan obligation (CLOs) and then sold to investors.

8. Northern Rock was one of the United Kingdom's largest mortgage lenders before it suffered a run on the bank by depositors who had lost faith in its capability to pay them back. The British government was ultimately forced to take over the bank to quell the run in September 2007.

9. This is also known as fair value accounting and is defined by the Financial Accounting Standards Board in FAS 157. www.fasb.org/st/summary/stsum157.shtml.

10. The credit controls were imposed in a failed effort to stem the period's high and accelerating inflation. The logic behind the plan was that a consumer borrowing binge was fueling spending and price pressures. The plan was quickly jettisoned as the economy quickly began to sputter and recession ensued a few months later.

Chapter 12

1. See www.federalreserve.gov/newsevents/press/monetary/20061212a.htm for the FOMC statement from the December 12, 2006, meeting.

2. This statement was made after a speech to The Committee of 100, a business group promoting better Chinese relations. See http://uk.reuters.com/article/marketsNewsUS/idUKWBT00686520070420.

3. The press release announcing the plan is available at http://portal.hud.gov/portal/page?_pageid=33,717219&_dad=portal&_schema=PORTAL. The FHA also announced the adoption of risk-based premiums for FHA insurance beginning in 2008. In theory, this allows the FHA to provide mortgage credit to more financially stretched households.

4. More precisely, LIBOR rates spiked relative to risk-free Treasury rates. The bigger the difference in LIBOR and Treasury rates, the greater the angst among banks.

5. Commercial banks, thrift institutions, and domestic branches of foreign banks are permitted to borrow from the discount window.

6. The same financial institutions that can use the discount window are also permitted to use the TAF.

7. Similarly big moves in the funds rate occurred in the early 1980s, but during that period of hyperinflation, the Fed was managing policy by targeting the growth in the money supply, not the funds rate.

8. Bernanke's first public reference to "recession" occurred in the Q&A period during testimony before the Joint Economic Committee of Congress on April 2, 2008. See www.federalreserve.gov/newsevents/testimony/bernanke20080402a.htm.

9. More precisely, the real federal funds rate is equal to the difference between the funds rate and inflation expectations. Inflation expectations as measured in the market for Treasury Inflation Protected Securities have remained low and stable at close to 2%.

10. The package satisfied the criteria for a well-designed economic stimulus plan— namely, that it was timely, it was a one-time cost to the government, and the benefits were targeted to those households most likely to spend them quickly.

11. This estimate of the job impact is similar to that determined in "Fiscal Stimulus Plan 2008," Mark Zandi, *Dismal Scientist*, 22 January 2008.

12. The stimulus plan also authorized states to issue more tax-exempt bonds to fund efforts to refinance hard-pressed homeowners into new, more manageable loans.

13. The new mortgage loan caps vary by metropolitan areas and equal 125% of the median-priced home in the highest-priced county within the metro area, but cannot be greater than $729,000.

14. OFHEO is the Office of Federal Housing Enterprise Oversight.

15. The 12 member banks of the Federal Home Loan Bank system are normally permitted to hold no more than 300% of their capital in mortgage securities; this was increased to 600%.

16. Although Fannie and Freddie's regulator, the Federal Housing Finance Agency, put them into conservatorship, the Treasury Department made the ultimate decision regarding their fate.

Chapter 13

1. A recession is defined as a broad-based and persistent decline in economic activity. A committee of economists at the National Bureau of Economic Research determines whether a recession is occurring based on a wide range of economic data. The rule of thumb is that a recession is defined by two consecutive quarters of declining real GDP. This is a rule of thumb, however, not a rule.

2. Consumer price inflation peaked at more than 14% in early 1980, and the unemployment rate peaked at close to 11% in late 1982.

3. Despite the 1987 stock market crash and the tech-stock bust at the turn of the millennium, stock prices had risen by more than 10% annually during the period. Despite the housing crash, house prices had risen 5% per year.

4. This was a period of double-digit inflation. Real house prices fell modestly, but nominal prices did not.

5. Residential investment's share of GDP was briefly higher immediately following World War II, when homes were built for returning U.S. soldiers.

6. This is the median homeowners' equity; half of homeowners have more equity in their homes, and half have less.

7. A 25% peak-to-trough decline in house prices would wipe out $5 trillion in homeowners' equity.

8. The saving rate calculations are based on data from the Federal Reserve's Flow of Funds and Survey of Consumer Finance using a methodology described in "Disentangling the Wealth Effect: A Cohort Analysis of Household Saving in the 1990s," by Dean Maki and Michael Palumbo, Federal Reserve Finance and Economics Discussion Series, April 2001. www.federalreserve.gov/pubs/feds/2001/200121/200121abs.html.

9. Each group of households accounts for about one-third of the population, but renters account for only about one-tenth of total consumer spending, homeowners who have never tapped their equity account for just over half of spending, and homeowners who have done so account for the remainder.

10. This is the real trade deficit. The nominal trade deficit had also fallen, but not nearly as much, given the rising prices for oil and most other imported goods.

11. This is the price for a barrel of West Texas Intermediate.

12. Adding in residential investment—which is not counted as consumer spending even though it is a household decision—the share of GDP rises from 66% in the early 1980s to 76% at its peak, at the apex of the housing boom in 2005.

13. GDP equals the value of all the goods and services produced by the economy and, thus, is a good proxy for the income generated by all the economy's assets.

14. Wealth is measured by net worth, which is equal to the difference between all assets and liabilities. This data is based on the Federal Reserve's triennial Survey of Consumer Finance. The survey was conducted before 1989, but significant changes in the survey make the results difficult to compare to the survey results beginning in 1989.

15. This culminated in the late-2005 bankruptcy reform legislation, which, among other things, implemented an income means test to determine who was eligible for a Chapter 7 liquidation or a lender-preferred Chapter 13 workout.

16. The Federal Reserve's Survey of Consumer Finance is also the source for these statistics.

Chapter 14

1. As discussed in Chapter 10, the Federal Reserve was granted this authority under HOEPA.

2. In addition, federal foreclosure should eliminate strict foreclosures which are available in a few New England states in which the lender files a lawsuit to take possession of a property without an auction.

INDEX

FINANCIAL TIMES

In an increasingly competitive world, it is quality
of thinking that gives an edge—an idea that opens new
doors, a technique that solves a problem, or an insight
that simply helps make sense of it all.

We work with leading authors in the various arenas
of business and finance to bring cutting-edge thinking
and best-learning practices to a global market.

It is our goal to create world-class print publications
and electronic products that give readers
knowledge and understanding that can then be
applied, whether studying or at work.

To find out more about our business
products, you can visit us at www.ftpress.com.